*A World
of
Differences*

A World of Differences

ONE WOMAN'S STORY

MARIE ADLER KESSEL

The University of Arkansas Press
Fayetteville   London
1990

Copyright © 1990 by the Lawrence and
Marie Kessel Foundation, Inc.
All rights reserved
Manufactured in the United States of America
94   93   92   91   90   5   4   3   2   1

DESIGNER: *Nancy Lindsey Burris*
TYPEFACE: *Linotron 202 Bembo*
TYPESETTER: *G & S Typesetters, Inc.*
PRINTER: *Braun-Brumfield, Inc.*
BINDER: *Braun-Brumfield, Inc.*

The paper used in this publication meets the minimum requirements of the American National Standard for Permanence of Paper for Printed Library Materials Z39.48-1984. ∞

Library of Congress Cataloging-in-Publication Data

Kessel, Marie Adler, 1915–
A world of differences / Marie Adler Kessel.
p.   cm.
ISBN 1-55728-119-X (alk. paper). —
ISBN 1-55728-120-3 (pbk. : alk. paper)
1. Kessel, Marie Adler, 1915– . 2. Arkansas—Biography.
3. New York (City)—Biography. 4. Sheep ranchers—
Arkansas—Biography. 5. Interior decorators—New York
(City)—Biography. 6. Social workers—New York (City)—
Biography. I. Title.
CT275.K45868A3   1990
973.9'092—dc20
[B]   89-36163
                       CIP

To my grandsons, Alexander and Daniel Shlomm

They have known me only as a doting grandmother. I want them to know me from my first day, as I have known them from their days of birth. I hope I have included all the things we so often wish we had asked our grandmothers and didn't.

Contents

Preface ix

Part One 1
   1   Getting Started 3
   2   Up and Rolling 6
   3   Learning How 26
   4   School and New Adventures 34
   5   Back to the Heights 48
   6   Joining Up 70
   7   Central High School, Little Rock 82
   8   Aftermath 93

Part Two 101
   9   Starting Over 103
  10   Honeymoon 116
  11   Down on the Farm 123
  12   Special Projects 132
  13   First Born 144
  14   Children and Animals 155
  15   Pigs and Ribbons 164
  16   Joining Clubs Again 170
  17   Paul 175
  18   Triumphs and Disasters 183

Part Three 193
  19   New York, New Life 195
  20   Change of Life 204
  21   Other Parts of My Life 215
  22   On the Job 218
  23   T-Groups 230
  24   New Adventures 240

25	Two New Homes and a Grandson	247
26	Lawrence	252
27	Alexander	256
28	Joys and Sorrows	260
29	The Computer and I	266
30	Summer's End	272

Preface

I wrote this book because I believe that our times should be shown through the eyes of the common people rather than just the lives of the celebrities. I felt that my account of five generations living in the United States would be of interest.

At some time during the past seventy-four years, I have lived on a farm, in a small town, in a medium-sized town, in a large city, and in a foreign country. I have lived through the Dust Bowl era, and I have survived the Great Depression. Every experience has left its mark.

I've been Christian and I've been Jewish. I have had successful careers in widely diverse fields. The people I have known intimately range from prostitutes to professors.

To have had psychoanalysis with a Freudian analyst is an enormous advantage. Because of this profound experience, I am able to recall my earliest years, not just the events of those years, but the emotions that accompanied each happening. I have tried to show how my traits of character were set at an early age and have continued throughout my life.

It is my hope that you readers will enjoy meeting the people who were so much a part of my life.

The book begins at a time when there were no radios and the movies were silent and jerky. It ends with the era of TV, video tapes, cassettes, compact discs, and personal computers. I have used and enjoyed all of them.

I am much indebted to Betty Filer, who through her friendship has seen to it that my time was made free to write this story of my life.

I am also most grateful to Rom and Ila Ermann, who were good enough to read the book chapter by chapter as I wrote it. They were the ones who encouraged me to keep going.

It has been fortunate for me that I married a man who wanted me to expand my interests and to do whatever was necessary to live a fulfilled life. Without his support, both financial and moral, I would not have been able to accomplish as much as I have.

Part One

CHAPTER 1

Getting Started

On October 9, 1915, some years before my mother had a chance to teach me that punctuality is the courtesy of kings, I decided to make my entry into this world on time, ignoring the fact that the house was quarantined due to Mother's ill-timed scarlet fever. Even the doctor could not arrive before I did. He was greeted at the front door by my lusty yelps from the second-floor bedroom. Luckily, Sally was there. All through my childhood, the story of my birth was her favorite. I loved to hear it over and over.

Sally also liked to tell me how she molded the shape of my head by rubbing it and how she forced Mother to breast-feed me every time I cried. I was a colicky baby, but Sally would carry me to Mother and say, "The poor little thing is hungry." I was probably overstuffed.

Mother had her own problems with scarlet fever. She was pretty annoyed that this baby cried so much. Nevertheless, Sally's story of my birth gave me the life-long conviction that being born was an exciting event and that life in general should be a series of adventures.

Our family was quite typical for the year 1915. There were Daddy and Mother and my sister Ray, who was twenty-two months older than I and thought that I was a duck because of the sounds I made. My grandfather, Daddy Albright, lived next door with my uncle Billy Ramsey. It was hard to sort out all these connections, but eventually I would figure out that Daddy Albright was my mother's father, and Uncle Billy was his brother-in-law. Grandmother Albright had died when my mother was a girl of sixteen.

In my list of family members Sally was certainly the most important as far as I was concerned. Sally had been born a slave and was five years old when Mr. Lincoln set her free. She amused me with her stories of how the slaves got back at their masters. When she was fourteen Sally had gone to work for Grandmother Adler as my father's nurse and had been in the family ever since. When Daddy's sister got married and had a baby, Sally was sent to be my cousin Ralph's nurse.

Sally couldn't read or write, and all successive infants in her care were required very early to take a solemn oath that when they went to school they would bring their newly acquired knowledge home and teach her to read the Bible. I'm ashamed to admit that I joined the ranks of those who preceded me in breaking that promise. Actually Sally had a much better talent than reading words: she knew the art of picture reading. She would hold me on her lap with a copy of the *Saturday Evening Post,* which always had great pictures on the cover, and point out all the details of the picture by making up a story. I helped to figure out what was happening and was praised if I noticed some small detail that she had not mentioned.

I liked this kind of "reading" better than the kind my mother did. There always seemed to be a lesson in the stories Mother chose, such as the one about little Harriet who played with matches and ended up as a heap of charred ashes. That was meant to scare me enough so I'd keep out of harm's path, but actually it drove me into controlled experimentation. By that, I mean I took the matches outdoors onto the concrete driveway and carefully struck them. I knew they were dangerous because whenever there was a fire in town it was always said that it had been caused by mice chewing on matches. Now, mice, there was something else I could add to the list of things to fear. I also thought about how hungry the poor little mice must have been to chew on matches. I don't remember ever tasting them myself.

There was a time when Sally had an accident because of matches. It was really Mother's fault. At least, I blamed her. Mother, having decided that the wood stove was no longer good enough, had bought a gas stove. It had just been installed. Sally turned on the gas and ambled across the room to find the box of matches. When she finally struck the match, there was a huge poof followed by a terrible odor like singed chickens. Only it was poor Sally who had been singed. I didn't know what had happened until I got up from my nap. By then, Sally was already back on duty with her whole face wrapped in ghostly white bandages and only her big, black eyes and ample mouth showing. It was scarier than a Halloween mask. As I ran screaming from her, she kept following me, pleading with me to understand, saying, "It's Sally. It's Sally." I didn't care who it was, I just wanted IT to go away.

Mother took advantage of the situation and decided to hire a white nurse so that Sally could devote herself to making lemon meringue pies and churning the butter. I knew immediately that I had overreacted. As soon as the bandages came off, I only wanted to be with Sally. I loved all the chores she let me share. It was really fun to shell the peas, string the beans, crank the ice-cream freezer, and even churn butter.

There are so many more memories of the early years in Batesville. That was where I learned about death, God, separation, punishment, and sorrow. There were days of joy, too, but joy is not something we have to learn.

CHAPTER 2

Up and Rolling

No one believes that I can remember learning to walk, but I swear I do. I had an enormous wooden hoop on wheels that rolled on the floor. A much smaller hoop attached above it held a cloth with leg holes. Seated in this contraption, I was able to propel myself across the floor at breakneck speed.

I was allowed to be in my hoop only in the attic. The floor there was as smooth as in the rest of the house, but there was no furniture for me to bang into. Some of our toys were up there too. One day the phone rang and Mother went to answer it. Before leaving, she told Ray to watch me carefully to make sure I didn't go near the stairs. What a challenge. When the time was right, I made a dash for the top of the steps. Knowing nothing of gravity and its dreadful pull, I nonetheless hurtled through space like Newton's apple and made a thunderous landing that got Mother off the phone in seconds. Before I knew what had happened exactly, she had gathered me in her arms and was screaming that my nose was broken. I had never seen her that excited before. She kept saying, "She can't even cry."

Why should I have cried? I didn't feel anything, and it was so much fun to be the center of all this commotion. To cap it all, Ray, the good little girl, the angel, was being loudly scolded for dereliction of duty. It was truly a day of triumph and glory. Little else was talked about. When Daddy came home, the story was told all over again. For once in my short life, I was being taken for the innocent victim.

I was given to understand that my religious training could not begin until I learned to use the pottie. In Mother's words, I wouldn't be allowed to go to Sunday school until I was able to "keep clean." This was a very hard way to learn the road to God, but I was determined. Ray was called for each Sunday by a neighbor, Codie McCormick. My sister was so proud in her party clothes that I was sad to be left behind while she pranced off to play with baby Jesus in his cradle and to deposit her nickel in the collection box. Every time I was successful in the pottie, I would ask if I had earned my right to rock baby Jesus. Mother always said, "We'll see."

It was due to this same pottie training that I learned my first adjectives. Mother's tone of voice really told me the most. I'm not sure when I really understood the words themselves, but at each inspection she delivered a critical comment such as "Mmmh good." "Mmmh nice." Once when Mother had a visitor downstairs, I was left on the pot to perform. She seemed to have forgotten about me and didn't respond to my shrieks that I was done. After a lapse of time that seemed endless, I toddled over to the banister and called down to her. "You don't have to come. It's nice and soft and hard and firm." Those magic words got her there on the double.

Finally, the day arrived when I could go with Codie and Ray to Sunday school. Codie carried me all the way in her arms. The moment Codie put me down on the floor I made a beeline for the cradle, but I was skillfully intercepted by the teacher, who explained that this privilege was reserved for children who'd had a birthday that week. I swore I'd just had a birthday. Here I was for the first time in the house of God, and I was fearlessly telling a fib (lie was a forbidden word) to achieve my ends. Naturally Ray and Codie were asked to testify on my behalf, and just as naturally my witnesses spoke against me. I then weaseled out by claiming not to know what a birthday was. Such humiliation.

Before this, my fibs had been known only to the family

and to God, who was busy recording them in his big, black book. According to Sally, God was a very careful bookkeeper who wrote down all of my fibs. If his book was too full, I wouldn't be allowed into heaven. This was a terrifying thought. Even though I wasn't so sure I would particularly like pearly gates, streets paved with gold, and winged angels playing harps and trumpets all day long, I didn't want to be left out if everyone else in the family was going to be there. I was careful in questioning Sally. Was Mother good and would she go to heaven? Sally was sure that Mother would be there. Was Daddy good and would he be there too? Again, she was sure Daddy would get through those pearly gates. My conclusion was that God wouldn't leave me out since it would make my parents sad to be in heaven without me. Having solved this problem to my own satisfaction, I went merrily on with fibbing whenever it suited me, with no further concern about what the bookkeeper in the sky was writing down.

While I'm on the subject of going to heaven, it seemed that I had a number of relatives up there who were waiting for me. For one, there was Aunt Rosa, who was Grandmother Adler's sister. There was going to be a day when Gabriel was going to blow his horn, and all of the dead were going to rise up out of their tombs, and there was going to be great tumult and rejoicing. I wasn't at all sure that I wanted to be around for Judgment Day. I argued that I wouldn't know Aunt Rosa if I saw her. Remembering how Sally had looked in her bandages, I decided it would be frightening and that I would rather not meet Aunt Rosa. I liked my living relatives, and I was satisfied not to add to their number.

Uncle Billy Ramsey was a constant source of interest to me because the second finger on his left hand was missing two joints. He said he had cut them off himself with a hatchet when he was young. I couldn't see why anyone would want to do such a thing, but I was careful never to get near a hatchet, not even when we drove out to the countryside to choose a tree to cut down for Christmas. Uncle Billy didn't seem to have any fear of hatchets. He went right on using carpentry tools of all kinds. In fact, he always had fascinating projects underway.

One project occupied Uncle Billy for a long time—building a new ferryboat to take cars across the White River between the two shores of the Ramsey Bottom farm, which was on the edge of town. This large farm had been in the family since about 1800, long before Arkansas became a state. The old ferryboat could only carry wagons and mules, but already there were several cars in town. Uncle Billy was looking forward to expanding his business. Not that he was going to run the ferryboat himself. He was interested in building it and getting someone else to run it.

Speaking of cars in Batesville, Daddy liked to tell me about his first car, a Hudson. It had been the first one in town, six years before I was born. Daddy had hired a mechanic to make a trip with him to visit Grandmother Adler, who was spending the summer in Kennebunkport, Maine. It was lucky he had the mechanic with him because he had fourteen punctures and had to drive through cornfields when there were no roads. He actually made it to Maine, but on his return trip he ran into a tree and damaged the car so badly, when he went over a bluff, that he ended up shipping it home on the train from Kentucky.

Just as Uncle Billy was thinking he needed to have a bigger ferry, the town was talking about needing to pave the streets because the cars would make too much dust with their speeding. I remember the car we had then was a Maxwell; it had isinglass curtains that Daddy put on when it looked as if it might rain. They were hard to put on because the holes on the curtains had to be right over the knobs that locked them into place. They were yellowish and foggy, which made them hard to see through.

Daddy Albright loved to take me with him on his daily rounds of our small town. I noticed he always asked my mother for permission. She always asked where he was going before giving her consent. I wondered if when I grew up my mother would ever ask my permission to do anything. She seemed to be the boss of everything. Rounds of Batesville, Arkansas, were always fun because Daddy Albright knew everyone and the world seemed such a friendly place. The sidewalks were cement, but the streets were still just dirt. He would pick me up and carry me to the other side so I wouldn't soil my white shoes.

We usually began at the icehouse. Daddy Albright owned the ice business, but he had someone else see to things. There was nothing in the world so delicious as the chips of ice I was allowed to gather and suck. Then we were off to the picture show house, where the manager would hand Daddy Albright a grocery sack and they would pass a few words about how many people had come to see the show the night before.

After that, we walked to the bank building on the corner and gave them the paper bag. When they'd opened it and counted out the money, they would give Daddy Albright a slip of paper with numbers written on it. He always put it into his pocket and said, "Well, that's that." It seemed that he owned the bank building but not the bank. It was difficult to understand.

Our next stop was the telephone building. Here again it was complicated because Daddy Albright owned the building but not the telephones. This seemed to be a purely social call. All the operators (I think there were four) gathered around to chat with us and admire the clothes I had on.

My mother was a regular dress factory. Sewing was her grand passion, and she kept my sister and me "dressed to the nines" (whatever that meant). We wore freshly polished, white high-buttoned shoes summer and winter. This was supposed to give us slim ankles when we grew up. In summer our socks were short and hand-embroidered with rosebuds; in winter we wore long, white stockings that on really chilly days hid the long underwear Mother considered necessary to keep us from ever having rheumatism. We were forbidden ever to sit on stone or concrete for the same reason.

Although I was pleased that Mother took such an interest in my clothes, I sometimes got the feeling that she was "playing dolls." I was supposed to return home as neat and clean as

I had left, and that was not possible. Too many fascinating rocks and sticks and flowers waited in my path to be gathered and examined.

Mother never made her own clothes, but she kept up with all of the latest fashions by poring over the pattern books. She was a beautiful woman with warm, dark-brown eyes and dark hair, which she wore drawn softly back in a knot. When she was deep in thought, her eyes had a dreamy look as though she were far away. When she and Daddy went to a party or ball, I loved to play with the yellow ostrich fan that she carried. That was the only time I was allowed to touch her clothes. I was comfortable with her at times like that, but when she got into one of her furies her whole face changed and her eyes grew larger and her jaws clenched. Her hands made fists. Then I was afraid.

Daddy Albright was the one to whom I ran when Mother got too angry and I felt I might need protection. He carefully asked why I thought she was mad. (He let me use that word mad though I wasn't allowed to use it in front of Mother, who said, "Dogs go mad and people get angry.") Daddy Albright had a whole list of things he would ask me. At the end of the list, after I had answered no to every one, he asked, "Did she take a broomstick to you?" When I said no again, he would say, "Well, than, I don't think she is as mad as all that. Come on now and I'll go home with you." I always ended up laughing at the idea of her taking a broomstick to me. But only with my grandfather at my side was my fear gone.

Actually, I was much more afraid of Mother, the Grand Inquisitor, than God because she was apt to deal out very swift and painful punishment whenever she caught me in one of my misdeeds. Corporal punishment must have been in fashion then, because it was a daily occurrence as far as I was concerned. It was usually just bare hand against bare bottom, but one day, after Ray and I had been dressed for a party, I was left alone for a few seconds. Profiting from the time alone, I slid down the grass terrace in the back yard. When discovered, I had grass stains on my white shoes and ruffled panties. With great solemnity, Mother went to the small peach tree and carefully selected a switch. She tested it to see if it had the right amount of bend, then she pulled all its leaves off while I stood watching her every move. When she was fully prepared, she put the switch between my legs and started whipping away so that both legs were stinging. I couldn't believe what was happening, and I began to run and holler that she was hurting me. She said, "I mean to hurt you so you will remember." And so I did.

I was very curious about the difference between boys and girls. The answers I got on this subject were far from satisfying. People would say such silly things as, "When boys grow up, they have beards. Girls don't."

Naturally, my retort to that was, "But when they are little, how do you know they are going to have beards when they grow up?"

They would then tell me that little boys wore pants and little girls wore dresses. Well, if that was all there was to it, why couldn't I wear pants and be a boy? Someone told me that if I kissed my elbow I would turn into a boy. It's a wonder I didn't put myself permanently out of kilter from the contortions I went through trying to achieve this result.

There was also the explanation that boys have short hair and girls have to let their hair grown longer. That one had an easy remedy. A secret scissors session could aid in the alteration. Fortunately, I was caught before the self-mutilation had gone too far. Since no one would give me real answers, I invented my own. I decided that dogs were boys and cats were girls. Horses were male and cows were female.

I then began having terrible nightmares in which a bristling cat perched on the branch of a tree only slightly beyond the reach of a lunging dog. Freud would have loved this one. I suppose he would have declared it was caused by witnessing the primal scene, but to me it was a nightmare. Every night I would pray to have good dreams, and I always had this same horror. Finally, I decided that God was stubborn like me, so I thought I would fool him and pray for bad dreams. It worked. The spell was broken, and the dog and cat disappeared from my dreams.

Breaking the spell may also have had something to do with timing. About then, Ray and I were moved into our own bedroom. Although our house had three bedrooms, my mother had kept Ray and me sleeping in the same room with her and Daddy until we had been vaccinated for smallpox. I never knew why she chose this time to evict us, but she did. Until then, we were never left alone there. If my parents went out at night, Sally sat with us in a rocking chair and nodded. If I woke up and asked where my parents were, she said they were in the mahogany room, the room with the mahogany four poster bed. This piqued my curiosity. What happened in the mahogany room? I began to be afraid of it. Fortunately, Ray and I were moved to the green room, and I had nothing against the move. In fact, I felt a certain relief and freedom.

Batesville had a population of only about five thousand people, so anything that happened there created a lot of interest. If the fire whistle blew, all of the people went out into their front yards to see what part of the sky was red and to guess, from the direction, what had caught fire. They would listen to hear how far the fire engine drove with its siren on. Lots of them broke into a dead run to see the fire. The more settled folks would be satisfied to stroll over, stopping to visit with their neighbors on the way.

One evening the sky turned a bright, streaky red, but the fire whistle didn't blow. There was no way to know where the fire was because every part of the sky was lit up. I was sure that this was the end of the world, but I didn't want to be a Henny Penny and run around scaring people. Then someone walked by and stopped to chat. He declared the red sky to be "a roar-a bore-a Alice." Although I knew each of the words, strung together they didn't make much sense to me. I knew "a roar" (what lions do); "a bore" (the circular motion grownups make as they recite, "I want to bore a little hole. I don't know where. I think I'll bore it right in there."—after which they poke a finger in your belly button); "a Alice" (a girl in town). I didn't know this long word, but it sounded better than doomsday. I had been afraid that was what it was. From then on, I proudly announced to all comers that it was the "a roar a bore a Alice." Everyone seemed to love to hear me say it. I was asked to repeat it over and over for all new arrivals in our front yard.

I was much older by the time that I learned that what I had seen were the northern lights known as the aurora borealis. After that, I gave up being so afraid of Judgment Day. I had already undergone the worst and had attracted lots of unexpected attention. I pretty much decided that learning to say big words was worthwhile even if you didn't know what they meant. That night, Ray was green with envy. She wanted to know how I'd learned the big word so fast. I couldn't understand why she hadn't learned it. Probably, being older, she hadn't heard the three simple words that I'd heard.

I was not much interested in dolls. As soon as I was given a doll, I stripped it bare to find the difference I was always hunting for. When the sailor doll proved to be just like dolls in dresses, I abandoned it where I had disrobed it. Ray loved dolls, and her collection of beauties had eyes, with long eyelashes, that opened and closed. Under each doll's long, curly hair, I could feel a soft spot that let me know there was an open hole in the head.

Ray once made a big mistake. She went to a birthday party for five-year-olds. No three-year-olds were invited. I would never have a better time to investigate how those eyes worked. As soon as I heard the door close and was sure Ray and Mother had left, I grabbed Ray's favorite doll from the doll's bed and sat down with it in the interest of science. It was really quite a simple device. The two eyes were attached to each other, and there was a lump of lead between them that I could push up and down to make the eyes do what I wanted. I was able to work it so the eyes would close with the doll sitting up. No one else knew how to do that. They thought the eyes closed only when the doll was lying down.

I got very excited about making the doll do this trick. All of a sudden her eyes were out of her head and in my hands. I tried very hard to put them back and make them stay in the right place, but it was beyond me. I scurried around with this now wigless and eyeless doll looking for a place to hide her so that my dreadful crime would not be discovered. I finally managed to climb on the piano stool and lift the top of the upright piano. There was the perfect burial place for this maimed thing. With the hiding carried out, I went off to more innocent play and to water the sand so I could make a birthday cake.

A few minutes after Ray and Mother returned, I was summoned to come inside and asked where the doll was. I made them describe which doll they were talking about. That gained a few minutes. Then I denied knowing anything at all about that doll's whereabouts and asked if I could please go back to the sandpile. No, I couldn't. I was to sit down while they searched the room. The search was extended beyond the room to the whole house. By this time, Mother was talking to herself. She kept saying, "Where could that child have put that doll?" After a very long time she announced in desperation, "I have looked everywhere for that doll."

With great innocence, I asked, "Have you looked in the piano?"

There was a brief time lapse. Shrieks came from the living room as Ray caught sight of her "favorite." Mother called to me, "You come down here this minute. You are going to get the whipping of your life."

Mother was so mad, she didn't take time to go to the peach tree, so it was back to the bare-bottom treatment. It was worth it to know the anatomy of the eyes.

Although I didn't much care about dolls, I did love my pets. All three of them were ill-fated. They were a motley assortment—a goldfish, a nanny goat, and an Easter baby chick. I wasn't very clever at naming my pets, so they were just Goldie, Nanny, and Chickie. I don't remember who gave me Goldie, but one day I discovered her doing a headstand and whirling about in that position. She was very smart, I thought, to be able to stand on her head like that. I had been trying hard to stand on mine, but I always toppled over and had to announce that I had meant to do a somersault anyway. The next day I found Goldie floating on top of the water in her bowl. I tried to coax her into doing another headstand, but she was beyond hearing. I slipped downstairs to tell Sally what had happened. She was very gentle with me, saying that Goldie was dead and we must have a funeral. She answered my question about meeting Goldie in the hereafter. That made the loss bearable.

I dashed over to Daddy Albright's house to beg a cigar box that could serve as Goldie's coffin. By the time I got back to my room, I was almost gleeful at the prospect of putting on a ceremony for Goldie. Just as I went through the door, I caught a glimpse of Mother dumping all the water in Goldie's bowl into the toilet. I shrieked for her to stop, I was too late. Her hand was already pressing on the handle, and Goldie disappeared forever in a great flush that whirled her about for a brief second and then sucked her under. How could my mother have no feeling for my loss, and how could she deprive me of building a cemetery for MY fish?

Daddy gave me Nanny because when he was little he'd had a goat and also a cart so the goat could pull him around town. Mother refused to let me have a cart. She said they would never be able to find me if I had such easy rides at hand. She was probably right about that. Actually, I think she didn't like Nanny. When I came indoors she always remarked, "Whew, you smell like that awful goat." I liked the way Nanny smelled, and she was very soft to hug and pet.

One day I noticed Nanny chewing something. I was sure she had found some chewing gum. I asked her politely to spit it out. I told her she should be willing to share with me. She went right on chewing and ignoring my requests. My patience was running out. I began to threaten that if she didn't spit out the gum I would hit her with a brick. I did. Goats being built as they are, with very hard heads, she took no notice of me and just kept chewing. A few days later Mother told me that Nanny had died in the night. She said she had been poisoned from eating berries off the China Berry tree. But could she have climbed the lattice fence to get to the berries and, besides, where was her body? She was too big for Mother to have flushed down the toilet, and yet she was gone. Mother said "they" had come to get her. It was all so mysterious.

Some time later, at the other end of town, we passed a yard filled with children and *there was Nanny* in the middle of the crowd. I couldn't believe what I saw. I was ready to jump out of the moving car, but I couldn't get the door open. Mother kept denying that the goat was Nanny, but she wouldn't stop so I could see at closer range. In any case, my faith in Mother was shattered. She had fibbed to me. No, she had lied to me. Now I wasn't too sure about getting into heaven riding on her coattails. I wasn't even sure she was going to make it there herself.

Then there was poor little Chickie, so young to die. I literally loved her to death. She was such a soft little piece of fluff that I liked to hold her tight. Also, I wanted to make sure she didn't run away. I guess she was hungry, because she never stopped peeping and chirping. I searched for worms for her to eat as I had seen robins do. I don't think she liked them much. The day after Easter, I clutched her in both my hands and squeezed her tight, while uttering endearing words. Suddenly, her eyes seemed to bulge, and her head fell to one side, limp and lifeless. Oh, unspeakable horror. I flung her away from me and ran for Sally.

I was learning about death very early. Then came a more important kind of death. Sally's sister Laura worked for Daddy Albright. One day there was a big to-do. Laura had been taken sick at work, and Daddy Albright had hitched up the horse to the buggy to drive her and Sally to her little house. When Sally didn't come back, Mother went to see what was going on. She gathered Ray and me inside, explaining that she had to leave us alone and we were to be good and stay in the house until she got back. It was the first and only time this ever happened.

At first it was fun to be alone with Ray. But then it started to get dark, and it wasn't fun any more. We both began to worry. Finally, I decided on a course of action. I stepped to the telephone and simply said, "Get me my mother." The operator assured me that Mother would be there very soon. She kept talking to me in a comforting way until I heard Mother drive into the garage. Laura was dead, and I didn't see Sally until after the burial. She dabbed her eyes with the corner of her long apron for a few days, and then we spoke of it no more.

Once when I was particularly angry with Mother I began to think of ways to hurt her. One idea I came up with was that if I died she would be sad and feel bad about how mean she had been to me. I could picture the scene. I would be in a coffin lined with satin, as I had heard them described, and there would be Mother weeping away. How sweet this vengeance would be. But than I realized it wouldn't be like pretending to be asleep in order to eavesdrop. Since I wouldn't be able to see or hear her weep, where would the fun be? I definitively gave up the project of dying for vengeance, and I have never again wished for death. It will have to come looking for me, not the other way around.

I don't want to give the impression that life was sad. There were wonderful days when I would be taken to visit my mother's cousins May and Ramsey Weaver. They lived a couple of blocks away, and something interesting was always going on at their house. They didn't have any children and repeatedly said they wished they had a sweet little girl like me. Why didn't their doctor bring them one, I wondered. It seems that May was always going to Chicago to see her doctor up there. Mother thought it a silly extravagance on May's part. There were perfectly good doctors in Batesville, and here was May frittering away all of Ramsey's money on train rides to Chicago. In any case, I loved to visit them because they let me feed their chickens.

May said she would take me up to her attic if I would tiptoe and not make any noise. She had turned the attic into a nesting place for canaries. Each of the yellow birds had her own cage. Some of them were sitting on eggs, waiting for them to hatch, and some already had very ugly baby birds with big eyes and beaks that were wide open and begging. I loved the big canaries, but I sure didn't like the look of their young ones.

May's house was just across the street from the very large house in which Daddy had been born and had lived all through his childhood. It was a two-story red brick Victorian home with a square block of land around it. Sally told me that the circus had once come to town and asked Grandfather Adler to let them set up the show on his land. He agreed to have them there for two days. When they left, they gave him one of their trick horses. Pretty soon my aunt, who was also named Ray (originally it may have been Rachel—my sister was named for her), took the horse out of the stable and tried it out. When they came to the fence, the horse went over it and Aunt Ray stayed on the other side. She hadn't known the horse was a fancy jumper, or maybe it was a tricky horse instead of a trick horse. She gladly gave up all her claims to this animal, and it became my father's favorite for a number of years.

In those days, parrots grew wild in northern Arkansas, and many homes had them as pets. Parrots were taught to talk and sometimes even began to say original things. Mostly, though, they just repeated what they heard. My grandmother was a very polite lady who would not hurt anyone's feelings. One day she looked out the window and saw the town gossip heading for her front door. She groaned and said, "Here comes that terrible Mrs. Jones." No sooner had Sally admitted the visitor to the entrance hall than Polly called out, "Here comes that terrible Mrs. Jones." I just loved that story and longed to have a parrot that I could train to do my insulting so I couldn't be punished for being sassy.

In the days when my father was a boy, there was a Chinese laundryman in town. All the boys except Daddy would tease him, chanting, "Chink, Chink, Chinaman eats dead rats, chews them up like gingersnaps." Although my father tried to make the others more respectful, they persisted in their ugly ways until they learned their lesson. When the Fourth of July came around, the Chinese man came to Grandmother's house carrying a large basket filled with all kinds of wonderful fireworks which he left for my father. He became the envy of all the boys. Nothing like those rockets had ever been seen before in Batesville. The laundryman had sent all the way to China for this wonderful display. There was a heavy moral to this story, but I liked it anyway. Sally was careful to train us never to use words like nigger or chink because she said they hurt people's feelings.

Sally had a great supply of slave stories about parrots. One was about a slave named Sam who was in the habit of taking biscuits and hiding them with the intention of eating them later or sharing them with other slaves. One of his hiding places was under the sofa. When the master came into the room, Polly called out, "Look under the sofa." The master looked and found Sam's biscuits. Sam was in a heap of trouble. He decided to get rid of this tattletale, so he took Polly out in the yard and wrung her neck. Evidently, Polly's neck was harder to wring than the chickens that Sally killed for our Sunday dinner. After Sam had left her for dead, Polly got up, shook her ruffled feathers a few times, and walked back into the house saying over and over, "Sam wrung my neck." No one seemed to understand what Polly meant by this, so Sam wasn't punished. Clearly, he would have to find another, quieter way of getting rid of Polly. Sam really was a clever fellow. He took a needle and thread and, as Sally said, "sewed up Polly's hole so she couldn't make dudu." For days Polly kept repeating, "I'm all sewed up." But again no one knew what she meant, and so she finally died. I thought the moral of that story was, "You will die if you don't make dudu." Maybe, on the other hand, it was that you mustn't be a tattletale.

Sally was indeed a skilled neck wringer. I wouldn't have missed her weekly performance for anything in the world. She firmly grasped the squawking chicken's head with one hand; while the chicken kept flapping its wings, she flung its body in circles until the neck broke and all she had left in her hand was its head. The real show then began as the headless chicken started its macabre run around the yard. I was always terrified that in its aimless dashing about it might bump into me, so my usual vantage point was high up on the back steps of the house. This ritual continued as long as Sally was with us, and it never lost its fascination.

I did have more ladylike occupations. With needle and thread I made necklaces by stringing red berries that I gathered off asparagus ferns. I also made costumes from the leaves of the tulip tree that grew in Daddy Albright's front yard. Tulip tree leaves have a stiff stem. I just broke it off and used it to pin one leaf to another. I made hats and dresses—almost anything I wanted. When I was really lucky, I could get a grown-up to reach one of the yellow-and-orange blossoms from the higher branches. This added a fancy touch. There were wonderful magnolia trees around town that had large, white blossoms among their shiny, dark-green leaves. I was always hopeful that someone would climb up and get me one of those blossoms, but everyone refused saying the flower would turn black if I touched it. I doubted that this would happen, but I never found out. I never got close enough to touch one.

Turning black reminds me of the little Casey boy's story, which I heard from Sally. When he was only two years old, he bit into a green walnut, turned black, and died. That happened way before I was born. His sister Kathleen was even older than my sister Ray. Kathleen's mother had a nervous breakdown after little Jack died, and pretty soon she died too. Kathleen was raised by her grandmother and her father. Sally also told me that Daddy used to take Mrs. Casey out before he met Mother. I loved to speculate on who and where I would be if he had married her. Would I be me or would I have been Jack? Would I now be dead or would I now be a half orphan? Would Kathleen be my sister instead of Ray? These were weighty questions that I didn't dare ask anyone. I always ended up being glad I was me.

At a very early age, I, like most children, liked to look at myself in the mirror. I woud kiss the mirror and pat it, saying "pretty baby." This was frowned on. Vanity was not in line with the Puritan upbringing I was supposed to be getting. Yet I noticed that Mother would swell with pride when anyone admired her sewing.

Once I did carry my self-admiration too far. I climbed on top of Mother's dressing table and sat in the drawer where she kept her powder and rouge. With my legs folded, I fitted in comfortably. Loading my hair with all the hairpins I could find, I tried putting on some lipstick. Then came the powder. At this point Sally appeared in the doorway. She froze in her tracks because she was afraid she'd startle me and cause me to straighten out my legs. If I'd done that, there would have been a crash of drawer and me and powder. She softly crept up behind me, and I was rescued before I knew I was in danger. I suspect that Sally came to my rescue more than once, but she never made any fuss about the trouble I caused her. She would just say quietly, "Now we've got to get your face washed up before anyone sees you." How many spankings did this dear soul save me? It's hard to say.

One day I talked Sally into taking me to see where Daddy worked. I knew he ran a bank, but it was not the one where Daddy Albright took his money. Daddy's bank was the First National Bank of Batesville. Grandfather Adler had started it back in 1880. When he died in 1904, Daddy became the new president of the bank even though he was only twenty-three years old. I had never seen the inside of Daddy's bank, and I wanted to surprise him with a visit. When Sally took me to the back office where he was, I couldn't see him behind the high piles of money on his desk. With a pen and ink he was signing every one of the bills. At that time, national banks were allowed to issue money. A bank ordered the amount it wanted from the Treasury Department. The money was printed up and then signed by the bank president. After that visit, when anyone asked, "What does your daddy do?" My unvarying answer was, "He makes money." Freud would set this down to concrete thinking, but in this case it was literally true.

I knew there was a war going on somewhere because I heard Mother talk about certain men being called up to serve.

I wanted to know if Daddy was going to be called up to serve. He said he didn't think so because he had two children. I then heard of someone who had four children and had been sent off. I was a little ashamed that Daddy was staying home on my account, but of course I was glad he wasn't going away. I remember the day the war came to an end. All the whistles in town were blowing, and all the church bells were ringing. People were dashing around yelling, "They've signed, they've signed. The war's over." I wanted to know what they had signed. My vocabulary got its second big word when they told me it was the ARMISTICE. I really made hay with that one.

Meanwhile, I kept on going to Sunday school even if I had lost interest in rocking the cradle of baby Jesus once a year. The teacher told me a lot of other interesting and scary stories that kept me thinking about things all week until the next Sunday. She told about the two boys in the fiery furnace. That was enough to make me panic. She also said that a rich man could no more enter the gates of heaven than a camel could go through the eye of a needle. That worried me more than the fiery furnace. I felt we were rich. So now it no longer depended just on the black book of fibs. I was going to have to be poor besides. How could I fool the system? Maybe I could give away all my money just before I died. How would I know I was going to die? What if I gave away all of my money and then got well? Could I get my money back? These were problems I couldn't seem to solve, but I tried, oh how I tried.

I liked when Daddy carried me around on his shoulders and tossed me in the air or held me by the hands and swung me in circles. I thought he was the strongest man ever. At home he would take off the celluloid collar that he wore when he left for the bank. Sometimes on Sunday he wouldn't shave. I didn't like that because it would scratch when I kissed him. His eyes were a light blue and had a very alert expression. He always had a twinkle as though he were thinking of a funny joke.

Daddy used to sing me a song. I suppose it was one they

sang during the war. I liked the song and thought it was written for me because it had my name in it. It went "*Oui, Oui,* Marie. If you do this for me, then I'll do that for you. *Oui, Oui,* Marie." Of course I didn't know they had thrown in a French word, and I thought the song was telling me to weewee. It seemed strange to make up a song about that, but I liked Daddy to sing it to me anyway.

I had a mania for planting seeds at this age, and miraculously some of them actually grew. They were inspected at least forty times a day so I could see if any progress had been made since the last time. My beloved garden was two feet square and exposed. One day the lumberyard delivered some boards (again it was Mother's fault) to be used for shelves in the garage. Finding no better place to stack the lumber, the men unloaded it on top of my garden. On my next tour of inspection, I could neither find the garden nor move the boards to search for it. Sally came to the rescue when she heard my cries of distress. Since all the plants were crushed, I was not consoled until I could put in a new planting. It was not the last time in my life that I had to replant a crop, but that story comes twenty years later in Olathe, Kansas.

Our house was unusually well built, with very thick walls to keep it cool in summer and warm in winter. It was also the only one I have ever seen with a sandpile built into it. One corner of the house, about eight feet by eight feet, was marked off by a stone post. Above the sandpile and supported by the post was my father's den, forbidden territory for me. This peculiar design was carried out for the sole purpose of always having the sand dry. It was a miserable idea, and again I blamed my mother for thinking that dry sand was better than wet. There is absolutely nothing you can do with dry sand except put it through a sieve and pretend it is flour. I was not allowed to carry water in my sand buckets, so I was forced to be inventive. Simply put, to get wet sand I would weewee. Then I could build castles and make cakes.

One day I went to Daddy Albright's back yard stable and took an ear of corn away from the horses. When I had shelled the corn, the kernels made lovely decorations for the sand cakes. A few days later I was amazed to see that one of the kernels had begun to sprout. Here in this dry sandpile was a green blade of corn. This was to become my secret garden, nourished daily by my own private method.

When the stalk was as tall as I was, a great bustling about began and I learned we were going to move to Little Rock about a hundred miles away. Daddy would be president of the White Diamond Fertilizer Company. I knew about diamonds but not about fertilizer. I wasn't too keen on leaving Batesville, but no one really wanted to know how I felt about it. As long as Sally was coming with us, I guessed it would be all right. Daddy Albright promised to visit any time he could hitch a ride. He kept his promise, but it was not the same as having him next door.

I gave Daddy Albright lots of instruction on how he was to water the corn. Of course, I didn't tell him how I had done it, and I didn't expect him to use my technique. Weeks after we arrived in Little Rock, I had a letter from him saying he'd had a roasting ear from my plant that had tasted like no other he'd ever eaten. Could it be—? I promptly dictated a reply asking him to send me a quarter for the roasting ear. I was a bit ahead of inflation, setting such a high price, but only I knew the uniqueness of that corn—the very special care it had been given.

CHAPTER 3

Learning How

By the time we moved to Little Rock, I was four years old. The house we moved into was much smaller than the one my parents had built in Batesville. It was a white wooden house with a front porch that had a railing not far from the sidewalk. The back yard had a tall persimmon tree that bore lots of fruit in the fall. A few days after we moved in, two girls, who looked to be about Ray's age or a little older, came and stood fidgeting on the sidewalk, looking as if they wanted to say something. Each urged the other with pokes and nudges. I can't remember how we finally broke the ice, but we formed a friendship that has endured all our lives.

Jane, the elder, was seven years old and had long, stringy brown hair that was soon to turn into a mass of long curls by means of the newly invented permanent wave. Without telling any of us what she was going to do, she spent the whole day at a beauty parlor with electric clamps attached to her hair. When her head got too hot, the lady fanned her with a towel. Even though we envied the results, Ray and I decided it sounded much too dangerous. Besides, Mother declared it to be a vain thing to do at our age. (Jane wasn't vain at all.)

Jane's sister, Anne, had blond hair and very blue eyes and a husky build. Both Jane and Anne Cockrill were already in Pulaski Heights grammar school, two blocks away, so we could only play with them when school let out and on Saturdays and Sundays. It didn't take long for them to invite us to the Episcopal Sunday School.

A few weeks after we started, the lesson was about Jesus Christ dying on the cross, crucified, according to our teacher, by the Jews. I made a big scene about that and said I was very sure the Jews hadn't done it because my father, who was a Jew, wouldn't think of doing anything so terrible. Nevertheless, I promised to tell my father what the teacher had said and to get the whole thing straightened out by the following Sunday. We didn't talk about it on the way home, nor did I get up my courage at the Sunday dinner table.

That afternoon we went for one of our long drives and, after thinking it over, I finally said, "Daddy, do you believe in Jesus Christ?"

He said, "I think he was a very fine man."

I was willing to settle for this answer, and the subject never came up again between us. Neither of us was particularly comfortable in talking about it. However, it came up with the children who lived next door to us. We had never played with them, but one day they started to chant a ditty, "Jew baby, Jew baby, sitting on the fence, trying to make a dollar out of fifteen cents." I ran into the house to report to Mother. She immediately dubbed them "white trash" and said we were to stay out of the yard on that side of the house. I began to sense that there was something unusual in a marriage between an Episcopalian and a Jew. In Batesville I had never heard anyone talk about differences between the two religions. I knew that Daddy never went to church, but neither did Daddy Albright or Uncle Billy. Maybe this was something women liked better than men did.

Next to the other side yard was a very big house with a glassed-in porch. Tied in a wheelchair on this porch was a grown man who couldn't talk; he made gurgling noises like a baby. In fact, he couldn't hold his head up, and it bobbed around. He had to wear a bib because he drooled. I didn't want to see or hear him, so when Jane and Anne came to visit we always played indoors.

I felt so privileged to be allowed to play with the older kids that I would do almost anything they said. I played at things I didn't really enjoy just to be part of the group. Since Mother liked to sew, she had a lot of pattern books showing the fashions for women and children. With very dull, blunt-ended scissors, we cut out these people and played with them as if they were dolls. We had whole families except for the daddies. In those days there were no male models, at least not in Mother's pattern books. The daddies in our games had always gone to work.

When anyone got an idea, she would say, "Let's play like . . ." This was usually shortened to, "Plike." Because it was so hard to follow the lines in cutting, my collection of paper dolls was very mutilated. Some were missing noses, and others had a shortage of fingers like Uncle Billy. Each player kept her collection in an old magazine. Several times I was caught making an unauthorized swap of dolls with Ray's collection.

Mostly, I behaved pretty well, for me. I knew that Ray had only to call out, "Marie is bothering us!" and I would be forcibly removed from the game without benefit of trial, jury, or witnesses. I didn't even like paper dolls, but I didn't want to be left out. The worst was when someone said, "Plike we are movie stars. I'll be Bebe Daniels and you be Ben Lyon." The others fed me lines to say, and I would always change the lines. I don't know if I changed the lines because I couldn't remember them or because I was just stubborn enough not to want anyone to tell me what to say.

I often had fallings out with Mother about saying what I was told. When we were invited to birthday parties, Mother liked to have a rehearsal of what we intended to say to the hostess when we left the party. First, she told me what to say. Then she asked me what I was going to say. I would answer, "I'll say what you said to say."

She would insist, "That's not good enough. I want to hear you say it. Now, what are you going to say?"

By that time, neither of us was about to give in. These sessions could go on a long time with threats that I couldn't go to the party at all if I wouldn't say my piece. I don't remember ever being kept home, but I do remember leaving the house with red, swollen eyes. On the other hand, Ray was very good about reciting what she was going to say.

For her sixth birthday, Ray was given a bicycle. I knew it was a sin to covet, but oh how I envied her that bicycle. Not only did she have a two-wheeler, but she had hours of Daddy's time on Saturdays. He ran up and down the block holding her onto the seat. Finally, when he thought she was getting the hang of it, he only held on to the back fender to help her balance. It didn't work. The minute he took his hand off the fender and yelled, "Keep going!" Ray would fall off. I was always on hand to tell her what she had done wrong.

Secretly, I began to take Ray's bicycle out and practice on it. At first, I sat on the bar and pushed as though it were a kiddie car. That way I got a feeling for its size and weight. Finally, I started trying to stand up and jump on the pedals while it was in motion. My struggles were many, but at last I did it.

When the next Saturday rolled around, I took up my usual post and function as Ray's uninvited coach. I must have been more insistent than ever because Daddy finally said, "You think it's so easy. Let's see you try it." This was just the invitation I wanted. I hopped on the bike and rode to the end of the block, got off, turned around and rode back to where Ray and Daddy were standing.

Instead of the expected praise, I got a terrible scolding from Daddy. He said, "You only did that to show up your sister, and I don't think it was nice of you." In spite of what he said, I think he was proud of me and also relieved that he wasn't going to have to struggle with me as he had with Ray. At least I was proud of myself and glad I had hung in there until I taught myself to ride. The pleasure of teaching myself to do things has stayed with me. I always seem to do better when there is no one around to know of my mistakes and struggles.

Like so many older sisters, Ray took pleasure in telling me that I was adopted. I still don't understand why I let her get to me in the way she did, because Sally had continued to tell me about how she had brought me into this world unassisted by a doctor. Maybe Ray was touching a sore nerve, because I did have fantasies about getting myself adopted in the future.

These fantasies came to me when I thought life was particularly cruel, and they always comforted me. In my daydream I would be standing halfway up the front steps of our church, dressed in my best Sunday school clothes, when, low and behold, along would come Mary Pickford and her husband Douglas Fairbanks. They were immediately struck by my charm and would remark to each other that they had never seen such an adorable child. They would ask me if I would like to live with them. Then each would take hold of one of my hands, and together they would lead me gently away as I glanced over my shoulder to watch Ray's mouth fly open. End of fantasy. It had everything!

At age five I had too many colds. Someone decided that my tonsils must come out. For once I was going to have something ahead of Ray; this time I was going to be FIRST. In those days, you were given ether through a mask that covered your nose and mouth. Going to sleep was a rather long, drawn-out time filled with scary dreams. In mine appeared the guardian angels that I had always mentioned in my prayers—you know the one—"two at my head and two at my feet to guard me while I sleep." I also had time to recall the prayer that always gave me nightmares, and no wonder: "Now I lay me down to sleep, I pray the Lord my soul to keep. If I should die before I wake, I pray the Lord my soul to take." How's that for a way to develop a world of insomniacs, people who are *afraid* to go to sleep. In this case, the ether had its way, and I did wake up—with the worst sore throat of my life.

Even the ice cream they offered me didn't really taste good, but it was lovely to have Mother's undivided attention. I do believe I deliberately stretched out my recovery in order to have her sit there and spoon-feed me.

When I had fully recovered, I was to suffer one of the worst embarrassments of my life. Ray was by now almost eight years old and went to school all day. She wanted to take her lunch like the other kids. Since we lived only two blocks away, Mother wanted her to come home for a hot lunch. I was sacrificed at the altar of compromise. I had to take her a hot lunch on a small tray, and she and her friends would sit on a big boulder, across the street from school, and eat. I wasn't allowed to sit down with them or join their chatter; I had to stand there like a deaf-mute with my hands in my pockets. I only submitted to this treatment a couple of times before rebelling so loudly and so effectively that Ray was allowed to brown-bag her peanut butter sandwich from then on.

Near where I had stood guard for Ray's lunches, the telephone men had been working, putting in poles. Sometimes they had to go through hard rock to make a place for the telephone pole. It was great fun to rummage around where they had been digging. I could always find wonderful crystals. My pockets bulged with these treasures. Other finds were copper wires twisted around with different-colored papers. These were perfect for making Indian bead rings. When mother didn't act quickly enough in buying colored beads, I would use beads from my secret source, our huge brass lamp from Constantinople. Its shade had a long bead fringe; a few strings from the fringe would never be missed. The only trouble was that they were all the same, a kind of sand-color glass, so the rings I made in hiding were not at all pretty and were certainly not worth the risk.

One Saturday night in June, Jane and Anne invited Ray and me to spend the night. It was our first "sleep over." Such excitement—to be packing a sack with our nighties. The next morning, quite early, Sally trudged over and said we were to come with her. She had a surprise for us at home. I told her she had wasted her time because Jane and Anne had the Sunday funny papers at their house too. Sally was very mysterious. Her surprise had nothing to do with the funnies, she said, and we must hurry because she couldn't stay away too long. She had a lot to do. There wasn't even time for us to get fully dressed. The weather was warm, so we just carried our shoes and socks and dresses across the street and down the block.

At home we were told to tiptoe upstairs to Mother and Daddy's room. There was "Junior," sleeping in a very fancy, ribbon-covered basket. I have to admit that with all my nosiness I had not had an inkling of this bomb that was going to be dropped on me. They had really pulled a fast one that time. Ray, too, was completely taken by surprise, and she was already eight years old. Even Jane and Anne didn't know a thing about what had happened or why. I know they didn't know, because when I was ten years old their sister-in-law Helen was looking so big in the belly that all of us noticed it. They told me she was going to have a baby in nine months. Well, that was the shortest nine months I ever spent, because inside of a week Jane and Anne told me they had a nephew named Sterling, after his father, and nicknamed "Ter-Ter." So, none of us had it straight yet.

When Junior was born, there must have been some talk about babies growing from seeds. I began to worry when I accidentally swallowed a seed of any kind. The worst seeds to let slip down your throat were watermelon. Suppose they grew inside you? How would they get our? Persimmon seeds were also very slippery, but since they were larger they didn't go down as easily. Even if they grew inside, it wouldn't be as big a deal as a watermelon. I wonder if I could have been spared some agonies had I felt free to ask all of the questions I would have liked to ask instead of being left to make up my own "scientific" theories. Having been labeled nosy at a very early age, though, I felt I should ask only what I absolutely had to know.

A few days after Nathan, Jr., was born, I walked in on Mother and Daddy in the living room. Junior was on Mother's lap with his diaper off, and I saw for the first time the difference between boys and girls. He was a bloody mess. They had just come from the doctor's office and were changing his bandage. I was thrown out of there without ceremony, but not before I had seen enough to make me happy that I wasn't a boy after all. I think I had already given up trying to kiss my elbow.

I was carefully told about the soft spot on the top of every baby's head and how dangerous it was ever to touch it. You could kill a baby just by a touch. Wow, what a thing to tell a kid like me. I thought often of the soft spot on Ray's favorite doll, the one I had examined so carefully.

I slipped unobserved in and out of the room where Junior slept in such innocence not knowing that the guardian angel at his head was in truth a little devil with not too well thought-out ideas of just lightly touching that spot to see what would happen. I don't know what stayed my hand, except that I had begun to grow a little fond of Junior. Jane and Anne always seemed to arrive on the scene just after Junior had pooped in his pants. Since they were so clever at nicknames, Junior became known to us all as "Smelly Boy."

CHAPTER 4

School and New Adventures

In October of 1921, the year Junior was born, it was finally time for me to go to school. I had been in a private kindergarten for a short time where we sang songs and acted them out. One of the songs was about a farmer scratching in the dirt. My acting was overzealous in that song, and I got a splinter under my fingernail. I had to be sent home so Mother could operate on it. After that, having decided I wasn't learning anything worthwhile, Mother kept me home.

My big daily event had been accompanying Sally when she wheeled Junior in his buggy, but that was abandoned when I marched off proudly to Pulaski Heights School to become educated. There was one small problem. On the corner of our block lived a very playful, large, bouncy puppy named Rags. He was delighted to see me every day because I ran past his house as fast as I could. To him this was a signal for a race. Mother had succeeded after all in transmitting her fear of dogs to me.

The schoolhouse was only six rooms built around a hall in the middle. You had to climb a long outer staircase to reach the front doors. One day when I arrived, all the children had disappeared from the playground, and I thought the bell had rung. Then I saw one of the teachers beckoning me to hurry inside. I was so relieved to find I wasn't late that I only half listened to the story of why everyone had been herded indoors. It seems a convict had escaped from the penitentiary a couple of miles away and had been seen in the woods behind the school. The only thing I learned that day was that grown-ups can be just as scared as kids. My teacher stayed at the window all afternoon except when she stepped into the hall to talk in a low whisper to one of the other teachers. At last, they told us the police had found the convict and taken him back where he belonged. All of us were sent home early in case our parents had heard the news. I don't know how they would have, because there weren't any radios in those days. I knew the police could always find escaped convicts because they wore coveralls made of wide black-and-white stripes so that people could spot them and report where they had been seen.

Mrs. Harris, my first-grade teacher, was determined to teach us to sit still. There were exercises for this. You sat with your hands folded on top of the desk and your feet firmly planted on the floor. Squirming, crossing the legs, rolling a pencil, and testing your teeth by biting holes in the pencils were forbidden. Breathing was allowed.

The punishment for not folding your hands properly was being put under the teacher's desk. Every so often, she would walk past and swing at you carelessly with a yardstick without looking. I was very quick at learning how to dodge these whacks. One day Mother came to visit my class. She poked her head in the door and looked around. Not seeing me, she was about to retreat when Mrs. Harris asked if she was looking for someone. Mother gave my name. Mrs. Harris ever so gently reached under her desk and helped me out, explaining to my mother that we had been playing a game of hide-and-seek and that I had been hiding. I hoped that God had his black book out and had written that one down against Mrs. Harris. I must admit that I didn't bother to tell Mother the reason I was "hiding."

A few days later, I was told that I was to be skipped from 1B to 1A. No explanations given, none asked. As usual, I tried to figure it out for myself. Maybe Mrs. Harris couldn't stand having me in her class and had given me to someone else to teach. To this day, I don't really know why I was skipped. Although I like to think it was because I was ahead of the others, there is still the nagging thought that it was because I was "bad."

In my new class I learned that if I wanted to go to the bathroom I had to hold up my hand for permission to leave the room. That was okay with me, but I drew the line at indicating what I intended to do when I got to the toilet. We were supposed to hold up one finger or two to indicate what business we had in mind. Whose business was it anyway? After a short time, I found that this was not worth a rebellion because when I held up my hand without giving the proper code I ended up being questioned out loud in front of the whole class. I learned to compromise and bend to the rules. Maybe I also bent the rules and didn't give the right hand signals, but who was to know? After first grade, I set aside the childish words for the body functions and they were thenceforth replaced by number one and number two.

I suppose I was learning to read at the same time as I was upgrading my vocabulary, but I don't remember much about it except a book about a boy and girl and a dog named Spot. One of the lines in the book said, "Run, Spot. Run." That reminded me of my daily chase with Rags.

I must already have been absentminded, because one day at recess, I just wandered off from school and went home. When Mother caught sight of me, she screamed. "*What* are you doing here?"

That brought me around. I rather feebly replied that I had come for lunch.

"Well," she said, "you just march yourself right back to school, and don't you come home until noon."

I'm sure Freud would have made a whole deal out of this, but I think it was mostly likely that I was hungry. Since I got back in time, my teacher never knew I was missing. Not only was Mother annoyed at my coming home in mid-morning, but she was probably a little frightened by it too.

There was considerable excitement in the neighborhood

when a house on the block behind ours was robbed while the people who lived there were at the movies. All the kids seemed to know or invent the details of the robbery. It seems that one robber stood outside as a "lookout"; he whistled signals to the robber inside the house to let him know if there was danger of getting caught.

After this I lay in bed night after night thinking I could hear the robbers in search of another house to rob. I slept on a screened-in sleeping porch and could hear noises from all directions. You've no idea how many people whistle at night. Maybe that's where the expression "whistling in the dark" comes from.

No matter how cold it got on the sleeping porch, I was never allowed to put my hands under the covers. Mother patrolled regularly during the night to make sure my hands were above the covers. Sometimes she went so far as to sniff my fingers to see if I had been so sneaky as to touch myself. I soon learned to sniff my fingers myself and then rub them vigorously on the sheets to get rid of any telltale odors. Between Mother and me there was always an undeclared war that was likely to break out at any minute if I even looked as though I might step over her invisible line. Only she knew where that line was drawn. Mother's reason, she said, for being so strict about touching myself was that she firmly believed this could cause you to go crazy later in life.

Jane and Anne Cockrill had four older brothers, some of whom had already married and lived in their own houses. They also had lots of cousins, both old and young. Their mother, Miss Jenny, seemed to manage her household from her huge four-poster bed. She often stayed in bed the whole day and read. She wasn't trying to get away from it all, because she loved to have everyone play in her room. We were allowed to play "dress up lady," which meant we could invade her closet and wear her shoes and hats and gloves.

My favorite thing to wear was a telephone shade. Telephones were still upright models, and they were hidden by fancy standing screens covered with gold lace and ribbons. Every self-respecting church sewing circle specialized in making these shades, but my use for Miss Jenny's telephone screen was to put it in front of my waist and pretend I was Queen Elizabeth. The heavy wires in the screen held it like the stays in a corset. Don't ask me how I knew about Queen Elizabeth. I had also heard of a queen named Marie Antoinette, and I liked to think I had been named for her until I learned that she had had her head cut off. Then I was willing to admit that I had been named for my mother's mother, who was called Maria. I didn't much like that name because the police wagon that came to make arrests, at that time, was called a "black Maria."

Jane and Anne's house was huge and built after the Civil War. All the rooms were enormous, and there were large central halls both upstairs and downstairs. Sometimes when we went to visit, we found the upstairs piled to the ceiling with furniture. Whenever this happened we would respectfully ask, "Who died?" Usually, it was some distant relative who had left her furniture to Mrs. Cockrill. A few weeks later we would arrive to find that all the furniture had disappeared. Then we would cheerfully ask, "Who got married?" The Cockrills never had to buy furniture because their inexhaustible supply of relatives left them their treasured possessions, knowing they would be handed down in the family.

It was hard to see how all these arrangement could be made from Miss Jenny's bed, but they were. When spring arrived, Miss Jenny would tell Jane and Anne to gather their friends together because she was going to get out of bed and take us all for a walk in the woods. She promised a prize to the one who found the most "velvets." Hunting for velvets is like hunting for four-leaf clovers. A velvet is a wild violet that has two very dark petals at the top; the other three petals are a much lighter purple.

The hunt itself was exciting, but the real treat came when Miss Jenny said it was time to go wake up Old King. She would lead us to a special hole in the ground. Sometimes we had to scratch away the leaves that covered it all winter. Miss Jenny would then tap on her hand near the hole and start talking to Old King, telling him that spring was here and that he should come out now. He must have known her voice and been waiting for her because soon this three-foot-long king snake would come sleepily out into the sunlight. He would stretch himself out to his full length and then curl himself back up again to enjoy the first light he'd had in a long time. He acted as if he wanted to keep on with his winter snooze. We were told not to frighten him, so we waved a timid good-bye and followed Miss Jenny to find wildflower plants to put into her rock garden. After we'd planted them all, each of us got a nickel as a prize. Miss Jenny could never choose just one winner. Having done her duty of waking up Old King, Miss Jenny could happily return to her own bed.

Jane and Anne loved to eat at our house because Sally made them a very special dish. With their talent for name giving, they called this dish the Ray-Marie steak. I was appointed to spy on Sally to see how she made it. She would gladly have told me had I asked, but it was much more fun to play spy. The recipe was very simple: She just ground up lots of meat (she even let me crank the meat grinder), then added salt and pepper and lots of cream. She had to mix it with her hands because that was the only way the meat could be made to take up the cream. After that she got the skillet piping hot and spread the whole glob of meat over the bottom of the pan. The real trick was to know when to turn it over and how to turn it without letting it break. When it was nice and brown on both sides, she put it on the table whole—like a pie—and cut it into pieces. I passed on this state secret to Jane and Anne, who in turn passed it on to their cook. Because she never had a success that pleased them, they thought I had left out something. So I might have. Even I have never been able to duplicate this simple delicacy.

In 1922, the second summer after Junior was born, we moved to another, larger house at the top of a hill on the other side of town. At the foot of the hill was a wide street that formed a boundary. On the other side was a colored part of town. From the top of the hill, the houses looked small and poorly built. There was usually smoke coming out of their chimneys in summer as well as in winter. They still cooked with wood or coal stoves. We were forbidden to go to the foot of the hill and certainly we couldn't cross that street.

In the fall we enrolled in the Mitchell school, which was about four times as big as the Pulaski Heights school. My first day in second grade, I fell madly in love with Edwin Dunaway. He was a chubby fellow with wonderful brown eyes. He had the tiniest of speech impediments that fascinated me, though he was probably not even aware of it. That night at the dinner table I talked of nothing but Edwin. I couldn't remember my new teacher's name, but I could already spell Dunaway and I knew where he lived because I had followed him home. Daddy remarked that Edwin must be the son of a man he knew named M. E., with whom he had done business. Anxious to glean any information I could about my new beau (who didn't know of his role), I asked Daddy what M. E. stood for. He calmly answered, "Maude Elizabeth." I explained that I wanted to know his father's name, not his mother's. Daddy assured me that this was his father's name. His parents had chosen it because they were hoping to have a girl. When a boy was born to them, they just used the name anyway. It had been a great embarrassment to him all his life, and some said it had affected his character. I never met him, so I couldn't judge.

I made some slight progress with Edwin. At least I got to the point of having him slow down to walk home with me; that is, he let me walk with him as far as his house, but he never walked an extra step in the direction of my house. This went on for the two years that I attended the Mitchell school.

I made friends with a girl six months older than I, who lived in our block. Digie, short for Virginia, had been taking piano lessons for two years and could play real tunes. I was so thrilled to have a talented friend that I wanted to start right away and learn to play like Digie. Alas, Mother was right when she went around moaning to herself, "That child doesn't have a talent to her name." If she was referring to my piano playing, she was accurate. She also was heard to mutter under her breath, "That Marie couldn't carry a tune in a basket." Was I really such a hopeless case?

The wonderful thing I learned in third grade from the kids at school was pig latin. This was a secret language you used when you didn't want grown-ups or younger kids to understand what you were saying. Of course, to learn this language you had to know the difference between a vowel and a consonant. Although Daddy also knew how to speak this secret language, at least Junior didn't understand it. Actually Junior didn't even understand straight English, though by our second summer in the new house, he was beginning to catch on to some things. I worked hard to teach him to walk, but he was a terrible coward. He was okay as long as I let him hold my hand. I reduced his grip to one finger, and he did just fine; than I held one end of a flimsy, thin switch, and he navigated all right; finally I turned loose my end of the switch ever so gently. Down he went on the sidewalk with a thud, a loud holler, and many tears. Mother was out of the house in seconds with her usual, "What have you done to him now? I can't even trust you for one minute. Did you push him down? Poor little fellow, it's no wonder he can't learn to walk with you knocking him over all the time." There was nothing I could say to defend myself. I had already been tried and judged and found guilty.

I was, of course, capable of these crimes, but I wouldn't inflict them on Junior. I was trying to bring him up to be strong and a fighter so he could do all the things forbidden to me as a girl. I wanted to help him grow up fast and not be a crybaby. I had, by this time trained myself never to cry, and I wanted to train him too. So far he had not been a very good pupil.

Digie and I now became such close friends that a couple of our dresses were even alike. We made early morning phone calls to decide which dress we would wear that day. There were times when tragedy struck and the dress we had agreed to wear was not yet washed and ironed, which meant more anguished phone calls. Ironically, I had detested Mother's insistence on always dressing Ray and me like twins.

I discovered playing doctor. I didn't get to play very often because something usually went wrong. There was the time

Digie was the patient and I was going to operate. First I had to give her the anesthetic. I remembered how they did it when I had my tonsils out, so I carefully put a handkerchief over her nose and told her to hold her head back. I then took Mother's bottle of perfume and started to pour it drop by drop onto the handkerchief. My hand wasn't steady, and I didn't exactly pour it drop by drop. Suddenly, Digie jumped off her stretcher and started screaming that I had poured the perfume down her nose. She was out the front door in no time flat, leaving me holding the bottle of evidence. She naturally refused to play that game with me again. So I became a doctor without patients. I did have a lot of fantasies about that time of boys bandaged from head to foot. I was always their gentle nurse. I'm not sure what part of my perverse nature those particular fantasies satisfied, but they were repeat numbers.

Digie's older brother, Billy, had a friend named J. B. (I no longer asked what initials meant.) Billy and J. B. each owned a horse; they kept them in stables attached to their garages. After dark they would dress themselves and their horses in long, white sheets. They rode slowly down the hill, crossed the street, and whipped their horses into a fast gallop as they rode through the colored town letting out Indian war cries. When they got back to the stables, the horses and the boys were in a lather of sweat. I'm sure the boys were more frightened than their intended victims. I don't think they ever did any real harm, though it was clear they were imitating the Ku Klux Klan. When Sally heard about one of those night rides she would say, "Those younguns are looking to get theirselves kilt."

There were four wonderful things about summer. First was lemonade and having a stand where we sold our cool drink. This was in the days before paper cups, so whenever we had the luck to snare a passerby, we had to take the empty glass inside the house and ask Sally to wash it for us. She was often too busy to mess with us, and we were told to find something else to do. On rare occasions we were allowed to make fudge, divinity, or taffy. None of these items was ever sold. They were consumed by the chefs before they could hit the market.

The second wonderful thing about summer was when it rained. We could put on our bathing suits, take an umbrella, go out in the yard, and stand in the rain. Since Mother was mortally afraid of storms, it seems strange that she allowed us to do this. She wouldn't even sew when it rained for fear that her steel needle would draw lightning and knock her dead. I can't imagine why she encouraged this particular pastime. I was so happy that I never questioned her motive, conscious or unconscious, at the time. I still like to walk in a summer rain.

The third wonderful thing was to go swimming in a small lake. This outing took place only about twice a year. There was not much time to learn to swim, but I managed somehow to tread water and thrash around and make enough of a splash to thoroughly annoy Ray. She was so busy covering her face, to protect it from the water I churned up, that she had no time to practice trying to stay afloat. I personally thought she was a natural-born sinker and that I was a natural-born floater. I don't know where I got ideas like that, but they made me feel good. Maybe I had some talent after all?

The word talent really confused me. In Sunday school I heard a story about two brothers who were each given ten talents. One brother buried his talents, and the other brother spent his. I don't remember what else happened, but there was some kind of moral about not burying your talents because then they wouldn't grow. Since I had none anyway, I guessed I didn't need to worry. Much later I heard about girls who had hidden talents. The boys used to snicker about them, but they refused to tell me what a hidden talent was.

The fourth delight on summer evenings was to stay up late enough for it to grow dark. Armed with mason jars we would catch fireflies in the yard. They were easy to find because they kept blinking their lights on and off, but they were hard to catch because by the time you ran to where one had flickered last, it had gone somewhere else. A really successful hunt might yield as many as a hundred in a jar. They kept on blinking in the jar, but gradually they weakened until their lights went out altogether.

Junior didn't know any more about gravity than I had known at his age when I went down the stairs in my walker. He would crawl right to the edge of the stairs, and you'd better be there to grab him by the seat of his pants or over he'd go. One day he was rocking peacefully in his little wicker rocking chair when he got a sudden notion to stand up in it backwards. The tilt went against him, and his chair went over. The chair was okay, but Junior's tongue was split down the middle. I had never seen so much blood, not even at a chicken neck wringing. Mother was so excited she even forgot to blame me for not watching him until after they got back from the doctor's. Then I caught it. All the time they were gone I wandered around the house reciting the old nursery jingle "Tattletale tit, your tongue will split, and all the dogs in town will have a bite of it." I was always good at picking the appropriate quote from my limited repertoire.

When I was in the third grade, Mother was asked to take part in a charity drive. My thinking was still pretty concrete at that time, so I thought she was going for a long drive somewhere and would be gone for a week. I was already making plans for my week of liberty when I learned that she was just going to go from house to house, calling on people on her list to ask for contributions to charity. Every night she told us about the houses and the people. She was almost always critical. Either their houses were messy, or she thought they were very stingy for such rich people. The stories of her charity drive amused me, but I resented that she no longer had time to think about what I should have for lunch. In the morning, when Sally asked her what to prepare, she would say, absentmindedly, "Give them some baked beans." By the time the drive ended, I was on the verge of explosion. I told her never to volunteer again because I didn't think I could go through another of her tours of duty. In this case, I recited the appropriate ditty of the day in front of her, and since she was the guilty one in this case she couldn't scold me.

"Beans, beans, the musical fruit. The more you eat the more you poot."

One night, everyone was awakened by a loud crashing noise downstairs. Mother didn't want Daddy to investigate for fear he would come face to face with the burglar. They decided to phone the police. At least the phone lines hadn't been cut. We all huddled in one room with the door locked. Daddy mustered the courage to let them in. He seemed calm enough, but a few seconds after he left us there was another big crash. We were all sure he had been attacked. It was a long time before he came back upstairs and assured us that he was okay. Mother had to drag the details out of him. The police thought a mouse was the culprit because there was a broken peanut butter jar on the marble counter in the kitchen. That had been the first crash. Then when Daddy went downstairs, Napoleon's white bisque statue on a rearing horse had gotten right in front of him and had been smashed to smithereens. Never had Napoleon met with such total defeat.

I was still determined to teach Junior to walk "lonie lonie," but he was still resisting, and we practiced on the grass. I had slipped off my shoes—strictly forbidden, but it was great to feel the grass on my bare feet. Suddenly under my foot I felt something I couldn't possibly describe. There was a slight peep, and I looked down to see, to my horror, a bald-headed, pop-eyed baby bird that had fallen from its nest. My end of the switch "fell to earth I know not where," and I was around the corner on the double. Junior was absolutely alone to walk or sit, as he chose. He decided to run too. This accident served two purposes. Junior learned to walk, and I learned to keep my shoes on.

I didn't dare sneeze around Mother, or she would whip out her cold prevention formula. Someone had given Daddy a whole case of whiskey that was already old before the World War. To prevent or cure a cold, I had to take whiskey mixed with crystal rock candy. I loved the candy and hated the whiskey, but they definitely had to be mixed in order to work their magic. I used to get into the candy between sneezes, so it sometimes happened that I sneezed and mother went to the cupboard and found it bare. How could she hit a sick child? She could, that's all.

My day always included a maternal working over. If it came early, I was relatively safe for the rest of the day. If it didn't, it hung over me, and I kept wondering when I would do something to tip her scales. Sometimes I deliberately tried to annoy her so we could have done with it for the day. At least she never threatened to get Daddy to do her dirty work. I think she knew that he would not be her second in this duel of wills. On his own, however, Daddy was quite capable of spanking me. I know because he did it twice. One Sunday morning, I had been told several times to take off my Sunday clothes when I returned from Sunday School. I had ignored these orders from Mother. Sally was also distressed with me. I kept poking my finger into whatever she was cooking, and she was trying to get ready for Sunday dinner which was served at noon. She had called upstairs to say that dinner would be late if they didn't keep me out of "her" kitchen. I hadn't known Daddy could run so fast. He surged up in front of me, bedroom slipper in hand, and gave me a few smacks across the backside. He hurt my feelings much more than my rear. How could he too turn against me for such a small thing?

The other whipping had been when we still lived in Batesville. I had hidden when it was time to say good-bye to him and Mother as they left for the picture show. He explained later that he'd punished me not because I hid but because of *where* I hid. We had a nine-and-a-half-foot grandfather clock with a glass door, and I sat—folded double—on the floor of the clock, underneath the pendulum and the three brass weights. They hadn't found me until I stood up and set off the chimes (they bumped into each other and made a terrible clatter). Daddy stayed calm until he had me safely out from under the weights. Then he taught me a lesson. At least he was honest about it and didn't say it was hurting him more than me. That was Mother's line.

We had lived in the house on the hill for nearly two years when Mother and Daddy bought a lot out in Pulaski Heights.

Jane and Anne Cockrill had been giving us the news about the school there when we saw them each Sunday. We knew that our old grammar school had been replaced with a brand-new, larger building because so many people were moving to the Heights.

The lot on which my parents were going to build our new house was full of lovely trees. Mother and Daddy went to visit the lot one day, carefully marked a couple of scrub oaks that they didn't like, and ordered the contractor to cut them down. A few days later, for the first time in my life, I felt sorry for Mother. She had visited the lot again and had discovered that the only trees left in the front yard were the two that she had marked for destruction. All the really pretty trees were cut down by mistake, and Mother was in tears. I wanted to comfort her, but I didn't know how.

CHAPTER 5

Back to the Heights

Mother was deeply involved in designing the new house. Evidently, Daddy had been in charge of building the house in Batesville, and he had hired the best architect from Little Rock to design it. Just a few years ago the Batesville house was put on the National Register—not because my father had lived there, not because I was born there, but because Daddy had had the good sense to hire Mr. Charlie Thompson's firm as architects. Maybe they liked the built-in sandpile better than I did.

Now, Mother wanted to have a go at it herself. She had seen a house that she liked when she visited Aunt Ray in Kansas City. Somehow, she arranged to buy the blueprints of this house from the owners. Her Scottish blood was showing. She was delighted to be saving so much money by not having an architect. It was a red brick colonial house with a center hall and a graceful stairway that had windows at the top of the landing. There were three bedrooms and two sleeping porches, one glass-enclosed and the other just screened with pull-down awnings in case a storm came up during the night.

This was an era when there was a fetish about fresh air. It took a long time to get dressed for bed, what with nightcaps and night socks and flannel gowns and hot-water bottles to warm the sheets before we could get between them. There were plenty of nights when I never uncurled from the fetal positon; if I straightened out, I would have touched cold spots in the sheets and could not have gone back to sleep.

Daddy kept trying to get Mother to plan a second bathroom, but she was certain that one bath upstairs and a half bath downstairs would be enough. She was dead wrong, but she never admitted it. There wasn't enough heat in the downstairs toilet. It was as cold as an outhouse on a farm. None of us would go there except under direst necessity.

When we moved into the house, I was nine years old and ready to go into the upper half of third grade. I was surprised at how few kids I knew in the school. After all, I had only been away from Pulaski Heights two years. This was time enough for the old six-room grammar school to be torn down and replaced by a much larger building. There had been a great movement to the Heights, so there were very few old-timers mixed in with all the newcomers. I was more comfortable with my old friends Jane and Anne, but they were miles ahead of me in school, and I was forced to make new friends in my own class. After a couple of weeks, we elected class officers. A boy who'd had his eye on me proposed me for president. Another boy, not to be outdone by his rival, seconded the nomination. There was so much snickering that no one thought to mention any other name, and I was unanimously elected to office. I think the election was held as a lesson in democracy because it didn't seem to serve any other purpose. I never had any duties as president, though once the teacher put me in charge when she had to leave the room. That was it.

We began to study geography, and everyone was told to find out where their ancestors had lived before they came to America. My classmates mostly came from just one country. I was proud that I could name four places of origin. I told them that I was Scottish, Irish, German, and Jewish. Ray and I had a big argument about this. She said Jewish wasn't a place, but I stuck to my guns. I knew it was a place because Moses had taken the Jews there. Ray was already showing signs of not wanting to be Jewish. I told her I guessed I had gotten all the Jewish blood and she could say whatever she wanted in her class. In my class I would be what I wanted to be. My ideas were fuzzy, but I had a great fondness for Grandmother Adler and Aunt Ray and Uncle Arthur; I wanted to claim kinship to them in my geography class. All we did was stand up and recite while the teacher found the places on a big map. She didn't have any trouble finding where Jewish was; it was just as I'd said, where Moses took the Jews.

We learned long multiplication and long division. One weekend we drove up to Batesville to vist Daddy Albright and so Daddy could see the man who was farming the Ramsey Bottoms place. On the way, I asked Daddy how many city blocks there were to a mile. I also asked him how many miles were left before Batesville. He said there were sixteen blocks to the mile and that we still had seventy-five more miles to drive. For the next ten minutes I was very busy multiplying these two numbers in my head and writing with my finger in the air. Finally, I announced that we were twelve hundred blocks from Batesville. Daddy said, "Yeah, that's right."

How did Daddy know that my answer was right? It had taken me so long to figure it out, and he had checked my answer in less than a second. I thought he must know some shortcut or trick that they hadn't taught in school. What was the trick? Daddy was very patient in explaining that seventy-five was the same as three-quarters and that sixteen was really four times four. To get the answer, you just multiplied three times four and added a couple of zeros. The rest of the seventy-five miles were spent in mulling over the lesson he had just given me in fractions. It's good he gave me that lesson. It is the only one I ever had on fractions because the teachers decided to skip me again, and the fourth grade was where they taught fractions and percentages. I thought I was very lucky to have a Daddy who knew shortcuts and tricks. Look at how fast you could do problems this way in your head. I was not as generous as he was; I never would tell my teachers or any of the kids how I did arithmetic without a pencil. They might have been able to use the tricks against me in the contests we were always having.

Once we were asked to find out what work our fathers did. No one's mother worked in those days, so they only asked about the fathers. Daddy had resigned the presidency of the bank in Batesville to become president of the White Diamond Fertilizer Company in Little Rock. When I attempted my assignment of interviewing him about his job, though, he was most uncooperative and told me to say he was a rakeman. He probably thought I was preparing to brag in front of the class. Both he and Mother were big on not showing off. Mother even carried modesty to the extent of wearing her diamond ring with the stone turned in to the palm of her hand so no one could see it. The logic of this baffled me and still does. Of course I didn't tell the class that Daddy was anything less than the president of his company.

When my teacher heard about fertilizer, she wanted me to bring her some for her collection of plants. She thought it would do them a world of good. I approached Daddy, who said he would be happy to give her whatever she wanted. He said it should be applied far from the roots and in very tiny amounts or it would burn the plants. In my excitement at making this contribution, I forgot to relay these instructions. Many of her plants visibly sickened, and some even died. I knew it was my fault, but I never owned up. I just brazened it out, though I hated to enter the classroom every morning and see what had befallen the plants overnight. I was glad to be promoted out of that class.

Next I went into Mrs. Overholtzer's fifth grade class. She didn't have any children of her own and was very partial to well dressed, clean children. She would call us up to her desk, and give us a big hug, and say, "Who loves you?" The answer was supposed to be, "You do." I would do anything to make the class laugh. It always set up my day when I could pull off a joke successfully. So once near Christmas, when I was called up for my hug and her question, I answered with a straight face, "I hope Santa Claus does." That was the last hug I got, but my day was made because the class got in an uproar, and it took a long time for everyone to settle down. The truth was that all of us considered ourselves too big for this embarrassing baby stuff. Mrs. Overholtzer always smelled like marshmallows, and she felt like a bag of them. Some of us thought she looked like a marshmallow. Kids can be so cruel, and I was a ringleader.

Miss Jordon, in sixth grade, was a no-nonsense kind of person. The first day she told us the story of a girl who went to college and took notes on everything she was taught. After four years, the girl graduated and came home with all her notes in a trunk. The trunk was lost, and the girl sat down and wept, saying, "There goes my college education." Miss Jordon wanted us to store everything in our heads so it wouldn't matter if we lost our notes. It was good advice, and I liked her for it even though I also got in trouble with her.

There was a big boy, much older than the rest of us in the class. He had been left back several times. I was minding my own business one day when a note arrived on my desk. I slipped it in my pocket to read later, thinking it was from a certain boy I liked. Miss Jordon's eagle eye was too swift. She called me up and asked me to hand her what I had put in my pocket. I did. She opened it halfway and went red in the face. She began questioning everyone to find out where this "note" had started and how many kids had seen it. Mother was called to school and asked to question me in front of the teacher. They finally decided that this particular time I was innocent, that I really didn't know what was in the note. By then, my own curiosity considerably aroused, I did a bit of questioning on my own. It turned out that in the folded paper was what looked like a white balloon rolled up flat; it was shaped like a doughnut only much, much smaller. Everyone thought it had come from the older boy. He wasn't going to pass sixth grade anyway, and so he was expelled. No one really cared what became of him.

I quit taking piano lessons as soon as Mother bought a baby grand player piano. It was so much more fun to let the music rolls do all the work. I would just make believe I was playing. Instead of taking piano lessons, I went to Miss Ramey's dancing classes. She called it "aesthetic dancing," but Daddy pretended not to understand the name and called it "pathetic dancing." He was probably right. Nevertheless, I was delighted when I was allowed to get toe slippers and join that class.

Mother made me wonderful costumes for being a snowflake and a chrysanthemum. I don't know how she did it. For once, I was willing to stand still for the interminable fitting sessions. She made some lovely costumes for Ray too, but Ray never got to wear hers. On the day of the recital she always shot a fever and was unable to perform. This happened year after year, with recovery timed for the morning after. I used to have great dreams of glory as a ballerina. I was stagestruck and already getting into arguments with Mother, always my adversary, about how I intended to go on the stage as a dancer. We could have saved our breath because when I was eleven years old I broke my ankle out in the yard climbing over a slide. Mother seized on this as an excuse to stop my "professional training."

Jane and Anne's grandmother, Mudda Cockrill, died in her bed. All of us wanted to know what her last words were. There was always a lot of curiosity about people's last words. It was as though the living expected to get a message from the other world by listening to the words of the dying. There were rumors that the dying would go back to the language of their infancy or show signs that they saw a loved one, long dead, welcoming them into heaven. I waited a few days before popping the big question, and was I in for a surprise. Mudda had said, "Leave my teeth in so I can bite the tail off the devil." Now there was a quote that had everything. It was funny, it was defiant, it was fearless, and it sent her off stage with a laugh. What could anyone ever say to top that one? It made me sorry I hadn't known her better. I wondered if my own grandmother, when her time came, would go back to talking German.

The summer when I was seven, Ray and I visited Daddy's family in Kansas City. I tried to get Grandmother Adler to teach me German. I hadn't gotten any further than "*Ich liebe dich*" when I broke out with scarlet fever. She did tell me stories about when she was growing up in Germany. She even gave me a sampler she had made when she was four years old with all of the letters and numbers done in cross-stitch. I hesitated to tell her, after all these years, that she had forgotten to put in a "j," but I knew she would forgive me so I told her. She was pleased, I guessed, because it gave her the chance to tell me that the German alphabet of that time used an "i" for both letters and didn't have a "j." That made me want to learn the German alphabet. This was more fun than pig latin.

I begged Grandmother to tell me stories of her life as a little girl in Germany. One story, about the day she was sent to the next village to get the mail, made me sad. It was hard to imagine a place so small that they didn't even get letters delivered to their front door. Grandmother found a letter in her father's handwriting. She was so curious that she opened the letter and read it. She learned that her father was in America. The sudden realization that he was so far away terrified her, and she sat down on the road under a tree and wept. Her tears stained the letter. She couldn't deny to her mother that she had been disobedient and opened the letter. (It was comforting to know that I wasn't the only little girl that did things like this.) It still made her sad just to tell the story. There was, however, a happy ending. Her father sent tickets for the whole family to join him in New York.

Grandmother was twelve when she came to this country. There were no classes to teach her English, so they put her in a class that was studying German, and she was supposed to do the opposite of everyone else. It must have been a good system because she spoke beautiful English.

Just before I got sick in Kansas City, my cousin Ralph asked his friend, who lived across the street, to help him take Ray and me to Electric Park. His friend was nineteen years old and was home from Harvard for the summer. He agreed to help Ralph out if they could make an early evening of it, because he had a real date for later. Ray and I had a glorious time riding on all of the crazy cars and the steam trains while the boys stood tapping their feet, impatient to get rid of us. When we got home Aunt Ray asked if we had been good girls. Ralph's friend answered, "Yes, except I couldn't get the little one off of the train." Eleven years later I went on another train trip with Ralph's friend. His name was Lawrence Kessel, and we were beginning our honeymoon.

After I got scarlet fever, Daddy came up and took my sister Ray back to Little Rock. I never in my life had so much loving attention. Ray Ray, as I now began to affectionately call Aunt Ray, let me fall asleep using her arm as my pillow. When her arm went numb, she would slip it quietly out from under my head. I was so glad that if I had to be sick I didn't have to be at home. Mother would just have handed me some crayons and a coloring book and told me not to scratch. Then she would have left me alone. In Kansas City, I was the absolute center of everyone's attention. When I was nearly well, Grandmother personally went into the kitchen and baked a batch of caramel rolls called schneckens—the German word for snails, because they curled around and around like snails. She made them just for me!

When I got well, the house was fumigated so no one could catch what I'd had. I think special candles were burned. In fact, the family had just sold the house and was getting ready to move to a new apartment in the Bellerive Hotel. The apartment was going to be much smaller, so they needed to get rid of some furniture. I made sure they wouldn't sell any of my favorite things. Grandmother had a pair of pink-and-white Dresden figurines that looked like George and Martha Washington all prettied up. She and Grandfather had received them as a wedding present. They were the only dolls I had ever loved. Grandmother not only didn't sell them, she made sure I would someday have them.

To make me feel grown-up, Ray Ray said I could help her sell the furniture. She told me the prices of everything. I was in my element. So many people answered the ad that an extra salesgirl was really needed, and I was it. There I was, seven years old and coining money.

On Sunday mornings I would go for a drive with Uncle Arthur. These drives with Unc were more interesting than the ones my whole family took with Daddy. I was his only passenger. Unc was in the mortgage business, and we drove according to a list of addresses he carried in his pocket. He started by showing me a house on which he had loaned money. He was very open about telling me all the figures. We drove past each house that had applied to him for a mortgage during the week, and he would ask me to compare it to the first house. He would give me all the details, the number of rooms and so on. I would give him my ideas as to whether it was worth more or less than the first house. He always acted as though my thoughts were very important to him and would influence what he told the poeple the next day.

On these Sunday morning drives, I always sat in a kneeling position, to make myself look taller, in hopes that anyone who saw me would think I was Uncle Arthur's wife sitting next to him. He drove a big, maroon Cadillac that he said he'd bought for Ray Ray. Since she was too small to drive it, he bought her an "Electric" instead. She used to let me help drive that. It didn't have a steering wheel like other cars, but a long bar that you held onto. I was never really in charge, but I was allowed to keep my hands on the bar.

Uncle Arthur Fels was a very handsome man except for his teeth, which were a little crooked. He had curly hair, but he always slicked it down. He went to veterans meetings wearing his old World War uniform. I loved to watch him winding khaki-colored bindings around his lower legs. They gave him such a neat look. He hadn't fought in the war, because his eyes were not so good, but he had been on the board that examined the young men for the army, and he still had something to do with recruiting even though the war was over.

Sometimes Unc would allow me to stand behind him and brush his hair into ringlets all over his head. The deal was that I could curl his hair if I would listen to him recite from his favorite book. He reread *Alice in Wonderland* every year. I can hear him now. "The walrus and the carpenter were walking close at hand." Or better still, from Gelett Burgess: "I never saw a purple cow, I never hope to see one, but I can tell you, anyhow, I'd rather see than be one." Personally, even when I was older, I was never able to read *Alice* even once, but he thought it the greatest, and I would have done anything to curl his hair. I wished I had curls like his instead of hair that Mother described as "straight as a poker."

My parents seemed in no hurry to get me back. Daddy didn't come up to get me until it was time for school in September. Years later I learned from Ray Ray that mother had had a kind of breakdown that summer. She had been so depressed that she couldn't even pull herself together to make our new school outfits for fall. At the time, I didn't know any of this, and as long as Daddy wrote to me, I didn't mind much that Mother never wrote me. When I got back to Little Rock, I told Jane and Anne that Mother hadn't written. They said that when their three older brothers had been in college, their mother had never written to any of them. Miss Jenny argued that if she wrote a letter to one of her six children, the other five would expect letters too.

Sometime that fall, Daddy got a telegram at the plant telling him that Uncle Billy had died that afternoon. He knew that Mother would take the news very hard, so he got in his car and drove home from work to tell her about it. Uncle Billy, like his father and his sister and his grandfather before him, had just dropped dead. It was something that ran in the Ramsey family. Since there had not been time for any last words, we didn't know if Grandma Albright had come down to help him find his way to heaven. Daddy had been right to come home with the news. Mother really did feel terrible.

I had last seen Uncle Billy when he came down to Little Rock for a very special meeting with Mother. He wore a wig. When the fringe of his own hair began to show under the bottom of the wig, he would drive the hundred miles from Batesville to Little Rock to have Mother trim his hair. He didn't want anyone in Batesville to know he wore a wig. That particular barbering session, I had burst in on them and caught sight of his bald head. I don't know who was more embarrassed, Uncle Billy or I. Anyway, I'm sure Mother saw to it that he was buried with his wig on.

This left Daddy Albright living alone in that big, old house. He was lonesome, so he began driving down to see us more often. Then he wrote that he had bought a new car to make the trip easier. We were expecting him one day, and it was getting late when the phone rang. It was Daddy Albright, who gently explained to Mother that he wouldn't be coming down that day because the car couldn't make it.

Mother got all excited and shouted, "What do you mean the car can't make it! It's a brand-new car! Why doesn't it run?"

Daddy Albright was still trying to break the news to her nice and easy, so he answered, "It's not that it can't run but that it can't swim."

"What on earth do you mean?" Mother said. "Why should it have to swim?"

"Well, because it's at the bottom of the river," Daddy Albright answered.

Mother finally got the story out of him. He had put the car on the ferry boat to cross a river on the way. When the boat landed on the other side, he got in the car and started the motor before the boatmen tied up. Since he wasn't used to the car, he accidentally stepped on the gas instead of the brake and shot into the water. He could swim, but the car couldn't. It was as simple as that. He guessed they would just have to leave the car there. No one seemed to know how to get it out, and it wasn't in anyone's way.

A few weeks later, Daddy Albright finally came down for his visit driving still another new car that replaced the one at the bottom of the river. Leaving the car in the river reminded him of something he had left behind him once before. He told me the story of his twenty-first birthday. He was out in back, chopping some wood, and he got to thinking he didn't want to spend the rest of his life not knowing how to read or write. As he chopped, he got madder and madder to think that he had never been to school a day in his life. Finally, he got so mad that he just stuck the ax in the piece of wood and, without saying good-bye to anyone, walked to the nearest town (about five miles away) and went to the schoolhouse and told the teacher he wanted to come to her school. What could she say? On his twenty-first birthday, he enrolled in the first grade.

We both had a good laugh when he described how he looked and felt with his long legs bent like a grasshopper, trying to sit at the desks built for little kids. Since it was a one-room schoolhouse with grades one through six in the same room, he made very fast progress. By the time he was twenty-three he went to Fayetteville to the University of Arkansas. As he put it, he only went for two years, because he had to quit and earn his keep.

He was full of stories that day. I was able to get a lot out of him. I wanted to know for whom he had been named. He told me that in 1853, when he was born, country folks were in the habit of naming their children after the president of the United States. Franklin Pierce was president when he was born, so that was why he was called Franklin Pierce Albright. Every family had their own system of keeping track of their "chillun."

The Albrights were a hardy lot, and *The Arkansas Gazette* once ran a picture showing six of Daddy Albright's brothers and sisters who were all over the biblical age of three-score-and-ten. The newspaper also gave a history of the Albrights, saying they could trace their ancestors to the Hapsburgs and had three fleurs-de-lys in their crest. Not knowing who the Hapsburgs were, I didn't brag about the connection. It is only recently, since I have become a history buff, that I have gone back to the "scrapbook" and reread the article.

The summer of 1925, when I was ten, we took a trip to Long Beach, California. For weeks we talked about the wonderful train we were going to ride. The arrangement was that Daddy Albright was to accompany Mother, Ray, Junior, and me, and Daddy would follow us out later. This special train had a shower, and I told every one who would listen that I was going to take a shower on the train. I had to eat my words. When Mother found out there was an extra charge to take a shower, she said, "Since you hate so to bathe, I don't see any reason to pay good money because we are on a train. You can just take cat baths until we get there."

I really needed the cat baths. The cinders made everything sooty and were always getting in my eyes because I liked to look out the windows. It was on this trip that Mother decided she wanted us to stop calling her father Daddy Albright. She had a vivid imagination and was afraid people would think she was a young woman who had married an old man for his money. It was decreed that we should henceforth call him Grandfather. I didn't notice anyone on the train listening to what we called him, but we had four days of close supervision on the train to make sure we didn't make a slip and call him by his former name. I found that habits die hard.

We arrived in California looking pretty shaggy because Mother had been looking forward to all of us having real haircuts. She said that the barbers in Little Rock were butchers and didn't know how to cut hair. She'd been letting our hair grow so we could get California bobs. Mother had stopped cutting our hair herself when we left Batesville. Talk about butchers—she was a real one. Many a time she had nipped my ear and said it was because I squirmed. She had also had a lot of trouble getting the bangs straight. When she got one side the way she wanted it, she found that the other side was too long. In the interest of evening things out, I sometimes ended up with practically no bangs left.

We were sitting in the California barber's chair when he got chatty and asked where we came from. When he heard that we were from Arkansas he was delighted. He was from Arkansas too! When Mother heard that, she yanked the cloth from around my neck, grabbed me by the hand, herded all three of us out of the shop muttering to herself, "I didn't come all the way to California to have you butchered by an Arkansas barber." I glanced back and saw the poor barber staring at us from the window. He didn't know what had hit him.

Grandfather was going to get the most out of this trip. He said that since he was seventy-two years old and this was his first time out of Arkansas, he intended to see all he could. There were buses lined up in the center of town early in the morning. Men were standing beside them trying to persuade people to choose their particular bus for a free trip. They even gave a free lunch. What they wanted was for you to buy some of the land they had for sale. Mother kept saying, "Papa, now don't you let them hoodwink you into buying property way out here." She was so afraid that a slick salesman would fast-talk him and get all of his money. Grandfather knew exactly what he was doing. He was seeing the country and being well fed, and it wasn't costing him a red cent.

When Daddy arrived, I had recovered from a terrible sunburn and had already peeled. Ray hadn't suffered because she had obeyed when mother told her to get under the beach umbrella. I got no sympathy from anyone. They were unanimous in agreeing that I had gotten just what I deserved. Even Junior went against me, and he was usually my ally. I called him at traitor, but he didn't care. He didn't know what traitor meant anyway.

Now things began to happen. We took real sight-seeing trips to Hollywood film studios and to see the homes of the movie stars. When we went past Pickfair, the mansion of Mary Pickford and Douglas Fairbanks, I was particularly interested in seeing where I might have lived if my fantasies of a few years earlier had come true. We saw the theater with the famous footprints in the cement. The guide pointed out the flags of all nations, which turned out to be someone's laundry drying on the line. At first I thought that was very funny, and then I began to think he made this same remark every day and that getting a cheap laugh like that couldn't be all that much fun for him.

When we got back to Little Rock, it was almost my eleventh birthday and time for me to begin junior high school. This was a big adjustment because the kids came from several other grammer schools and didn't know that I was a queen bee. They didn't know to nominate me for president of the class, let alone elect me. We had to go from class to class now, instead of staying put and letting the teachers move from room to room. I hadn't changed. I was still absentminded and apt to forget where my next class was. Did math follow Latin or was it the other way around? I couldn't even attach myself to another pupil and have her guide me because everyone had a different schedule. My record for being late to class was pretty bad. I didn't dare say that I had forgotten where I was going, so I always gave the same excuse—that I'd had to go to the bathroom. If my teachers thought about it at all, they must have thought I had a real problem with my body functions. I suppose they didn't really care where I had been.

We had a special class for art. I never got beyond drawing a tulip in a vase. It was not possible to get the two sides of the vase to look alike, so I gave the eraser a lot of work. By the end of class, the paper had grown so thin you could see through it, and still the two sides of the vase didn't match.

Then there was the music class. I never got the hang of that either. I loved it, but when we sang songs in rounds I was always singing with the wrong group. The teacher would decide that I was an alto and would put me in among the altos, at which point I suddenly began to sing soprano. She said she had never before had anyone like me in her class, and she gently suggested—though she would pass me anyway—from here on out, I was just to move my lips without making any sounds. In that way the class could make progress, and she wouldn't have to waste her time moving me around.

My English teacher fascinated me, not because of her subject but because of her nose. It was absolutely unique. It was a double nose that was split down the middle, and she spoke with a slight lisp. I wondered if maybe her tongue was split too. I had heard of babies being born with their tongues tied: they'd had to have them clipped. I was full of my usual scientific speculations as to why my teacher lisped and whether it could have been corrected when she was a baby if they had sewed her tongue together.

In seventh grade I began the study of Latin. Miss Mason was careful to explain that it was a dead language and that we would not be expected to learn to speak it. That was a relief. We would, however, have to learn all the parts of speech, to conjugate verbs, and so on. In two more years we were going to read Caesar. I had a good friend who got me through Latin by reading the lesson to me before class. To me, finding the nominative, etc., was like figuring out a puzzle. I just wanted to get the story line right and find out what happened to Caesar with all his wars, but reading just one paragraph a day was pretty discouraging. By the time I read one day's lesson, I had forgotten what happened the day before. It may have been the right way to teach Latin, but it was not the way for me to learn about Roman times. It was then that I made my first academic decision. I would not enroll for Cicero or Virgil. I didn't ask anybody. I just told my parents that I now knew all the Latin I would ever need to know, and that was that.

I had a violent crush on my math teacher. I knew he was married, but that didn't stop my fantasies. I spent a lot of time cooking up schemes to get to ask him a question or somehow attract his attention. I found out that he liked to play tennis. Nothing would satisfy me until Mother arranged permission for me to play on the private court that was just behind our house. She didn't realize that this sudden interest in tennis was for the sole purpose of having my math teacher all to myself. I had visions of just the two of us playing. It was all so romantic. The day I had invited him to come, he arrived looking very sporty in his white trousers but carrying both his racket and his wife's. When she got out of their car, my heart went into my mouth and stayed there all afternoon. I could hardly manage to introduce them to Mother. Afterwards, Mother commented, "He seems like such a nice man." I simply replied, "Yeah, he's okay." He didn't get another invitation even though he hinted a few times. From then on, Ray and I played together, and there were the usual accusations of cheating and that the ball was NOT out. I loved to serve, because then I could slam the ball with all my might and pent-up anger. It wasn't actually all that pent-up. I was a fairly active volcano that erupted frequently.

Mother was finding me increasingly difficult to deal with. She had finally told me I was too big to spank. All she could do now, she said, was try to reason with me. When I exasperated her more than usual, she would take me to the screened-in sleeping porch, point to the insane asylum on a high hill about two miles away, and declare, "That's where you're driving me."

Why was she so sure she was going to lose her mind? For

some reason, she thought that her father had been drunk when she was conceived. It was a common belief that this could cause insanity. I never saw Grandfather take a drink, so I didn't believe her theory. Why didn't she just ask him? Wouldn't that have been the easiest way to find out? I had another idea of why she was so afraid. Maybe her mother hadn't been as strict about sleeping with her hands on top of the covers as she had been with me. I had the feeling that if she ever did break down I would get the full blame. I really did try not to upset her, and Daddy would always ask me not to worry my mother, but somehow there was always friction between us.

The summer before I was twelve, I finally got to summer camp for two months. A lady had organized a large group of girls from Little Rock to go to a camp in North Carolina. I went there for four consecutive years. I was very ignorant about many things, but in looking back I realize I was exposed to a lot of things that a well-brought-up Puritan girl shouldn't have been seeing, hearing, or learning. The counselors slept on the back porches of the cabins, away from the bunks of the campers. After the campers were supposed to have gone to sleep, the counselors would visit each other by climbing over the back railing. The next morning before reveille blew, each would return to her proper bed. We weren't allowed to disturb them unless we fancied we were having an appendix attack or something equally serious.

We were always snooping around to hear what was going on. There would be lots of heavy breathing and low, moaning sounds. If those sounds stopped, we made a dive for our bunks for fear they had heard us at the keyhole, our listening post. We were more interested in the act of spying than we were in really knowing what made them emit such noises. These were senior counselors. They came from all parts of the south, where in winter they were important teachers and even heads of departments in their schools.

I only once had a pass made at me and that was by a junior counselor I admired because she was so sporty in her plus-four knickers. She suddenly grabbed me in front of a lot of people and bent me over backward, saying, "This is the way Rudolph Valentino kisses." My confusion was total. On the one hand, I was flattered that she had chosen me for her demonstration. On the other hand, I had never before been kissed on the mouth by anyone either male or female.

This was yet another thing that mother forbade; she said it was for reasons of hygiene so we wouldn't get germs. Even Grandmother had to kiss us on the back of the neck. This was considered a safe spot. And here was this handsome, masculine girl planting a long kiss squarely on my mouth. While I was staggering out of my stupor, a whole bunch of campers were lining up and shouting, "Show me too."

I spent a lot of time hanging around the horse stable. In fact, I was supposed to do some chores to earn part of the extra fee that was charged for horseback riding. Although I loved the horses, I had to overcome my fear all over again every year. We were taught how to ride by a former captain in the U.S. Army cavalry. He put us through all the drills he had used in the army. We had to learn to ride bareback like Indians. At a signal, we had to lie back with our heads on the horses' rumps. From that extremely awkward postion, we had to get the horses into a trot. We also had to ride well enough to go down the side of a mountain so steep that the horses sat down and slid on their hind legs. There were, of course, the easier exercises; doing figure eights on the track and making your horse change his lead hoof each time he changed direction. When we could pass all these tests, we were allowed to go on an overnight camping trip. This was what we strove for all summer.

I was always trying to kill two birds with one stone, and since I was anxious to improve my sunburn, I put on my bathing suit under my jodhpurs and shirt. A few miles out of camp I started stripping off my outer layers. The other girls were jealous that they hadn't thought to prepare in this way. In those days, swimming suits were made of wool. Before long the suit began to itch, and their admiration for my forethought turned to derision at my discomfort. Something else to add to my growing list of things to remember not to do again.

Once we were taken on an overnight hike. We camped by some big rocks over which the water rippled. There were old wild grapevines overhanging the stream. The shape of the grape leaves reminded me of the leaves from the tulip tree in Grandfather's yard, so I started making a costume of grape leaves. I looked like a young female Bacchus standing on a big rock in midstream. Someone ran for her Brownie box camera and took a snapshot of me. When the picture was developed, everyone wanted a copy. I made a deal with the photographer to split the money with me. We took orders and did a thriving business. It was a lot more profitable than my old lemonade stands.

I clearly enjoyed making money, so the following year I came to camp with a trunk full of sweaters that I had tired of or outgrown. When the new, inexperienced campers showed up shivering on their first cold night in the mountains, I sweetly offered to sell them each a sweater from my cache. They were very grateful; they hadn't known how cold the Great Smoky Mountains could get in midsummer. With the money I earned, I bought my first pair of high-heeled shoes. They were beige leather with dark-brown polka dots, and they had ankle straps. When I limped off the train in Little Rock wearing them, mother let out a war cry, "Where in the world did you get those shoes?"

I was so taken aback that I stammered that someone had given them to me.

To this, mother had a ready answer, "I can see why. She gave them to you because her mother wouldn't let her wear them, and neither will I."

This was my greeting after two months away. I was just off the train, and we were already at each other's throats. I couldn't even tell her about my business success, and she didn't notice that the full outbound trunk had come home more than half empty.

I learned other things at camp besides the usual swimming, canoeing, diving, and tennis improvement. I learned to smoke and hitchhike and drink. Of course, the camp had strict rules against all these things. That was what made them so inviting.

Several of us would go into the woods that surrounded the camp. We were armed with boxes of matches and tins of Lucky Strike flat fifites. We were such heavy smokers that buying ordinary packages of twenty cigarettes was out of the question. We used only one match each, to start our first cigarette. Thereafter, we lit the next cigarette from the one we had just finished smoking. We thought it was very sophisticated to chain-smoke. It was our proof that we were grown-up. Besides, they did it that way in the movies.

When we hitchhiked, it was in groups of three or four, and we usually weren't going more than a few miles down the road to get an ice cream soda or some such delicacy. Once we went as far afield as Asheville which was twenty-five miles away. We had such a hard time getting back to camp and into our bunks by the time taps were blown that we decided not to do that again.

As for drinking, we were curious to know what everyone meant when they talked about being drunk. None of the four of us who started off one afternoon had ever had a drink except as medicine. We knew there were lots of "stills" in those backwoods hills and that if we stopped in enough farmhouses we would eventually find someone who was willing to sell us something that would get us drunk. We were right. About the third try, an old hillbilly said he had some wine he would sell us but it wasn't quite ready to drink. We would have to promise him we would wait another two weeks, until it was ripe, before we drank it. We swore we would do this and then took our jug of wine off to the camp council ring, usually used for night meetings of the four Indian tribes into which the camp was divided.

We sat down in the leaves and began to drink and compare notes. We commented on the taste and declared that we felt nothing at all. We thought the old man had cheated us. Maybe it was just grape juice after all. Then someone said she felt kind of sleepy, and we thought we'd just take a little nap while waiting for the state of drunkenness to descend upon us. All four of us fell fast asleep. When we woke up, none of us could stand up, and it was pitch dark with only a few stars out. We knew we had better get back to camp before those infernal taps blew. We finally decided to crawl on all fours. That was the longest quarter mile I ever traveled.

We all had a good throwing-up session in the john and crawled into our bunks, where we stayed for three nights and days. No one came around to see why we were absent from our scheduled activities. We were left strictly alone. On the morning of the fourth day, one of us ventured to the dining hall and brought back some cold biscuits. This was the turning point. We ate them and knew that we were going to live after all. There has been divine retribution for this sin. I have all my life had an allergy to wine. Doctors explain that tissue has a memory and that my whole system goes crazy if I accidentally have wine in a sauce. I don't know much about tissue having memory, but I sure know about my having memory, and this was a bad one.

We were always playing tricks on each other, making "pie beds" or putting something revolting between the sheets. I had gone to take a shower one night, and when I came out all that I could find was my towel. My clothes had been whisked away. Whoever pulled this trick expected me to stay endlessly in the shower waiting for help to come. That wasn't my style. I'd show them. Instead of putting the towel around me and making a dash for my cabin, I began a spring dance in the nude, waving my towel in the air like a Greek maiden's scarf. Astonished eyes peered around the corners of cabins. Someone yelled a warning that one of the head counselors was coming. I quickly wrapped the towel securely around my body and walked primly back to my cabin.

Next day I was called before a powerful group of counselors to explain my actions. They let me know that being sent home was in the balance, but in any case my mother had to be informed. I hoped God didn't have his big book out because I was about to tell one of the biggest whoppers I had ever tried to pull off. I swore I had been viciously maligned. I had gone directly to my cabin, and the towel had never been anywhere except covering my nudity. I also felt I had an ace of trumps in my hand: sitting on my jury were two of the counselors who I knew were swapping beds at night. Either I truly put on a convincing defense, or the counselors just wanted to make a show of scaring me, but they decided not to send me home. They did write Mother about the "incident," but for once she was amused by my antics and didn't even scold me. We were separated by seven hundred miles, and I felt closer to her then than ever before.

CHAPTER 6

Joining Up

One fall day Grandfather phoned to say he was driving down from Batesville. He had some news. All of us were speculating about what the news could be. Daddy thought that maybe there had been an offer to buy the Ramsey Bottom farm, because for quite some time there had been talk about building a bridge over the White River that would cross our farm at the point where Uncle Billy's ferry boat had its landing on the Batesville side. That would be big enough news to drive a hundred miles to tell in person. Mother didn't think that was it. In fact, Mother seemed worried. This time she had a right to be. Grandfather tried to stay calm as he explained to Mother that ever since Uncle Billy died he had been "rattling around in that big, old house alone." That was it.

Mother fairly shouted, "You're not going to sell the house, Papa."

No, he wasn't going to sell the house. In fact, he was going to build a small house in the side yard. He had been seeing a widow woman with grown-up children, and he was building the house for her parents because he and Myrtle were going to get married, and this way her parents would be living right next door. Mother, in her usual considered, diplomatic way, blurted out, "What in the world could she want with an old geezer like you?"

He kept his cool and just answered, "Well, I don't know the answer to that, but she seems to think she wants to get married, and her kids don't object, so that's the way it's gonna be." He stayed overnight, and Mother kept pumping to find out what Myrtle was like. Was she tall? Was she fat? Was she pretty? The answer to most of her questions was, "Middling." Ray and I got the impression that he hadn't much noticed many details about Myrtle, but he knew he didn't like being alone.

As soon as Mother got hold of herself, at Daddy's urging, she became obsessed with the question of what to give Myrtle as a wedding present. After coming up with dozens of ideas, all of which she discarded, she hit on making a pink frilly negligee for Myrtle. It was a little difficult. She was used to interminable fittings, and here she was making an intimate garment for a woman she had never seen and didn't know anything about except that she was "middling" in every way. We children were not invited to the wedding because we would have had to miss school, but Mother and Daddy drove up with the pink negligee carefully giftwrapped. When they got back, I asked mother how Myrtle had liked the negligee. Her strange answer was, "Who cares what she likes."

Thank goodness Mother took the occasion to go through Grandfather's attic and to take whatever she wanted. She came back to Little Rock with four oil paintings of her ancestors. When I came home from school and first caught sight of the portrait of Allen Ramsey, I shouted, "That's who I look like!" I was so happy to find someone in the family whom I resembled. Whenever we had visitors, they would declare that Ray was the spitting image of mother and Junior was a dead ringer for Daddy but Marie was a puzzler. Whom did she look like? Now I had the answer. I looked like my great-grandfather, and what's more I had some of his other characteristics. I was absentminded as he had been. There was a family story about how he would ride his horse to town and when he'd finished his business he walked home. He wouldn't remember his horse until he went to give it some oats, and then he had to trudge back to Batesville to get the poor, tired animal that had been hitched to a post all day. I could sympathize with doing a thing like that. I had been known to leave my bike somewhere and not remember where. Mother used to say it was lucky that my head was firmly attached to my shoulders.

Mother did well to rescue those portraits because very soon Myrtle decided that she was going to do some fixing up, and she didn't like all of those antiques that Grandfather had. This was the time when the big fashion was raffia furniture. In the cities, the style was probably wicker, but in Batesville they were selling the cheaper version, called raffia. Myrtle threw out all the Victorian antiques and replaced them with tables, chairs, lamps, sofas, and bookcases, all made of brown raffia. Mother thought it was tacky (one of her favorite words). Paper flowers dipped in paraffin, of which I produced bouquet after bouquet, were tacky. Ribbons on dresses were tacky. But smocking, which she loved to do, was very elegant. Personally I hated it, and when I went to high school I let her know that she could go on smocking to her heart's content but I would never again wear anything with smocking on it. At fourteen, I didn't know if it was tacky or not, but I knew I felt silly in those babyish dresses.

Grandfather went along with Myrtle's redecoration. After all, there hadn't been a woman to care for the house since Grandmother Albright's death when Mother was sixteen. It was okay with him if Myrtle wanted all that newfangled furniture. Their marriage seemed to be going smoothly when Myrtle made a fatal mistake. She told Grandfather that she had seen a diamond brooch at the jewelry store and would like him to buy it for her. That did it! This time it was Myrtle that got thrown out. He didn't have to throw her very far. She just moved in with her parents, who lived next door in the house Grandfather had built for them. They went on living peacefully as neighbors for the rest of their lives.

Grandfather let a family named Wallace move into the big house and live there rent free as long as they would give him supper every night. He thought their kids would liven the place up, and they did.

In Little Rock we stayed friendly with Jane and Anne Cockrill and spent a good deal of time at their house. Their youngest brother, Howard, had become a handsome, tall boy, and we liked hanging around him. We were not welcome nor were his sisters. He was very involved with playing jazz on his clarinet, which he called his licorice stick. He would put a record on the Victrola and accompany it as best he could while wandering about the room. We were awed by his musical talent. When he decided suddenly he had had enough of our moony-eyed glances and wanted all of us out of there, he would take the licorice stick out of his mouth and yell, "Scram, vamoose, or I'll give you the boot." Real he-man stuff, and we loved it!

Anne and I referred to ourselves as the Baddy Bads and considered ourselves united in mischief. We called Ray and Jane the Goody Goods (not to their faces of course)—we did think they were awfully prim. From this beginning, we began to form clubs and invite others to join. The clubs really had only one purpose: initiation. New members had to pay an initiation fee and undergo an initiation ceremony. We gave a lot of thought to the horrors we dreamed up for new members. Sometimes they had to walk blindfolded, in their bare feet, over raw liver. Once each had to eat a slice of laundry soap between crackers. Another time it was a raw pod of garlic. The worst I remember was having to swallow a tablespoon full of Vicks VapoRub. Right after we had collected all of the initiation fees and put everyone who was gullible enough to join through the ceremony, the club would fall apart, and we would organize another one.

Once we were invited to join a club formed by the downtown girls. They were more sophisticated than the Heights kids and were going to charge us five dollars each to join. We were required to earn the money ourselves. We hit on a scheme to run a beauty parlor in the playhouse in the Cockrill's yard. It was a one-room house with a front porch. On the inside it was about six feet by seven feet, with two windows and a door but no running water. This was at a time when the best beauty parlor in town would give you a shampoo and marcel wave for a dollar. Our shop gave you a cold water shampoo for a dime. We had to carry the water from the garden hose into the playhouse. We also did manicures for a dime. We only had pale pink or a pumice cream that we buffed to a high gloss. We had customers lined up waiting for us to open. That was the power of word-of-mouth advertising.

In the midst of all of this ten cent stuff, Mary Brack called up and said that her uncle was visiting her mother. Could she bring him over for a manicure? It was our only telephoned appointment and our only grown-up client, so we did some extra scurrying around to find a real chair and table for him instead of the child-sized furniture we were using for our other customers. Mary arrived with her uncle, whom she proudly introduced to all of us beauticians as "my uncle, Senator Sims of New Mexico."

I was elected to do the honors. My hands were shaking, and I knew I would never get the liquid polish on straight, so I suggested he let me just buff his nails. There, my shaking would be an asset. He was so pleased with my job that he gave two dollars to the general kitty. We thought the two dollars might be a kind of bribe. Mary never wanted to be left out of anything, and she hadn't been invited to join this particular club. I was very impressed with Mary's senator uncle, but Jane and Anne just pooh-poohed his importance. Everyone knew that their great great grandfather had been Chester Ashley, the second U.S. senator from Arkansas.

Guess what those downtown girls did to us at the initiation? They poured molasses and feathers in our hair. This time our mothers had to do the shampooing, and they swore they would never allow us to join another club. All these social clubs were child's play, just a prelude for the day when we would go to high school and join a national sorority.

At that time I directed most of my questions to Daddy, who was always thoughtful when he answered me. He wasn't annoyed by my incessant curiosity as mother had been. He never once told me it was curiosity that killed the cat or that I was trying to open Pandora's box. I remember asking him why we didn't have a railroad pass that would let us ride free to any place in the country. Jane and Anne and all their family had passes because their father was the lawyer for the E. L. Bruce Lumber Company.

All of our friends could go anywhere they wanted without paying. Actually, the only place they went to was Ludington, Michigan, where their families owned a colony of cottages. They invited us often to come for a visit. Since I knew Mother would consider the trip a gross extravagance, I was approaching it from the angle of having Daddy get a pass too. I pointed out to him that he was probably entitled to a pass since his company did a lot of shipping. He said, "That's precisely why I won't accept one. I've been offered passes many times, but I want to be completely free to negotiate on the rates for shipping fertilizer. I don't want to have my hands tied because I accepted a favor from the railroad. That pass they would give me wouldn't be worth more than a few hundred dollars, and it might cost thousands in the rates I'd have to pay. It simply would handicap me. Does that make sense to you?"

I had to agree that he was right. The business ethics he taught me were a code I would live by all my life. Don't be bribed.

Another question I asked Daddy was: Would he consider joining the Little Rock Country Club? All our friends belonged. Each of them invited us twice during the summer, but there was a rule that the same guest could not be invited by the same member more than twice. I felt like a charity case always having to wait for an invitation. I thought it would be much simpler if Daddy became a member. This time he was almost grave when he answered. "In the first place, I doubt that I would be accepted as a member because of my race. They have a rule against admitting Jewish members. In the second place, if they made an exception, I would not feel comfortable joining a social club that did not accept my people. So the answer has to be: No, I would not join." His answer made me very sad, and I think he was sad too. He was a very generous man and liked to give his family anything within his power, but this clearly was not.

Mother had evidently been listening from the other room.

As soon as Daddy went off to read his paper, she came into the room and said to me, "I don't want you to worry about not belonging to the country club. I know how you feel because I don't like to always be a guest when I play bridge there, but when you grow up you and Ray can join in your own names." She meant to console me, but she made me feel even worse. I had just heard Daddy say he felt loyal to his people. I felt they were my people too, so how would it be right for me to join and thus deny "my people?" I never let on how hurt I was that she would sabotage Daddy in this way.

When I was much younger I had often used being Jewish as a weapon to hurl at Mother when I was particularly angry with her. I would shout, "I demand to be sent to synagogue." This really got under her skin, I knew, but she just answered by telling me not to be ridiculous. I don't know what I would have done had she ever taken me up on my demand. I loved Sunday school and being with all my friends in the car pool. The day we talked about the country club was the day I realized that there were deeper dimensions to the problem and that I was going to have to learn to cope with it.

One day, Daddy announced he had been invited to join the Rotary Club. I had no idea what that meant, but I waited impatiently to learn if he was going to accept. He thought it sounded interesting. He would meet prominent business men at the luncheons, and he liked the idea of listening to their speeches, so he decided to join. I was relieved.

Another time he came home looking upset. This time he had been invited to join the Ku Klux Klan. He was at a total loss to understand how they could have made the mistake of asking him to join. I hung on every word we could get out of him as to how he had handled this very awkward situation. He hadn't wanted to anger the committee that came to see him at the fertilizer plant, nor had he wanted to encourage them to believe he thought as they did. He had put it to them simply. He said, "Gentlemen, it is my understanding that your organization is against the Negroes, the Catholics, and the Jews. You may not have been aware that I am Jewish, but now that you know, I'm sure you will want to withdraw your invitation, and there will be no hard feelings."

They all shook hands and said good-bye. Daddy would never tell us who his visitors had been for fear we might one day blurt out their names. Daddy had taken us once to a KKK parade at night. It was scary to see how many men had dressed themselves in their ceremonial garb—with masked faces and tall, pointed hats—and were parading to show what a large and powerful organization they were.

I'm not saying the KKK had anything to do with it, but there was a lynching in Little Rock. A Negro was accused by a white woman of raping her. I didn't know what rape was, but I did know that no Negro man was allowed even to touch a white woman; that if they were both walking on the sidewalk, the Negro had to step off the curb into the gutter when he passed a white person. The morning after the lynching, the newspaper was filled with stories and pictures. They had strung the man up in a tree, poured gasoline on him, and set him afire. That day at school, one boy said he had been at the lynching. He wanted to show everyone a piece of charred hair that he claimed was from the head of the hanged man. The boys were curious and wanted to see his ghoulish souvenir, but all the girls fled when he came near.

The whole business had a nightmarish quality. The newspapers continued to focus on this lynching. All the papers in the country ran stories about it. The editorials were concerned with the image of Arkansas before the whole world, but none of them moralized about a mob taking the law into its own hands without giving the man a chance to defend himself before a court of law. I was beginning to understand that there were different rules for blacks and whites. Mother wanted Daddy to get a gun. He said he didn't need one and that if he had one he wouldn't use it. Besides, one of the children might accidentally get hurt. Daddy could be very firm with Mother about something he thought was important.

Sally had been pensioned off by that time, so I couldn't talk over the lynching with her. She had gone to live with the postman's sister. There she was looked after, and she didn't have to do any work. Mother was happy with the arrangement. It enabled her to hire a young and vigorous maid. As long as Sally was around, she had managed somehow to get all of our maids to quit. Sally herself was no longer strong enough to do the work, but she was jealous of anyone else's doing it. There had been a series of girls hired, most of whom were straight off the farms. After a day or two, mother would declare them to be "green as grass and not trainable." The fact was that mother had no idea of how to train them. She herself only knew how to make angel food cake. That was her entire knowledge of cooking. She had been spoiled by having Sally who had been trained by my grandmother.

Before coming to Grandmother, Sally had had a rough life. She had worked as kitchen helper on a Mississippi steamboat. She'd also had to wait on table and had been taught to pass the food so fast that none of the men would have a chance to grab what she was passing. She would enter the dining galley of the boat with a plate of butter in her hand and start racing around the table saying, "Have butter, have butter, have butter?" She would almost get stabbed by the men's knives that were poised waiting for her entrance. When she got to the kitchen, she would be punished if anyone had managed to take some of her butter.

Another of Sally's tales of life on a steamboat was of the captain who was diagnosed as having a tapeworm. There really is such a thing, and he had one. The cure at that time, Sally said, was to starve the tapeworm. To do this, you had to starve the person too. After a week or more of no food, the person would be weak. His mouth would be propped open and a piece of raw meat held in front of him. The starving tapeworm would then come up to get the raw meat, and the person sitting guard would grab the tapeworm by the head and give a strong yank. It was the kind of job that required you to be awake all the time. Sally had to take a turn every so often. She was glad she hadn't been on duty when the worm came out, but she said the captain got all right after that treatment. Such was my trust in Sally, that to this day I can't bring myself to doubt the story. Improbable as it may be, Sally told it to me for true.

Mother finally found a maid who suited her and who had been trained by someone else. Cary was given the house out in the back yard and was allowed to entertain her boyfriend out there. She even had parties once in a while. She once asked if she could cook some chitterlings down in the laundry room. Mother wasn't sure what chitterlings were, so she said it was okay. She regretted it the minute she got the first whiff. It took days to get the house aired out.

Cary's boyfriend was called Big-To-Do. He was known to have killed three or four men, but he had never gone to jail for the killings. It seems that if you only killed your own kind then nothing would be done about it. We would see Big-To-Do when he arrived after supper. He was always gone before morning. One night we heard lots of noise and shouting going on in Cary's room. Mother wanted to call the police, but Daddy just went out on the sleeping porch and shouted, "Quiet down there." That was the end of the noise. Such was the power of the white man's voice that he could control a known killer with just three words. I'm not saying this was good or bad. I'm just saying this is how it was.

Daddy was a mild-mannered man. The strongest words I ever heard him speak to my mother were when he disapproved of what she was saying or doing. He would say, "Now, Helen." It was how he said it that calmed her down and got her off her high horse. There were obvious points on which the two of them disagreed. For instance, Mother was wild about bargains. She went to every sale in town. She adored buying remnants of materials. She was always sure she would find something to do with them, and she usually did make something clever out of these short pieces of fabric. It would never have occurred to her to come home from a sale empty-handed. She bought dozens of pairs of shoes in the hope that she or Ray or I could fit into them. I would try them on and declare loudly that they hurt and that no matter how pretty they were I couldn't walk in them.

Daddy would overhear the discussions and get involved by

saying, "Helen, if the girls need shoes, why don't you just take them to the shoe store and have them fitted?"

She would answer, "Nathan, you don't understand. I bought three pairs for the price of one. They were a real bargain."

He would counter with the argument, "They are only a bargain if you need them and if they fit."

At that point, he would leave the room, and Mother would turn to Ray and me and say half under her breath, "Well, you'll just have to wear them anyway."

Ray did, and she has bunions to prove it. I didn't wear them, and I haven't got bunions to prove I didn't.

We heard that Sally was ailing, and I wanted to go see her, but something always interfered. I guess I didn't want to go badly enough. Then one day we had a phone call from the postman's sister telling us that Sally had passed away in her sleep. I was filled with regrets that I hadn't at least gone to say good-bye. I had always known her love for me was constant and unquestioning. Someone very wonderful had gone out of my life, and I would never find a replacement for her. To add to my terrible guilt, Sally had left all her hard-earned savings to me—all two thousand dollars.

Daddy sat me down for a serious talk. He said I could have the money, but he wanted me to think hard about how I used it. He said that Sally's people were generally poor and he thought I should consider some good I could do for them with that money. He reminded me of how much her church had meant to her and suggested that maybe I would like to contribute to it.

I was in great conflict. Sally had given me the first money I'd ever had in my life, and Daddy was telling me to give it to her people. I asked for time to think it over. My fantasies of having a blue rumble-seat roadster when I was sixteen, in a few more years, were being shattered. I would never again have the chance to be so utterly frivolous. I vacillated between keeping the money for myself and doing what Daddy had suggested. After about a week, I went to him, close to tears, and quietly told him I had decided the money should go to Sally's people and I hoped he would arrange it for me, because I really didn't know how to go about it. He gave me a big hug and said he was proud of me. That was enough.

Shortly after my big sacrifice, Daddy told me that he had been saving money in my name ever since my birth. He had put money in the bank on each of my birthdays, for Christmas, and on other holidays. He wanted me to know he was buying stocks with that money and asked if I would care to follow the stock market with him to keep an eye on my money. I had already learned in school how to read the stock page so I was very excited to actually own some stock. This was about 1927, and he had bought me a few shares of U.S. Steel. What fun we had together watching that stock go up, up, up! Every day was a day to celebrate—until. Suddenly Daddy didn't like that game any more, and he stopped bringing home *The Wall Street Journal*.

CHAPTER 7

Central High School, Little Rock

High school at last. I was not quite fourteen in September 1929. I had never had a real date, but there had always been gangs of boys skating or biking over to hang out in our front yard. There was even a bunch of Heights boys who between them owned a model-T Ford. On sunny days they would arrive in it. I say sunny days because the car had no roof, and for that reason it could carry twice as many passengers as other cars, but not in the rain. As many as ten boys might arrive at once and disappear just as quickly when someone gave the signal by saying, "Let's see if there is anything happening at Mary Brack's." I hated losing them to her.

We were not allowed to invite the boys into the house during school days, but weekend nights were a different story. Our house was fully equipped to make Ray and me popular. We had progressed from the crank-driven Victrola with bamboo needles to an automatic record-changing electrical player. The Radiola Superheterodyne that Daddy had assembled himself, with miles of wires strung around as antenna, had been replaced by a radio that didn't squawk and squeal but brought you music by Rudy Vallee. There was also the baby grand player piano. Sometimes all three of them were playing at once, and Daddy would poke his head over the banister and call, "Cut it down." As if all this musical paradise were not enough to lure the fellows, we invited four or five more girls as added attractions. The hook was baited on weekends. Even so, we only knew boys from the Heights.

When I arrived at Central High School, I felt utterly lost. There were over two thousand students. I had a hard time finding anyone I knew. I could walk endlessly through the long corridors without seeing a single familiar face. I liked my teachers, and I felt comfortable when I was in class; but when the bell rang and all two thousand people surged into the halls, I was alone and frightened. It was like being in the crowd at a circus, but without a parental hand to hold.

This phase didn't last long because rush week began early in October. All five fraternities and two sororities decided whom they wanted to have as new members. They began to gather up the chosen ones and tell them all the reasons they should join their club instead of going with the competition. I was enormously relieved when I got bids from both sororities. I had been afraid that I would be invited only by DBS, which was Ray's sorority. I didn't want to join DBS for two reasons. First, I didn't want to feel I had been voted in just because I was Ray's younger sister. The other, more important reason, was that as a "pledge" I would have to obey all the members, doing whatever they told me to do, and this would include obeying Ray. There was no way that I would submit to being her slave. For me the choice was easy. I joined DAD.

There had been a lot of negotiating for terms. We pledges had made a deal that there would be no initiation, just a Fool's Court. That should have made Mother very happy after the molasses and feathers of a few years earlier. It didn't make her happy. She worried about what people would think of a sister who was so disloyal as to join a different sorority. I did not explain. I just told her I liked the girls in DAD better and to leave me alone.

As pledges we were supposed to salute all the sorority members by dropping our books on the floor whenever we saw them in the halls. This could be very time-consuming. We carried books for every subject, and gathering them up again could even make us late to class. So from wandering the halls looking for a familiar face, I began to walk with my eyes cast down to avoid encountering a member and having to "salute." Some of the members were very nice and would signal me not to bother spilling my books all over the place, but others were strict and determined not to let the pledges get by with anything. I decided that I respected the members that didn't build their self-esteem by making others feel small. I decided to be like them when I was a full member.

Meanwhile, the boys had been chosen by the fraternities, and they too had made their decisions. There began to be get-togethers and dances for fund raising. Blanket invitations were issued to all the fraternities so the group became an elite one of around two hundred. This made a crowd of manageable size, and one got the sense of belonging instead of feeling lost. I never questioned what was happening to the eighteen hundred kids at school who had not been asked to join. I imagined that they had also made friends. At any rate, I had found my niche.

The officers for that year had already been elected. The meetings were held on Sunday afternoons, each week in the home of a different member. Most of the "business to come before the house" was talk of why the treasury was so flat broke and how much we would have to be assessed for the Christmas dance. Should we raise the dues, or was it a matter of having members who were in arrears? The treasurer didn't seem aware of who had paid and who had not. Along about February, a movement for impeachment was afoot. Having heard of the dissatisfaction, the treasurer graciously resigned saying it was too much bother. This left the second most important office wide open. Not many people wanted the job. I did. I don't remember the details of my maneuvers, but I triumphed.

I very proudly told my father that I was the new treasurer. His response was stern: "You know it's not just an honor, it's a responsibility. You will be handling money that doesn't belong to you, and you must be accountable for every penny." He helped me set up a book containing all the members' names and listing all the months next to the names. He taught me how to make out a deposit slip for the bank. He required me to hand him a deposit every Monday morning; he dropped it off at the bank for me and gave me the receipt that night. In addition to recording the members' payments in the dues book, I wrote on the back of each deposit slip the names of all the members whose dues were included in that deposit. Now I began to wonder why I had wanted the job and also to understand why there was so little competition.

Every Sunday, at the meeting, I would give a report whether or not they wanted to hear it. In the end, they became enthusiastic as they saw the treasury grow. I was learning more through this experience than I was learning in my algebra class. I understood its application to real life better than I understood how I was going to ever make use of algebra.

Having gotten my social life settled, there remained the question of academics. I was much happier with French than I had been with Latin. After all, French was a live language. I would not have admitted it then, but the little Latin I had learned in spite of myself was proving useful in guessing the meanings of French words. I liked my teacher, Miss Mary Murphy, the head of the French department. She spent all her summer vacations studying in Paris. She lived with her sister Celia, who was head of the English department. They were both splendid, dedicated teachers who cared about their students. Miss Mary not only cared about the students' progress in French, she cared about their progress in whatever romantic involvements they might be having. She was incurably romantic and got great vicarious pleasure from keeping track of her pupils' love affairs.

I kept Miss Mary pretty busy just tracking me. We never knew who was the source of Miss Mary's information, but it must have been someone who later joined the FBI because not a trick escaped her. Miss Mary even knew what none of my boyfriends knew. She knew I was wearing four fraternity pins at the same time. Of course, I didn't wear them in the open. It would have been a declaration that I was going steady.

I wore them inside my bra. That kept me chaste—I had an extra reason for not letting any boy put his hand inside my bra. If a boy had ever gotten that far, he would have thought he'd found a hornet's nest. This was a dangerous game, but lots of other girls were doing the same thing. Who knows, maybe the boys were giving away more than one pin too. At any rate, I considered myself an operator and one of the last big-time virgins.

Since my parents didn't allow me to date just one boy, I arranged it so I had a regular date for Friday nights. Then there were two other boys who alternated dating me on Saturday nights. Naturally, someone had to pick me up after the sorority meeting on Sunday and take me for a coke before depositing me at home. There I was, locked in except for school until the following Friday night.

There was an absolute taboo on necking in parked cars. I interpreted this to mean that necking was okay but that the car had to be in motion. A number of assaults had been made on couples in parked cars, so we always arranged to double date, taking turns at who was at the wheel and who was having fun in the back seat. Both ways it was exciting. Either we were listening to the other couple, or they were listening to us.

Speaking of assaults on people in parked cars reminds me of a tragedy that befell Little Rock. A seven-year-old girl disappeared. There was a wide search. It was such an unheard-of event that the police didn't know where to start their investigation. There were no clues—no pieces of clothing or lost shoes. Nothing. Everyone was petrified. Mother reported that her sewing circle in the Presbyterian Church had offered prayers for the safe return of the child. Then the morning paper carried a banner headline. The child's poor little body had been found in the bell tower of the very church in which Mother and the sewing circle had been praying. Just thinking about it gave us all the shivers. The janitor of the church was found guilty, and life settled back to normal.

With all my dating, note writing, and hanging on the telephone at night, there wasn't much time left for study. I always made time for my math lesson because there was no possibility of faking that. I was a master at bulling through the other subjects. The only time I was called on the carpet was a few weeks after the whole school had been put through a battery of aptitude tests. The teachers discovered simultaneously that there was a big discrepancy between my aptitude and my achievement. They called me in for a pep talk on how I was capable of so much more than I was giving them. Today, they would label me an underachiever and do something to make me begin studying.

Miss Mary did try to get me to work. She said she was going to have to flunk me if I didn't start learning my vocabulary lists. I knew she really liked me a lot, so I didn't listen to her threats. She wouldn't dare flunk me. Not *me*. But she did! I went to summer school to make up for what I hadn't done all winter. It wrecked the summer, so I decided not to let that happen again.

The English curriculum was strict. Each semester we had to read one Shakespeare play and two chapters of the Bible. In addition, we read and memorized a number of poems by the English and American poets. I'm surprised at how often those poems come to mind at appropriate moments. It sometimes takes a long time to piece them back together in my memory, but I feel rewarded when I can manage it. I got a big kick when my grandson had to memorize "Ode to a Daffodil" and I was able to recite it to him after at least fifty-five years.

Sorority life continued, and I was elected twice more as treasurer. The DADs were becoming the richest club in town. I loved watching the bank account grow. Each year we had a house party in June, right after school closed and before anyone left for summer vacation. The house party was really a series of parties over a weekend. There was a big luncheon, generally followed by a swimming party, followed by a treasure hunt in cars. Then there would be a supper dance. The following day, an equal number of exhausting events would take place. My ambition was to have enough money in the treasury so that in my senior year I could tell them: "This year we're going to have our big bash, and we don't need any assessment because the treasury can afford to pay the whole tab."

Several interesting things happened in the sorority during my senior year. Mother asked me to propose the young daughter of one of her friends for membership. Actually, the girl's father was a business acquaintance of Daddy's. I agreed to do it, though I thought I might be in for some problems. Quite by coincidence another girl was also being proposed. I'm going to fake their names for obvious reasons. The girl I was to propose I'll call Julie. Julie's parents were both Jewish, but they had sent all three of their children to the Episcopal Sunday school where I went. I had succeeded in having my boyfriend, who was the minister's son, get Julie's brother a bid to his frat the year before. That made my task in regard to Julie a little easier. The other girl being proposed I'll call Martha. It came out in the discussion that Martha had been adopted as a baby by a Jewish couple.

The meeting devoted more than an hour to the religious status of the two girls. It was decided that Julie was really Jewish even though she had been brought up as an Episcopalian. It was decided that Martha was really Christian because it was rumored that her real mother had been a Christian and that even though she had been brought up in the Jewish faith she was in truth a Christian. They voted on Martha first, and she got in. I held my breath. Then they voted on Julie. They decided that even though she was Jewish, she had a swimming pool that they would need for next summer's house party, and therefore they would take her in too. After all this talk, I was curious about what the discussion of religion had been when Ray and I were voted on for our sororities.

My senior year was rough. Most of my boyfriends had gone away to school. The year before I had been all dated up for months in advance, and now I was sitting home many weekends. It gave me more time to study and prepare for college, if my parents could afford to send me. Ray was already in her sophomore year at Sweetbriar College, so she was not really aware that the 1929 stock market crash had occurred. I had become aware of it because Daddy had stopped bringing home *The Wall Street Journal* to read with me. It was now three years later, and the financial market was still down.

Daddy gave me a book on bankruptcy, which he asked me to read. He said we would talk about it when I finished the book. I rushed to read it because I knew how worried he was and I was pleased he wanted to take me into his confidence. I had begun to say that maybe I would rather go to secretarial school instead of to college. He wouldn't listen to that. When I told him I had finished reading the book and was ready to talk about it, he said there was no need to talk about it because he had already made up his mind. I knew better than to push him if he didn't want to talk.

Mother had stopped making new clothes for me. Her last big project had been getting Ray ready for her freshman year at Sweetbriar. She had sent her off to school with thirty new dresses. Even after Ray left that fall, I had to stand in for her during those awful fitting sessions as Mother continued to make and ship her still more dresses. Daddy finally noticed that I hadn't had anything new in a long, long time. He suggested to Mother that if she was too tired to make me a dress, she should take me to a store and buy one. She couldn't even rally to that, so Daddy handed me a twenty dollar bill, and I went downtown alone to buy my first "store-bought" dress. I thought it was the best looking dress I had ever had, but Mother found that the hem didn't hang right. It was uneven, and she could fix it, but it wasn't worthwhile for her to touch it. I knew there had to be something bothering Mother for her to let me out of the house in a dress with a lopsided skirt.

During my senior year I was elected to be rush captain. We were very successful in pledging a group of terrific girls. The pledges, in turn, chose me as their pledge mistress, with the duty to act as a go-between for the members and the pledges. One afternoon in February when the business meeting had concluded, one of the members asked me to go upstairs and bring down the pledges. She wanted to beat them. I said I would not bring them down for that purpose. She insisted. I refused. I finally said I would go upstairs and tell them what the situation was. I came back downstairs with my hat and coat in hand and told the sorority that I was resigning because I did not want to be a member of an organization that would beat a pledge. If they wanted to beat the pledges, they would have to fetch them themselves. I turned and walked out.

It was Monday noon, and I didn't know where to sit for lunch. For two-and-a-half years I had sat with the same girls at the same table, and now I had deliberately isolated myself. I went to a far corner of the cafeteria with my bowl of chili and my Hershey bar and asked humbly if I might sit at this table of total strangers. They consented in a befuddled way. A few DAD members sought me out to tell me they hadn't beaten the pledges after all and that I should feel free and welcome to come back to their table. I told them I was glad they had not been brutal, for everyone's sake, but I would not come back without a written apology from the ringleader. A lot of messages were sent back and forth. She would apologize in private, but not in writing. I stood firm. Negotiations took all week, while I had my lonely bowl of chili in a far corner. Finally, the note came, and I was able to rejoin my sisters. This was my first battle of conscience on behalf of the underdog. It was not to be my last.

One Sunday morning in March 1932, Daddy woke me up at six o'clock. I was groggy with sleep, but he was bright-eyed and enthusiastic as he said, "They're pulling into Grand Central Station at this very moment."

I turned over, still half asleep, and muttered, "Who?"

He pretended shock as he answered, "Why, your sister of course. Have you forgotten her spring vacation begins today, and she and her friends are just arriving in New York? I bet her eyes are big as saucers." He was delighted that she was having this trip with Jane and Anne and a few other girls from college. Every day for the next two weeks, he speculated as to what the girls would be doing that day. He was enjoying their trip in his imagination.

Two weeks later, we were having Sunday dinner when Junior looked out the window and, across the street, saw Mr. Harris watering his lawn. All of us were surprised to see him. A week earlier the newspaper headlines had reported Mr. Harris's attempted suicide with pills. The paper said he had been found in time, and his stomach had been pumped. Now here he was doing an ordinary chore.

Junior and I chattered on about whether or not Mr. Harris would make another attempt at killing himself. I didn't believe he would because his family would now make him realize how much more important he was to them than the insurance money would be. Junior agreed with me. Daddy hadn't quite caught what Junior said and asked him to repeat it. Junior said, "I think anyone who has been that near dead and has come back to life won't ever want to try again." Rather grim conversation for the Sunday table, but there had been quite a number of suicides in town during the aftermath of 1929. One man had driven onto the railroad tracks so his family could collect double indemnity for an accidental death, but everyone in town knew that he had done it deliberately.

That night when I was studying, Daddy came to my desk and said, "Would you think your dad was a country bumpkin if he went to sleep with the chickens? I'm tired, and I have an important day tomorrow." He kissed the top of my head and went off to bed very early.

The next day began like any other Monday. Daddy took the laundry out to his car. He asked me for the deposit for the bank. He just forgot one thing: he was supposed to take me to school. It didn't really matter because Mother would take me.

During the course of the morning, Mother had a phone call saying Jane and Anne's father had died suddenly at home, and the family was going to try to reach them on the train from New York so they could transfer in Washington and get the train back to Little Rock from there. Mother naturally phoned Daddy to tell him the sad news. He said he hoped they had been able to reach the girls and hung up.

At noon all the men of the greatly reduced staff at the plant went out to lunch. While they were out, Daddy sat down at his desk and wrote Mother a letter. It began, "How strange that Mr. Cockrill should die on the very day that I had picked to go." He explained that he had waited until Ray's vacation was over because he didn't want to spoil it for her, but that he had a large premium due on an insurance policy that he had been paying on for twenty-odd years and he wasn't able to meet the payment. Rather than let it lapse, he was taking this way out. He had then carefully put his gold watch and diamond ring away with a note to Junior and had gone into the chemistry lab. He drank a bottle of carbolic acid that he had secretly taken from our bathroom, hidden in the bundle of laundry. When the men returned from lunch, they found Daddy on the floor. He was barely breathing. They called an ambulance, but he died on the way to the hospital. Here was a man who loved life, loved his family, and yet chose death at age fifty.

Someone else picked me up at school and drove me home so that Mother could tell me about Daddy herself. She gave me his letter to read. There was a postscript on it saying, "I had intended to write a separate note to each of our children, but now that the time has come I find I can't. Kiss them for me."

His Masonic Lodge arranged the funeral. He had indicated that he wanted them to do that for him. It was a very large funeral, and Mother kept saying over and over again, "I never knew that Nathan had so many friends." In a sense they had lived their separate lives, she with her church sewing circle and he with his Rotary Club. Neither knew the other's friends. Now Mother was going to have to live without him, and she was numb as she began to realize her loss.

Ray arrived home in time for the funeral. John Collins, the executor Daddy had appointed to handle his estate, called us all together at the bank to hear the reading of Daddy's last will and testament. During the reading, Mother put her hand on my knee and said, "I hope you are listening, because you are the one who will have to decide everything from here on. I can't."

CHAPTER 8

Aftermath

Aunt Ray stayed on with us while sister Ray went back to Sweetbriar to finish her spring term. Mother never got dressed anymore. She complained constantly that the pills the doctor was giving her so she could sleep were making her feel peculiar. She was always repeating herself, but I didn't think there was anything strange in that behavior. She had always told me to do something and then, before I could act on it, she would tell me again. Under the circumstances I learned to control my anger when she did this. I was having trouble dealing with sorrow and responsibility.

I continued going to school every day, only now I drove Daddy's car; after all, I was sixteen and had my license. The beginning of May was approaching, and there was so much to do. Get ready for final exams. Finish the plans for the DAD house party. Meet with Mr. Collins to keep posted on what he was doing with Daddy's affairs. Daddy had left him a book with each of his holdings written on separate pages. On every page he had clipped notes with his recommendations to Mother and to Mr. Collins on whether to hold or dispose of each stock. From the dates on these notes, we realized that he had made his decision back in December of the previous year and had known all that time that April 4, 1932, would be on his grave marker.

Mother kept repeating that Daddy had sacrificed himself for all of us just as surely as Jesus Christ had died on the cross. I hated that analogy, and I knew that Daddy wouldn't have liked it either. I was torn between feeling angry with him for what he had done and feeling angry with myself for not having insisted on discussing the book on bankruptcy that he had asked me to read. Maybe together we could have worked out another solution to his financial problems. It was like working on a jigsaw puzzle. Many of the pieces were coming together. I was learning things that he had never talked about at home for fear of worrying all of us. He had always tried to protect us, and he saw this final act as another means of caring for us financially. I couldn't see it that way, nor could I really give vent to my anger at him for abandoning us. I began to turn against God instead.

Ray Ray was visibly tired from the whole ordeal. We didn't argue when she said she had to return to Kansas City. I drove her to the train and thanked her for staying with us. I sent my love to Unc and my thanks to him for letting her stay away so long.

The day after Ray Ray left, I came home from school as usual. Cary met me at the door before I could go upstairs to see Mother. She said that Mother's friend Susan Goodnight had been there to see Mother and that she wanted me to come directly over to her house. I got back in the car and drove to the other side of town. Mrs. Goodnight came right to the point. She said, "Honey, I don't know if you realize it or not, but your Mother is not at all herself, and I think you should have a psychiatrist look at her. She just isn't making sense."

From her house I telephoned Dr. Brown, who was the chief psychiatrist at the Arkansas State Hospital. I happened to know him because his daughter Betty had been a friend of mine in grammar school. Dr. Brown was extremely kind and agreed to come to our house at ten o'clock the next morning. He suggested that I also have our family doctor meet him there. All this was arranged before I went back home. Mother didn't even notice I was late.

The next morning I sent Junior off to school, but I stayed home. Mother hardly noticed that I hadn't left on time. At a few minutes before ten, she looked out the window and saw the two doctors walking toward our front door. She let out a scream like a wounded animal, then started moving all of the furniture in the room to barricade the door so no one could get in. She was frantic and kept saying, "They're after my secret. Whoever knows my secret could make a fortune. Don't let them steal it from me."

I went down to let the doctors in. I described what was happening upstairs, and Dr. Brown said he had heard enough to know that she needed to be in a hospital as soon as it could be arranged. He thought it would be too upsetting for Mother if he went upstairs and started asking her questions. Dr. Dibbril agreed. They made a few phone calls and arranged for a trained nurse to come right away so that there would always be someone in the house with her.

Then I called Ray Ray to tell her what had happened. She said she was simply physically unable to come back down. I was to sit tight, and they would try to arrange for Mother to be placed in the Robinson Sanatorium in Kansas City. It might take a few days, but she was sure that Unc would come down to help me out.

I had been very frightened when Mother was so violent at the sight of the doctors. I was not reassured when the nurse arrived. She was a small, white haired, mild-mannered lady. I was sure Mother could overpower her even when in her right mind. In her present agitated state, she would be capable of annihilating the nurse. I talked to Cary and told her that I wanted her to spend the night inside the house, in one of the bedrooms, and that she was to have Big-To-Do, her boyfriend, ready to come in if she called him. Then I went upstairs, where everything was dead silent. I was able to push the door open a crack and see Mother lying asleep across the bed. Evidently she had exhausted herself. I kept checking back at the door until she awoke.

When she caught sight of me, she told me to come in and

said she would tell me the secret the doctors had wanted to steal from her. She said she believed that she could control how things happened by concentrating on them. She held a piece of paper to her forehead and said she was going to give me a demonstration of her new power. She was going to think about the clock chiming. She was going to will it to chime. She was triumphant when, after a few minutes, it went through its usual Westminster tune. Mother was convinced that with this power she could control the running of railroads. Was she also perhaps feeling that her thoughts had driven Daddy to kill himself?

I knew by this time I should not argue with Mother or try to talk to her in a logical way. I just went along with whatever she said. One moment she would say something sensible, and the next moment it was utter nonsense. I was the only person she would trust. Everyone else was trying to poison her. I had Cary prepare a tray for her, and I brought it up. At first she refused it, but then she said she would eat if I would feed her. What a reversal of roles!

I was trying to protect Junior from seeing Mother like this. She had grown haggard and old in the month since Daddy's death, but now, almost overnight, she had developed a wildness in her eyes that was frightening. It was easy to keep Junior outdoors during the daylight hours. When night came, I had to let him in the house. He was such a good kid that if I told him Mother wasn't feeling well he wouldn't insist on seeing her.

When it was time for bed, I asked him to sleep in the glass-enclosed sleeping porch in the bed further from the door. I slept in the bed nearer the entrance. I was able to fall asleep because the nurse was there, Cary was there, and Big-To-Do was at the ready.

I awoke with a start. A Lady Macbeth-like figure was hovering over my bed with her hair hanging in all directions. I sat bolt upright, and in a very commanding tone of voice I said, "Now you go back to bed." She turned silently and did as I told her. I was the only one who saw this apparition. The rest of the household slept. I did not sleep the rest of that night. I did not tell anyone about it the next morning.

Finally, Uncle Arthur arrived to take Mother to Robinson Sanatorium. The day before they were to leave, the nurse and I got Mother to let us bathe her. The next day I prepared clothes for Mother to wear. Nothing was to her liking. I kept showing her different outfits. She would have none of them. At last I persuaded her to try on just one dress to see if it still fit her since she had lost so much weight. Once I got her into it she decided to keep it on. So far, I had only said we were driving to the station to take Uncle Arthur to the train. I packed her bag in secret and hid it in the trunk of the car. All was in readiness when Mother balked. She sensed that getting her into the car was a trap. She would stay home while I took Unc to the train. When we overcame this obstacle, she wanted Unc to drive and me to sit in the back seat with her. The nurse also rode up front. During the drive to the station, Mother again placed her hand on my knee and said with lucidity, "I know where you are taking me, and you are doing the right thing for everyone." I've been glad all my life for that one statement. It was hard to be sixteen and making such big decisions.

When we got to the station, Mother got out of the car, and we walked along the sidewalk arm in arm. Suddenly she tore herself loose from my supporting arm and sat down on the curbing and began to weep. I sat down with her and talked to her in low tones, persuasive tones. It worked. We were again on our feet and heading toward the train. We had arranged for a stateroom large enough for the three of them. I stayed on the station platfrom waving good-bye through the window and wishing the train would please pull out before Mother changed her mind. Please God, move that train. He did.

I drove home alone in the big, seven-passenger Graham Paige. I felt like washing my hair and I did. Then I prepared my lessons and got ready for school the next day. It was the first time in a week that I'd gone to school, but it seemed like a year since I had been there.

I was welcomed back by all my friends. How could they realize that I was no longer the frivolous girl they had known, but a sober adult? I didn't talk about all that had happened during my absence. Now I had to try to get ready for exams and graduation. Mother had long ago bought the material and pattern for my special dress, but she never made it. It was to be white swiss voile with rosebuds embroidered all over it. My heart was not in it, but I found a seamstress to carry out Mother's plan. I was functioning like an automaton. I could have been a zombie going to class and making all those arrangements.

The month of June arrived. Report cards were out. My report card was the best I had ever had, and there was no one to show it to. No one to sign it as proof that I had brought it home. We were entitled to four tickets each for the graduation ceremony that was to take place on the football field. I said I only needed one ticket for Junior. He was only eleven and worried about sitting alone in that big stadium.

When we formed the marching line, I realized that I had forgotten to send myself roses. All the others had a dozen each, sent by their parents, to carry in their arms. Everyone felt sorry about my not having a bouquet, so they each contributed a rose. In the end, I had the largest bouquet of all, and it was mixed colors of roses. I cherished it as a sign of friendship.

The next day was the beginning of the DAD house party—the one for which I had been hoarding money during two-and-a-half years so there would be no assessment. This one was on the treasury. It was the fulfillment of an ambition. I would not be there. On the train with Junior going to Kansas City, I wondered if any of the girls missed me as much as I missed them.

When we got to Kansas City, I asked Ray Ray if I should go to visit Mother. She emphatically said that I was not to go because Mother would not recognize me and she surely would not want me to see her like that. I did not argue with that decision. I was glad she had decided for me.

On June twentieth, I was taking Mother home. She had died in the hospital—of acute nephritis—and I was taking her to be buried next to Daddy. Mr. Collins had arranged to have the funeral at Christ Church. Ray was with me on the train. I don't remember one thing about the funeral. I assume it was Reverend Witsell who spoke. He was the minister who, a year before, had confirmed me in the Episcopal Church. His son Charles was most attentive and kind, but we were no longer in love. At that moment, I just wanted to do what I had to do and get out of town. It was time to start a new life, and I wanted to get on with it.

Remembering how I had helped Ray Ray sell off her furniture when I was seven years old, I decided I knew how to close down the house. I chose the pieces of furniture about which I felt sentimental. I asked Ray to do the same. Then I had an appraiser come in to give me the prices that I should get for the rest of the furniture. It was the bottom of the Great Depression, so I wasn't to ask too much. In fact, I only got two hundred dollars for the player piano. The grandfather clock was carefully packed in four separate crates and put in storage. Hordes of people came to the house, some to buy, some to gawk, some to pilfer. I sat at a table by the front door to check people out. It was Mr. Collins who now made the bank deposits for me.

My friends were at a loss to understand why I was anxious to dismantle the house so quickly. Why was I burning my bridges? I had my reasons. A few weeks earlier, after Mother had gone into the hospital, one of her acquaintances asked me to come and talk about my future. Her husband worked for Mr. Goldman of St. Louis. In fact, Mr. Goldman had made him a very rich man. He and his wife lived in an enormous house even though they had no children. She was full of questions and unsolicited advice. Why didn't I hire someone, such as a school teacher, to come and live with Junior and me? What she was proposing would, of course, mean that I couldn't go away to college; but there was a junior college in town where I could learn secretarial work. I kept telling her that Junior would be better off in Kansas City with Ray Ray, and I would be able to find a college that would accept me even at this late date. She finally blurted out, "If you go to Kansas City, you will become Jewish, and we wouldn't want that to happen to such nice children."

I thanked her for her concern and made a dash for my car. I had never driven so fast in my life. I could hardly see the road. I was so angry. How dared she talk to me like that! She in all of her Christian virtue had not offered to give us a home in her fine, big house. In my eyes, her motives were unworthy of a true Christian. If she was an example of Christian charity, maybe I didn't want to be a Christian after all.

I definitely wanted to burn my bridges so that I could not return. I was forcing myself to start an entirely new life. I didn't ask Ray how she felt about what I was doing. I'm not sure I would have listened to her. Besides, she was going to return to Sweetbriar in the fall, and I was the one who would have to worry about Junior if we stayed in Little Rock.

While I was still in town, Mr. Collins wrote up a petition for the court to have my age disability removed. I was questioned by the judge, who found me mature enough to act on my own behalf and to be Junior's guardian. This being settled, and the house being put in the hands of real estate agents, I was on my way.

Part Two

CHAPTER 9

Starting Over

Ray Ray and Unc were living at the Bellerive Hotel, where they had moved ten years before. It was still one of the nicest apartment buildings in Kansas City, half hotel and half apartments. All the celebrities stayed there when they came to town for concerts.

Ray Ray's apartment had only two bedrooms, so we were crowded. Three beds in one room wasn't too bad—we were used to that because of our sleeping porch. But three of us with only one clothes closet and Ray with her huge wardrobe—there was the rub. It was not going to be for long. Ray and I would be going to college, and then Junior could have the room all to himself until Christmas when we would descend on him again for the holidays.

Ray and I were immediately accepted by the boys that Ray Ray had rounded up from amongst the children of her friends. Not so the girls. They didn't want to know us, and, what's more, we were on their turf.

My days were filled with writing letters to try to get into college. It would have been relatively easy for me to go to Sweetbriar, but there was still my old aversion to following in Ray's footsteps. It had begun in first grade when the teacher had greeted me with, "Are you going to be as smart as Ray?" It had been repeated in every class I'd ever entered. I was determined to put an end to that eternal question and deliberately chose a northern school. I had heard that Skidmore, in Saratoga Springs, New York, had a strong math department. Since math was the one subject in which my grades had been consistently good, I decided that I would like Skidmore. Evidently a Southerner had never applied before. Since all the schools were hot for geographic distribution, I was in.

That settled, I flung myself into a buying spree. I bought clothes regardless of the closet situation. We finally brought the wardrobe trunks up from the storage room and began living out of them. This had the advantage that when it was time to leave for college, the trunks were already packed.

I went for a routine medical exam that Skidmore required. The doctor called Ray Ray in great alarm to ask that I come for a rerun of certain tests. I felt fine. How could anything be wrong? He reran the tests four times. He had no further doubts. I was showing albumen four plus in the urine. At first, he said I was not to go away to school. I put up such a fight that he finally agreed to let me go if I would promise to have tests run every two weeks. I was ready to agree to anything. I just hoped he hadn't rocked the boat so that the school would now reject me.

The nights in Kansas City were very gay. Living at the Bellerive Hotel was terrific. It had a large dance floor and hired all the big name bands. Since we were regular guests in the hotel, we weren't subject to the usual cover charge. We always finished our evenings with a half hour of dancing in this dimly lighted ballroom. Ray Ray didn't seem to care about curfews. Mother had always insisted that I be in the house at eleven o'clock. Now, if I wasn't having too good a time, I would invoke the old curfew myself; but if I was enjoying the date, I was free to stay out later. Ray Ray was just glad we were having fun after so much sadness.

One evening Ray Ray's friends Laura and Paul Kessel invited all of us to see movies of their trip around the world. They were easy to be with, and the movies were interesting. I don't think I spoke a hundred words all evening. I learned later that Mrs. Kessel had written a letter to her son, Lawrence, that very evening. He was studying at the University of Berlin and was going out with one German girl in particular. His mother was petrified that he would marry her. In her letter to Lawrence she wrote, "I think you should come back to America. I have found the perfect wife for you. Ray Fels has two nieces living with her and you would like the younger one." He wrote back that she was to mind her own business and that no one had asked her to find him a wife. Besides, at twenty-eight, he felt he was old enough to choose for himself.

September came and I was again on a train. I was traveling with two girls I had never met before who were also Skidmore bound. We had to change trains in New York City. Then it was another three-and-a-half-hour ride straight north. Grand Central Station reminded me of the Sunday morning in March when Daddy had awakened me to share the excitement of Ray's arrival there. Just six months had passed, but oh the difference.

The entire town of Saratoga Springs showed that it was a famous resort. The Skidmore campus was in the same Victorian style as the hotels and all of the buildings in the center. It was like turning back the clock fifty years.

I can't say that registration went smoothly. Skidmore let me know that I would not be able to take calculus because they didn't have a professor for it that year. What would I like to take instead? I restudied the catalogue and decided that business law would help me to understand what Mr. Collins was doing. The registrar said business law was out of the question for a freshman. It was open only to seniors and in any case was already filled. I was not to be deterred. I let Skidmore know that if I couldn't be admitted to that course, the college would have to hire a professor to teach me calculus since I had come there especially because they offered it. When the powers that be heard how determined I was, they let me take the course in business law. It was the best course and the most useful information I had.

The problems my roommate and I were to have with our room were not immediately apparent because it was too early for the heat to be turned on. It was on the ground floor of

Hawthorne, the only room in the building that did not have an enclosed foundation. The wind would whistle under our floor and even send gusts up into the room. It was cold! It was my first year out of the South and no one let me forget it.

As freshmen, we had to wear bibs made of oilcloth. We painted our names and the names of our towns on the bibs so we could be easily identified. I still claimed Little Rock as my home. All the upper-class women would read my bib and tell me to talk Southern for them. Having heard my accent, they would call all their friends to assemble. I would have to talk for them too. I was very quickly a novelty on campus. I didn't like trying to say something different to each person, so I began telling jokes. I became a raconteur. Then they began to seek me out for the jokes as well as the accent. I knew a few really good ones, but looking back, they were pretty tame stuff.

When the first of October arrived, I got out my new fur coat. A furrier in Little Rock had gone bankrupt; this coat and two that Ray had at Sweetbriar were Mother's last bargains. My coat was muskrat masquerading as mink. I put it on, because it had suddenly turned cold and I was anxious to wear it after seeing it hang in the closet for over a year. When I put it on, an older girl asked if I had two fur coats. I confessed that this was the one and only. The girls warned me not to start wearing it so early unless I had another to wear on top of it—this weather was mild compared to what we might expect later on. I took their advice and nearly froze.

Meanwhile the steam had been turned on in all the rooms except ours. We reported this to the maintenance department, and they sent the plumbers. They tinkered around all day so we couldn't study and then went away announcing that everything was in good order. The next day at 4:00 A.M. we were awakened by a great banging and clattering. We couldn't sleep, and there was no heat. My roommate and I huddled together in a thirty-inch-wide cot to keep warm and to pool our blankets. Each morning was filled with "sound and fury signifying nothing." The first snow came. It helped things a little by sealing off the chinks around the windows so the wind couldn't come in, at least not through those particular ports of entry.

It kept on snowing. The sidewalk snowplows were out in full force. The street plows were throwing snow in another direction. Finally we were walking to class through canyons of snowbanks higher than our heads. Why had I chosen to come north to school?

Early in November a few bus loads of boys were imported from Williams College for a mixer dance to help the freshmen meet some boys. Since there were a lot more girls than boys, it was up to the girls to ask the boys to dance. That was not how it was done down south. I finally got courage enough to ask one boy. I got stuck with him, and it was so long before anyone tagged him that I had vision of our spending the whole evening together. We had long since run out of topics to explore. I was relieved when someone broke in on us.

The dating situation was at a very low ebb. A few of my friends were New Yorkers. Occasionally, someone drove up to see them and brought a few extra boys along. I would have been more than willing to have a blind date, but no one asked me. As I was never one to suffer in silence, I asked the New York girls pointblank why they were inviting other girls, whom they never saw during the week, to join them on blind dates on weekends. A girl from New Rochelle was honest enough to level with me. She said, "I don't think the boys would want to have a date with a Jewish girl."

What had happened? Had my passport expired? Wasn't I the same person I had always been? Was the decision no longer my own as to where I belonged? I hadn't changed my religion. All I had done was have a few dates in Kansas City with Jewish boys. It was 1932 and no one had heard of Hitler yet, at least not at Skidmore, but there it was, a full-blown case of anti-Semitism. I knew its symptoms.

The girl from New Rochelle then invited me to come home with her for the Thanksgiving weekend. There was a slight hitch: she was going to introduce me as Marie Alden, and under no circumstances was I to let her father know that I was Jewish. I thanked her but declined with grace. I would go to stay with Cary, a cousin of Ray Ray's who lived in New York City. Cary's children were far away at colleges and wouldn't be home, so there was plenty of room to put me up. I felt welcome to come and go. A Kansas City boy, an ex-Yalie, had arranged for his former roommate, Val, who was now in his second year at medical school, to take me out. Lightning struck both of us at the same time. But then I was lightning prone. Val was Catholic but not devout. He was so sophisticated that he knew how to step off the curb and hail a taxi. I was impressed. He wanted to show me everything. We went tea dancing at Central Park Casino to the music of Eddie Duchin. He handed me his handkerchief to smell, and I was gauche enough to ask if the scent was Vapex. He was kind enough not to embarrass me for this faux pas; he just said it was 4711, of which I had never heard. The boys in Little Rock didn't wear it. We even got into a speakeasy because he knew the password. We went to the Cotton Club in Harlem and heard Cab Calloway. What a lot of excitement packed into four days!

Cousin Cary wanted to show me a special exhibition at the newly opened Museum of Modern Art. They were having a one-woman show of the works of Georgia O'Keeffe. It was the first museum I had ever visited. This was something I had not seen on any calendars or even on the cover of the *Saturday Evening Post* that Sally had picture-read to me. Here were the paintings of a great woman, who was creating such beauty by showing the skulls of cows on desert sands with a gardenia lying next to them. It was all done in tones of white. Now I had something I could show to Val, my constant escort. When he picked me up that afternoon, I literally dragged him to the musuem. He said there were lots of museums in town. If I would come back for the Christmas holidays, he would show me all of them. It was very tempting, but I wanted to spend the holidays in Kansas City with what remained of my family. We agreed that Val would come at Christmas to visit his former roommate, who had introduced us. That way we could continue our great romance. I had rather neglected to tell Val that his old roommate also fancied he was in love with me. Like Scarlett O'Hara, I'd think about that tomorrow.

Back at Skidmore after Thanksgiving, I continued to have bimonthly examinations for albumen in the urine. All the tests were negative until suddenly it looked as if I had diabetes. I had indulged in a whole package of stuffed dates the night before. The doctors reran the glucose test. What a relief when the second test came back negative.

I can't remember how it began, but suddenly I was ghost writing letters for a number of girls. I seemed to have just the right romantic touch. Girls would bring me letters from their boyfriends. I'd ask what they wanted to answer and then write the response. The girls' correspondences were definitely heating up. They wondered if they could sustain the fever pitch in face-to-face encounters when they went home for Christmas. I gave each of them the same advice I gave myself, "Worry about it when it happens."

I was enjoying an introductory course in European history. Since it was the first lecture course I had ever had, my notes were an absolute shambles. I found if I listened carefully I couldn't write, and if I wrote I couldn't listen. I opted for total attention and doing my notes later. That helped. Most importantly, I was learning that a great history had taken place before America was discovered. A whole new world, the Old World, was just opening up to me.

At Christmas it was time to go back to Kansas City. I had lost my southern accent. I would have worried about it had I been going to Little Rock. No one dared come back to Little Rock talking like a Yankee.

My time was completely taken up by Val and his roommate. It was a weird arrangement. One night it was Val's turn and Ray was the roommate's date. The next night we exchanged dates. Were they wacky or was I? Or was I just in love with the idea of being in love? I didn't think I was hurting anyone. I was having enormous fun. I was a limit setter. I knew how far I would go, and they never pushed me beyond that point. By that time, I had stopped wearing four frat pins on my bra. They did not have to fear getting stuck. The "almost-a-doctor" persuaded me that there was no reason to be embarrassed if I let his hand go a bit astray, since he was used to examining women professionally. That was slightly sneaky, but I was willing to buy his argument.

Before the holiday ended, Val decided to go back to New York. He gave the feeble excuse that he wanted to spend New Year's Eve with his mother. Our parting was very tender. A few days later I received a seventeen-page letter. He had not realized when he came to visit that his roommate had serious thoughts of marrying me, and he didn't want to interfere with whatever plans were afoot. He knew I had not yet been approached on the question, but he felt that his leaving town would enable me to consider the situation more clearly. He said if I really wanted to know how he felt, I should read the lyrics to Schubert's "Serenade." I enlisted Unc's assistance in finding the lyrics. I read them and wept. How could I let Val go out of my life? He had indicated that if I didn't marry his roommate, he was still available. It was so confusing. Why would anyone propose marriage to a seventeen year old?

A few days before my scheduled return to Skidmore I finally got around to seeing the family doctor. He needed to test me again. I was relaxed about the whole subject because I'd had all the tests at school. When I heard that he had again found albumen at a high level, I was devastated. This time he was adamant. I was not to go back to school. He wanted me to go to bed for a month. He would look in on me daily. He said that what I had was serious. I must never consider having children; the strain on my kidneys during pregnancy might be too much for me. How could I feel so well and be so sick?

I agreed to stay home. I even agreed to stay in bed for the prescribed month, but I would not go to bed until the second of January 1933. I wanted New Year's Eve to be as gay as possible. I had a date with the roommate, and he had talked of a surprise. I thought it was going to be a ring, from what Val had written. Instead, it was the key (borrowed for the occasion) to a friend's apartment. We went there. The rhinestone strap of my evening dress broke, and we searched for a safety pin. I was frightened that he might bring up the subject of marriage. I was frightened that he might *not* bring up the subject at all. I used the broken strap as an excuse to have him take me home early instead of going to the dance.

On New Year's Day I had no date, but Ray's date insisted I come along with them to an open house for an old friend who was in town for just a few days. I went for lack of anything better to do. At the open house I remet Lawrence Kessel, Ralph's friend who had taken us to Electric Park when I was seven. He invited me to see Ethel Waters in a show at a matinee the next day. He didn't have tickets, and I didn't know who she was. We agreed that he would call me when he got the tickets. Instead he had his secretary call and get Ray Ray on the line. Then Lawrence got on the phone and asked Ray Ray, "Which one of the girls did I make a date to take out this afternoon?"

Ray Ray explained it was Marie, the younger one. She put me on the phone. Yes, he had gotten third-row-center tickets and would pick me up at one o'clock. The house was packed. How had he managed tickets at the last moment? He had his method. I later learned he had talked his parents out of their seats. They were so pleased he was taking me out that they were willing to sacrifice the tickets.

Ethel Waters was enchanting, and I was so engrossed that I was able to forget this was my last outing for a month. Lawrence, on the way home, asked me for a date the next day. I had to tell him I had a date to stay in bed. He said something to the effect that at least he would know where to reach me.

Lawrence was supposed to take his mother to Florida at the end of the week. He and his father usually took turns accompanying her because she had been ill and there was no need for both Lawrence and his father to be in the store at the same time. After the Ethel Waters show, he announced to his parents that he would not be going to Florida at all. He suggested that his father should go there prepared to stay the full two months. His parents didn't dare look at each other for fear that their confirmed bachelor son would pick up some eye signals. They waited until he left the apartment before they started patting each other on the back.

Why were they so happy to have me as a potential daughter-in-law? I wasn't the prettiest girl in town. I wasn't sure of my financial situation because Mr. Collins was still trying to figure out what would be left in my parents' estates if he paid off all the business debts that Daddy had left. I wasn't the most cultured girl around: I'd never even heard of Beethoven. I wasn't the healthiest girl: wasn't I going to spend the next month in bed? I had been told never to have children. Everyone knew my father had killed himself and my mother had died in a mental hospital. Maybe I, too, had some weaknesses in that direction. While I secretly worried whether I was worth marrying at all, Lawrence's parents were hoping that I would marry the most eligible bachelor in the Jewish community: their son.

Ray Ray was also rooting in his corner. He had always been a favorite of hers because of his kindness to her son Ralph during many operations to correct a limp caused by polio at age two. During the month I spent in bed, Ray Ray was the traffic controller. She arranged that there would not be too many visitors at one time. She wasn't very good at this task: she was never able to get one visitor out before the other one arrived. Rival visitors seemed to like each other's company; they stayed on and on. If I hadn't had kidney trouble when the treatment started, I was going to have it by the time it ended. I simply didn't know how to get out of bed and go to the bathroom gracefully while there were men in the room.

At first, Lawrence showed up only after work. Soon he began coming at noon also. Then he started looking in on me on his way to work. The month passed faster than I could have imagined. The groundhog and I reentered the world on the same day. The groundhog saw his shadow and went back into his hole for a few more weeks, but I was free at last. The other men sensed that they had been outflanked. When they phoned, they began defensively by saying, "I suppose you have a date with Lawrence Kessel tonight." I said they were right. This was their way of saving face. They hadn't actually asked me for a date.

On Valentine's Day, Lawrence sent me a corsage of green orchids because we were having dinner and going dancing at the Muehlbach Hotel. Going from the car to the hotel, I lost the corsage. We were seated at our table before I discovered that it was missing from my dress. I never knew if Lawrence really found it on the sidewalk or if he bought another one. He was gone quite a while. In the middle of dinner, after describing the beauties of Europe to me, he said, "I'd like to show you Europe."

With caution, I replied, "Do you mean the right way?"

He said he did. I wasn't playing hard to get, but I asked for time to think it over. There was still a boy in Little Rock I had not altogether finished loving. I wanted at least to go down there and take one more look at him before I made a lifetime commitment to Lawrence.

To my astonishment, Lawrence not only took me to the train but stayed on when it pulled out of the station. I was not the calmest person on the train. Did he mean to go all the way to Little Rock with me? After about twenty minutes, he said it was time for him to get off. I breathed easier.

I stayed with my old friend Jane Annis Cochran for the few days of my visit. She let me know that she had been dating the very boy I had come to check out again. She said she had arranged for him to take me out. She made it sound as though he were doing it only as a favor to her. What was going on? He picked me up that evening. When I said I had something serious to talk about with him, he suggested that we go to his house. Seated calmly on his sofa, I said I wasn't sure it would really interest him but I'd had a proposal of marriage and I wanted to tell him about it in person. He asked me to describe Lawrence, how he looked and what he did.

I said that Lawrence was twenty-nine, a Harvard graduate, six feet tall, had dark wavy hair and deep brown eyes. Finally, he said, "I'm only twenty-two and I'm just getting started in business. I never intended to get married until I was well established, but it looks like it would have to be now because I would do anything to stop you from marrying that JEW."

I don't know what I had expected him to say, but that certainly wasn't it. I tried not to show how hurt I was. Keeping my cool, I said, "If it is wrong for me, being half Jewish, to marry a Jew, then it would be twice as bad for you, who are fully Christian, to marry a half Jew. Feeling as you do, it would be only a matter of time before you would reproach me for it. Please take me home now."

It was still early in the evening. I phoned Lawrence and told him that I would be returning to Kansas City sooner than I had anticipated. I had accomplished my mission.

Lawrence got on the train at the same place where he had gotten off on my outbound trip. We fell into each other's arms. It was all settled except we decided not to tell anyone until his parents returned from Florida. There were a few other loose ends to be tied, but in principle we had an agreement.

Lawrence took me to St. Louis, where both of us went through extensive physical examinations. Dr. Alexander thought the history of albumen was utter nonsense. He said this simply wasn't the way it behaved. As for having children, he said I was built for it. He wished us well and gave each of us a clean bill of health.

Lawrence's parents returned to Kansas City the day Roosevelt was inaugurated for his first term, March 4, 1933. He insisted I go to the station with him to meet their train. We all got in the car together, and his mother wanted to drop by and say hello to her sister Beatrice. When we got there, the first words out of her mouth were, "How do you like my new daughter?"

By the time I got back to the Bellerive Hotel, Ray Ray was in a snit. She hadn't known we were going to announce the engagement that day. There was no ring to show. What was she to say to all the people who were calling her? When I was alone with her, I said that I too had been surprised by the announcement but hadn't know how to stop his mother. Ray Ray forgave me.

The next day a trip to the bank vault, to take out one of the diamond earrings that Lawrence's grandmother had worn, solved the problem of the ring. We went together to select the mounting. The wedding date was set for March 25. It took some bustling around to get me added to Lawrence's passport so we could use his visas. Each country required a visa. Because the wedding was set for a Saturday night, we had to have a civil ceremony at the county court house earlier in the week. That was wedding number one. Then we went to the home of Reverend L. M. Birkhead to rehearse what he planned to include in the service on Saturday.

Reverend Birkhead was a Unitarian minister and a close friend of Lawrence's. Sinclair Lewis had lived in Birkhead's home during the time he was writing *Elmer Gantry*. Lewis was there that day. He said he wanted us to get married then and there so he could sign our marriage certificate, as witness, and also so he could kiss the bride. That was our second wedding.

The third wedding took place, as scheduled, on Saturday night. It was a bit of an anticlimax because someone had given me an aspirin to calm me down. I had never had one before, and I broke out in hives. That night on the train, in our roomette, our third and last marriage was "consummated" by Lawrence's giving me a shot of adrenaline for the hives.

CHAPTER 10

Honeymoon

By the time we got to New York, all my hives were gone. Lawrence had to work during the days. I had plenty of time to explore the museums on my own. Ray was in New York again for her spring vacation from Sweetbriar. There were a number of other girls from Little Rock in town for their holidays, so I wasn't lost while Lawrence worked. He was doing the summer buying for his women's wear store.

At my urging, Ray telephoned Val to say she was in town and that Lawrence and I were also there. It was arranged that we would all meet at a restaurant in Yorkville and spend the evening together. I suppose Val was curious to see whom I had married. He brought along his friend, Alistair Cooke, who at that time was reviewing movies for a newspaper. He was utterly charming then, as now. He told us that he had been educated in his native England to be an expert in the management of forest lands but much preferred what he was doing. When he heard that we were going to spend a month in England, he graciously wrote out a list of good restaurants. He did this because Lawrence said he had never had a good meal in London. With Cooke's list in hand, we felt reassured. Nevertheless, I'm sorry to report that we ate mostly gray roast beef.

Cooke also told us about a friend of his who was playing in *Hamlet* in London. He wrote a note so we could go backstage to meet John Gielgud. We thanked him and said we would surely look him up even though we had just seen Leslie Howard playing Hamlet in New York. I had no idea that John Gielgud had the lead. We saw the play, but I was so awed by his performance that I was too timid to go backstage with the note of introduction.

We sailed out of New York on the S.S. Champlain. I couldn't believe the glamour of it all. We kept pretty much to ourselves as was understandable on a honeymoon. I'm sure there were interesting people on board, but we didn't meet them nor were we looking for them. Lawrence had told me about all the exciting adventures he'd had on other crossings. He said that a person alone was more likely to make chance acquaintances than people traveling together who appeared to be self-sufficient. I was always learning something from Lawrence in what began to be a Pygmalion relationship. He was my Professor Higgins; though he didn't need to correct my English, he needed to fill me in on subjects about which I knew zero. Not only was he a Harvard graduate, class of 1925, but he had done three semesters at different German Universities. I felt I was having excellent private tutoring under the pleasantest of circumstances.

The education of Liza Doolittle began in earnest when we got to London. Lawrence gave me a running commentary on the Italian paintings that were so abundant in the National Gallery of Art. He spelled out the characteristics of the various painters and how to recognize each of them. We began playing a game: we would stand at the entrance to a room and identify as many painters as we could. I realized that Sally's picture-reading had trained me to look at every detail and that this was an asset, maybe even a talent. Lawrence was delighted that I was catching on. I loved not only my teacher but the subject he was teaching me.

He took movies of everything we saw: the changing of the guard at St. James, Buckingham Palace, Whitehall, and the

Tower. No matter where we went, I wore the same dress. Mother wasn't around to tell me what to wear, and it was simply too much trouble to dig into the wardrobe trunk that Ray Ray had insisted I needed to take. It was such a nuisance. Lawrence had begged her not to send me off with so many clothes, but she would not listen. Ray Ray was convinced that every girl had to have a trousseau. She loaded me up with French lingerie even though we were going to be in Paris. She meant so well. She never knew until she saw our movies that I had lived in two dresses for five months.

A month was too short for London, but we had to move on to Europe or miss tulip time. In Holland many of the things we saw no longer exist. We visited Markham when it was still an island. Now the sea that was so rough to cross is filled in, and one can drive there. We saw the large private collection of Van Gogh's paintings when they were still in the owner's home in The Hague.

Brussels was supposed to be a mini-Paris. I adored it in its own right, but by then I was anxious to get on to the real Paris. I had seen enough Peter Paul Rubens canvases to last me a long time.

Leaving the station in Brussels on the way to Paris was a near calamity. I had grown so dependent on Lawrence that I didn't even carry a pocketbook. He put me on the train and told me to get two seats. He would follow with the porter and our bags. The train started, and Lawrence wasn't on it. I was headed for Paris without a husband, without a passport, and, worse, without a sou. The train was picking up speed as it left the station behind. It came to a halt and switched to another track. Then began the slow chugging backward. Our reunion was half joy and half reproach. We had both been so frightened, and we had both worried about my not having any money. Now I was saddled for life with carrying a pocketbook. Time to grow up.

Lawrence's sister Gertrude and her husband, Walter Bieringer, had been in Paris when we became engaged. They had made reservations for us in the Hotel Savoie on the rue de Rivoli near the Place des Pyramides, where the gold-colored

Me in my buggy.

Sitting still for a change.

Sally McDermott, born a slave, freed at age five. My adored protector. I was always safe in her arms or behind her ample skirts.

Daddy, Nathan Altschul Adler.

Mother, Helen Albright Adler. The photographer was intuitive in the way he posed all of us. I was more comfortable standing behind Mother.

Daddy Albright, Franklin Pierce Albright. Together we walked all over town and chatted with everyone.

My Grandmother, Emilie Altschul Adler. I was so comfortable on her lap. My only cousin Ralph Fels was with us.

My great-grandfather Allen Dunn Ramsey. This picture was painted around 1840 by an itinerant painter.

This is the bridge that crosses the White River at Batesville. It replaced Uncle Billy's ferry.

The three of us. Ray age twelve, myself ten, and Junior four. There has been a battle over pulling up the socks. I won.

My first store bought dress. I was sixteen.
Mother wouldn't straighten the hem.

A pastel portrait of me
done by Lawrence's cousin
Margaret Liberman.

My one and only,
Lawrence Reefer Kessel.
We were married
March 25, 1933.

Me as a young matron
of twenty-five.
One of the rare
occasions when I
was out of overalls.

First born, Paul Kessel II.

Lawrence and Paul coming in from the field.

Laura, taken just before she lost her first tooth.

Lawrence during his board member days.

Laura and her new husband, Boris Shlomm.

Me with the grandfather clock.

statue of Joan of Arc on her horse stands. As a practical joke, Walter had reserved a huge suite of rooms. The living room was so enormous and so formal that I couldn't imagine myself ever sitting there. We stayed one night and then asked the concierge for something smaller and cheaper so that we could continue to live there. We loved the location. We were practically across the street from the Louvre.

The concierge found us a smaller room with a dormer window just under the roof. There was a popular French song at the time called "*Sous les Toits de Paris.*" I learned the lyrics and would sing them in the bathtub when Lawrence went out. I still couldn't and wouldn't sing in front of any living person. Even this garret room was expensive for a long stay, but the concierge kept giving us the free theater tickets that were sent to him. He didn't particularly like the theater. He was a family man and wanted to spend his evenings at home. We got so many free tickets that we joked about not being able to afford to leave the hotel.

After we had seen all the plays in Paris, we moved to a *pension* on the Left Bank. It was run by a widow who had a teenage daughter. There were eight other paying guests, all of them students from foreign countries. That in itself added a new dimension to our stay. French was our only common language. I found that drinking a beer before the meal enabled me to converse rather fluently. It loosened both my tongue and my censor.

Lawrence thought we should enroll at the Alliance Française and work seriously on our French. I asked him to go and see if he liked it. Maybe I would follow in a few days. He went. He liked it, so I decided to accompany him the next day. When we walked into the classroom, the professor said in French, "How nice that you have brought your little sister with you."

"What's the matter with him?" I thought. "Doesn't he know a married woman when he sees one?"

At the Alliance, I had my *first* experience in mental telepathy. Lawrence and I were in a large auditorium listening to a lecture given in French. To follow what the professor was saying required extreme concentration on my part. In the middle of his talk, he asked the audience if anyone knew how many divorces there had been in France the previous year. Without any thought at all, I rose like a zombie to my feet, blurted out a number, and sat down. The professor said it was the exact number he had had in mind and that he would like to see me after the lecture. He was obviously shaken by the experience and so was I. Surely he was going to ask me how I knew the number, and I had no answer for him. It had just come into my head and was beyond my knowledge. At the end of his lecture I beat a speedy retreat because I didn't want to discuss it with him. I have subsequently had a number of such telepathic experiences.

Because of my experience with mental telepathy in Paris at the Alliance Française, Lawrence and I followed news items on the subject with interest. When we read later that Duke University was doing extensive research on extrasensory perception (ESP), we sent for their deck of twenty-five cards. The deck included five cards for each of five signs. One person looked at a card, another person attempted to say which sign was on it. Using chance alone, or just guesswork, one would probably call five out of the twenty-five correctly. That is exactly what Lawrence averaged. However, when I was calling the cards, my average was thirteen on each runthrough. Lawrence and I enjoyed playing this game and keeping score.

Several of Lawrence's friends from Germany had enough curiosity to come to Paris to see him and his "child bride." Having known him as a gay bachelor in Berlin, they wanted to see the girl who had caused him to cross the threshold. Hermie Rathenau, the nephew of Walter Rathenau, the ex-chancellor of Germany, was one of those friends. Under the guise of showing me the real Paris, he and Lawrence took me to such places as the House of All Nations, where each room was in the decor of another country. Some of the rooms had been left over from the World's Fair held at the time the Eiffel Tower was built. I looked on it as yet another museum until they brought out the girls, each with one breast exposed, for the men to make a choice. That's when I decided the game had gone far enough and the sightseeing trip was going to end. The madam made all kinds of offers in order not to lose her potential customers. My answer was loud and clear: "Get me out of here!" Lawrence was only half apologetic for having taken me there. He explained that he didn't want my education to be one-sided. It wasn't.

Eric Adler also came to Paris. Eric was a doctor of philosophy who had met Lawrence at Harvard. Years later they had run into each other again in the Berlin Opera house and formed very close ties. Eric didn't want to visit the nightlife places, but he did accompany us to Rouen, the chateau at Chantilly, and the cathedral of Beauvais. Eric told us years later that while he never doubted that Lawrence could educate me he doubted strongly that Lawrence would be able to keep me submissive for very long.

Lawrence and I wanted to see the chateaux of the Loire Valley. There were no bus tours at that time. Tourists were scarce due to the world depression. We ended up making a deal with a taxi company for a four-day private tour. We asked for a chauffeur who spoke good French so that we could practice what we had been learning at the Alliance. We got practice all right, but not in the way we wanted.

The chauffeur turned out to be a Russian refugee who spoke very little French. He was stubborn about asking directions because he couldn't understand the answers anyway. We got lost constantly. Once when we didn't know where we were, we saw some children picking wild strawberries. We joined them. I was wearing sunglasses; they had never seen dark glasses and wanted to know if I wore them because I had sore eyes. That was how we practiced our French. Another way was hiring guides to take us through the chateaux when we finally found them. We really got practice in listening; there is nothing in the world as garrulous as a French guide who is a frustrated history teacher. The guides seemed to think that the more they talked the bigger the tip would be. They were probably right: sometimes we paid to get rid of them.

When I see the packed tourist buses lined up at Chambord

today, it is hard to believe that in 1933 we were the only people in the entire chateau. There was not a single piece of furniture. We amused ourselves with the double staircase, the architectural wonder depicted in so many books. Lawrence made movies of all the chateaux. He told me that he had showed his world tour movies for many charities in order to raise money, and he thought these films of France would be very good for fund raising. It's hard to believe home movies were such a rarity that people paid money to see them. Now they would probably pay not to see them.

Lawrence thought I should learn to do the commentary explaining the shots. Of course, there were no sound tracks on these nonprofessional movies. I made the mistake of saying I would never in the world be able to stand before an audience and talk. Famous last words. That night he had me stand up on the foot of the bed and tell him the story of "The Three Little Pigs" in full voice. He had trained speakers at Harvard for La Follette's campaign for president and was training me in the same way. It worked. I have never since hesitated to speak in public.

Lawrence wanted to take me to Italy, but I couldn't tear myself away from Paris. Maybe we would go to Italy the next year. It was to be nineteen years before we returned to Europe.

When I began to repack my wardrobe trunk for the return trip, we both realized that in all of our months in Paris I had not bought a single souvenir. At Lawrence's insistence I finally bought a pair of pigskin gloves and a matching pocketbook. There was nothing I really wanted. I thought I had it all. Love, marriage, travel, intellectual stimulation, and best of all I had a husband who wanted me to keep learning.

CHAPTER 11

Down on the Farm

Honeymoon over, it was time to go back to real school. I enrolled at the Kansas City Junior College. It was quite a comedown from having had my own private tutor all spring and summer. Here I was confined to regular classroom work and slide lectures in the art history course. It was pretty mild fare.

We found a furnished apartment easily. Learning to cook was a bit of a problem. Lawrence's mother would have been happy to go on cooking for the two of us forever, but I didn't want to be treated like a child. I had better learn to take care of my own husband. Someone told me that cooking is just like doing chemical experiments: you follow a formula step by step. I must say that each meal was certainly an experiment. Some were good, but some were so bad we had to dump them in the garbage can and go to a restaurant. Lawrence never fussed about such culinary accidents. He was much more interested in our other biological appetites.

In the early spring of 1934, Lawrence began to get concerned about the possibility of inflation. Having been a student in Germany during their wild inflation of 1923, he had seen how worthless money could become. He thought common stocks and real estate were the best things to have during inflation. What kind of real estate, I wanted to know. Did he want to buy a house? No, that wasn't it. A house could not be income-producing. We or he decided that we needed to buy a farm.

I still don't understand how we made that decision because I was already part owner of a number of farms that were included in my parents' estates. Nevertheless, we began to spend our Sunday afternoons following lists given us by real estate agents. I was back to the Sunday afternoon drives with the family when I was little and Daddy wanted to see the customers' fields.

I was amazed at how much I had learned by absorption. I knew a good stand of alfalfa, and I could spot poor soil at a glance. Now it was Lawrence who was impressed with *my* knowledge. Not only was I choosy about the soil and the buildings, I wanted to have a nice house in the bargain. There were so many farms available, foreclosed by the banks and insurance companies, that one could write one's own prescription. Sometimes we didn't even bother to get out of the car and disturb anyone when I could see at a glance that the place was too run-down.

When we were beginning to despair, we found a beautiful farm of two hundred and forty-six acres all in Kentucky bluegrass. The house had four bedrooms, two baths, a living room with a huge stone fireplace and a vaulted ceiling. The ceiling was high enough so I could bring the grandfather clock out of storage and again hear its ticking, which to me was a heartbeat I had missed for the past two years. The outside of the house was a gold-colored, rough-hewn fieldstone. There were seven barns and a large silo. One of the barns was over two hundred feet long and was built of gunite, which is blown concrete. This was the farm I wanted, and it was to be ours.

We hired Jess Lauck to design some additions to the house. Jess had been the architect for some of the largest and best buildings in the downtown section of Kansas City. Now, because of the Depression, there were no buildings going up. We were his only clients. No one ever had more loving and expert attention than we got. Here was this wonderful and talented man spending his days supervising a job he wouldn't have sneezed at during the twenties. He gave us some great advice, too. He said, "Never finish your house. Always leave something that you want to do. When you finally do it as a project, it will renew your interest in the whole house."

He was so right. I pity people who do their houses to the last ashtray and have nothing further to look forward to doing.

We ran an ad in the *Kansas City Star* to find a farm manager. There was a three-bedroom white frame house for a farmer and his family. Unemployment at that time in our part of the country had reached twenty-five percent. Even so, we were not prepared for the deluge of applications that we received. When mail started coming in, I emptied out a whole dresser drawer to hold it. Then I emptied a second drawer, and still letters kept coming. I read them all. I penciled comments on the envelopes. I threw away those that began, "I've never done any farming before, but I'm willing to try." Hell, I didn't need to hire someone who was as ignorant of farming as I was. I needed someone with experience, and I needed him soon.

Our farm was located only two miles from Olathe, Kansas, the county seat of Johnson County. It was about twenty miles to Kansas City, and Lawrence drove to his store six days a week. It was obvious that I was going to be the farmer in our family. I contacted the county agent, who put me in touch with the Kansas State Agricultural College. They had an extension adviser who would look at your farm and evaluate the possibilities of raising various crops or stocks. The adviser did surveys to recommend projects with the best chances for profit in the coming year. Fortunately, with all the barns we had, we could pretty well follow the adviser's recommendations. Over the years this led me through the whole gamut. The first year they suggested we begin with sheep.

Mr. Ingersoll, our newly hired manager, knew all about everything to do with a farm, but nothing about sheep. None of the neighbors had ever raised sheep. There was an old Scotsman a few miles away who had a flock, but he didn't want to sell any of his animals. In the end, we sent to Colorado and ordered a train carload of merino sheep. There were about two hundred in the shipment, and we also bought four purebred Hampshire rams. We thought that should get us started. The Scotsman came over and admired our purchases; he promised to come back the next winter to give us a lesson in helping the lambs come into this world. He would then teach us whatever else we needed to know. He was being mysterious about the rest of it.

Meanwhile I had written to Washington, to the Department of Agriculture. I think I ordered everything they published and they published a lot. I even ordered their pamphlet on childbirth, just in case. The pamphlet on breeding sheep recommended painting the briskets of the rams with gentian-blue powder when you turned them in with the flock of ewes during the first cool nights of August. In this way, when the rams mounted the ewes they would leave their color marks on the rumps of the ewes. We figured one ram was responsible for covering fifty ewes. Fortunately, not all the ewes came into heat on the same night, or we would have found four dead rams in the morning. The rams knew their job and were diligent in performing it. After they got over fighting with each other as to whose turn it was, and once they realized there was plenty to go around, they settled down to the task at hand. When it was morning, we would separate them from their ladyfriends so they could fill their bellies and get some rest. They did both and by evening were raring to go again.

We changed the color on the rams' briskets every seventeen days. Next came Venetian red. If the ewe was already pregnant, she wouldn't get a red mark because rams don't fool around with a ewe that isn't in heat. After the red came lampblack. A ewe that got a black mark was sent to market. There was no use feeding a barren animal since there would be no dividend at the end of five months. Ruthless, yes. This was business, and the animals were merchandise.

All during their gestation period, I would take the ewes for long walks twice a day to make sure they got enough exercise. We had bought a black-and-brown Belgian shepherd. This breed of dogs is famous for being natural heelers. This means that when they work with sheep they force them to go in a certain direction by nipping at their heels rather than approaching their heads as some dogs do. Ted, our sheepdog, always went with me when I walked the sheep because he could keep them from straying off.

As lambing time came closer, I began to watch for signs that would tell me to put a particular ewe in a pen with fresh straw in case she had her lamb that night. I watched their gait, I looked to see if their bellies had dropped low, and I watched their vulvae to see if they were swollen or showing a discharge. Any of those signs and the ewe was put in a private pen.

Someone made rounds of the maternity ward every two hours to see if any ewes were in trouble. Lawrence, Ingersoll, his wife, his older children, and I each had our hour for patrol. No matter whose patrol it was, I was to be called if there was trouble because I had the smallest hands. If there were twins, one twin was sure to get into a position blocking the exit, and the other twin would be frantically butting his or her head against the first twin's belly. At the beginning, someone had to hold a flashlight so I could read the government pamphlet on what to do next. Eventually I could have done it blindfolded. With a well-greased rubber glove I went in and found the two front hooves of the exit blocker. I hooked one finger over his head, waited for the contractions to come, and gave a slow and easy pull. Usually, in less than ten minutes the ewe was on her feet and licking her twins to remove the gelatinous membrane that clung to them. She usually had a strong preference for the larger twin and, if left alone, would have ignored the smaller one. At this point, Ted was called in on the case. He would make the ewe just nervous enough so that her protective instincts would come into play and she would have a surge of maternal feelings toward both lambs. That settled it; she had two babies, and she had to raise both of them.

Once we caught on to raising twins, we found it more profitable. If left alone, sheep will produce twins ten percent of the time. We realized that if we could raise the percentage of twin births we would also raise our margin of profits. Lawrence had studied Mendel's law a bit. He advised using ear tags to mark the ewes who had produced twins. We retained them in the flock. By that time our flock was over four hundred females, not counting their lambs. We never kept the lambs for breeding because they were hybrids. If we bred the hybrids, their offspring would not have the same quality of rapid growth or vigor. I was finally able to get fifty percent of the ewes to have twins. Not only did they have them, but I forced them to raise the twins to market size.

In view of the multiple births that are taking place in humans now, I begin to wonder if another thing that we were doing may have contributed to our high percentage of twins. Estrogen had just been isolated, and its use had begun. My gynecologist and I decided to do some experiments with it on the sheep. I wanted to bring them in heat earlier than late August so that I could be the first to get them to market in the spring. We thought that shots of estrogen might do the trick. This was a great success, and we were than able to go through lambing in December. Now I wonder if my big success in producing twins may have in part been due to the estrogen.

I've strayed far ahead of that first crop of lambs when I still had so much to learn. My friend the Scotsman came back to give us a lesson on how to dock the lambs' tails and how to castrate them so the meat wouldn't taste too strong. The demonstration of how to cut off their tails was straightforward. There was an implement made for doing it, and it worked with a minimum of bleeding. When it came to explaining how to castrate, the Scotsman became embarrassed. He said that no implement made for the purpose was any good and that one really didn't want to cut the scrotum, but just crush the cord inside that led to the testicles. "Okay," I said, "but how do you do it if there are no instruments?"

At that point, the expert grabbed the lamb, bared his teeth, and bit the lamb where it hurt. No blood, no fuss, and the lamb ran off. I turned to our farmer and asked him if he thought he would be able to do this operation. He answered, "No, ma'am, I don't." I thought the farmer was just being squeamish, and I prepared to give him a pep talk. Then he added, "You see I ain't got no uppers." Sure enough, he didn't. We finally solved it another way. We found a Swedish device called an emasculator that was easy to use and effective.

We bought a flock of purebred Hampshire ewes so we could raise our own rams. These purebreds were terrible snobs. They were sent to the same pasture as the merinos but refused to associate with them. I guess they thought of themselves as elite. One can argue that because they had been raised together they preferred to stay together, but I think they felt themselves to be superior. It didn't matter as long as they did their job, which was to produce rams for our own use and for us to sell to other farmers. A number of other farmers had followed the county agent's advice and our example, so there was a market for this breeding stock.

We entered a pen of five of our lambs in the county livestock show. The judge spent only seconds looking at our pen. Then he spent a long time going from one pen to another and back again. Lawrence was getting anxious and kept saying the judge didn't like our lambs. I felt confident of my own eye as a judge. I thought that we were easily in first place and he was trying to decide second and third places.

When our pen got the blue ribbon, Lawrence was surprised and I was vindicated. This was the first time we had showed in competition. Until then we had been regarded as city slickers who didn't know what they were doing, but now our image began to change.

Raising sheep was really hard work. First of all, sheep have no will to live. If they become sick, they do their damnedest to die. They just want to lie down and give up. If they take it into their heads to die, you may as well let them do it their way.

Second, many things have to be done to keep them in good health, and all of them take work. Their hooves grow long and begin to curl under, so you have to throw them over on their rumps and take a sharp knife to trim their hooves. You do that to four hundred of them and you can say you put in a good day's work. Then they have a tendency to get stomach worms. You have to give them a liquid dose of nicotinic acid to kill the worms, and you hope you don't kill the sheep in dosing them. They fight you all the way when it comes to taking medicine.

Then there are insects called blowflies that love to lay their eggs in the wool tags that are just under the tail. You don't know the blowflies have made their deposits until the larvae begin to hatch and you see the tails start to twitch. Then it's time to do the worst job of all. You have to drench them in a strong chemical. That means picking them up bodily and putting them in a large tank full of the disinfectant that kills the larvae. The sheep hated this and so did I.

Another thing that the sheep detested, but I rather liked, was when we sheared the wool. There were itinerant shearers who had to be engaged far in advance. We prayed that when our turn came the weather wouldn't be too cold, because after the sheep were shorn they would be running around naked for a while. Besides their embarrassment, they might catch cold. The shearers taught me how to grab the fleece as it came off the sheep. I was to throw the tags from the tail area to one side so the whole fleece wouldn't be graded down and declared "dirty." Then I had to fold the wool from the legs toward the center of the fleece and get a cord around the whole thing and tie it. I had someone else ready to carry it away and pitch it in the wool bag ready to send to market. When it was time to sell the wool, I went along with it and watched while each fleece was graded separately and weighed. The money we got for the wool was supposed to be enough to pay for feeding the sheep all year. The profit, as I said, was in the lambs.

One year the *Kansas City Star* wrote an article about us or, rather, about our lambs. We had sent two truckloads to market, and the price we were paid was written up as an all-time high. We got fifteen cents a pound on the hoof.

One year we had a total disaster with the fine flock of twin bearers that we had built up. I began to notice some of the sheep were stumbling and staggering as they came in from the walk in the pasture. Some even bumped head-on into fences. It was getting near the end of their gestation period. No one had ever seen anything like it.

The Agricultural College sent experts to see what was happening. They analyzed what we were feeding. The diet was perfectly balanced. The sheep began dying. At first I personally did autopsies on them and sent the most important parts to a laboratory for examination. The closest diagnosis that the lab could make was that the cause of death resembled uremic poisoning in pregnant women. It affected only the ewes carrying twins and triplets. On autopsy, the kidneys looked like small balloons filled with blood. They were completely shot; even inducing early labor would not have saved either the lamb or the mother. The ground was frozen solid, so we couldn't bury the dead. Fortunately, the same cold weather froze the corpses so there was no odor. We just piled the bodies high outside the barn. We lost a third of the flock and never knew why.

We had defeats, but we also had triumphs. There was never a time when we weren't ready to start a new project if it held promise of being either interesting or profitable or both.

CHAPTER 12

Special Projects

Everyone seemed to be full of good ideas about what I should be doing on the farm. The neighbors, the family, the county agents all gave me advice. Some of it I solicited and some of it I took. There was also some very good advice that I failed to take and that I sometimes wished I had heeded. Aunt Elise Wolff of St. Louis, who was Grandmother Adler's sister, visited us on the farm when she was well over ninety. She said, "Marie, it occurs to me that you are learning to do many too many things. I just want to tell you that whatever you learn to do, you will be expected to do." She said it plainly enough, but I didn't understand her until it was too late.

The neighbors were always telling me I should have a large vegetable garden. When I fell for that one, they thought I ought to get a pressure cooker and can what I grew. They kept telling me how many quarts of beans they had put up or how much corn they had laid by. It began to be a question of keeping up with the Joneses. One of the neighbors egged me on with her favorite expression, "It'll taste mighty good when the snow flies." They would look in on me every so often to ask how many quarts I now had. When I finally hit eight hundred, I decided that I had run the course and that I had nothing further to prove to them or to myself on that score. I shut down the pressure cooker and never went near it again.

I made several big blunders. The first was not acknowledging that neither Lawrence nor I liked canned vegetables. The second was not realizing that we would have had to eat over two quarts every day of the year to get rid of all eight hundred quarts. I got a lot of empty cartons from the grocery store, packed the whole summer's production into our International pickup truck and took them to the orphanage in Kansas City. I hope they enjoyed eating them more than I enjoyed canning them, but somehow I doubt that they did. What kid likes vegetables?

Then there was the strawberry patch. I would spend the whole morning picking strawberries and the entire afternoon making preserves. By the next morning enough new berries would have ripened so that the whole process repeated itself. This time I got smart. I ran an ad in the Olathe, Kansas, newspaper saying that anyone who wanted to come and pick berries should bring a container. Pickers arrived by the dozens. They and their kids swarmed all over the place like bees. At the end of a few days, there were no more berries and no more vines either, so I didn't have to make any more preserves ever.

Speaking of bees, there was a shortage of sugar during the war. A beekeeper came to ask me if he could place some hives in my yard. He would watch over the bees and give me a share of the honey. That sounded all right, no work, and we would have a good sugar substitute. What could go wrong? What went wrong was that the beekeeper died shortly after he had deposited his large swarm in my side yard.

It was back to the government pamphlets. They told me how to burn rags to smoke out the bees while I robbed them. They just left out one small detail. At what time of day should one rob the bees? The word rob to me conjured up the image of a night prowler, so I decided to do the deed at nightfall. I dressed for the occasion. Lawrence had done some fencing at Harvard and still had his protective mask, so I put that on. I wore a coverall and put rubber bands around the sleeves and the ankles. High gloves completed my costume. Armed with my smoking rags, I went about my task.

Lawrence and our friend Ensign Dick Mintz were standing on the sidelines coaching me by reading from *Beekeeping Made Easy*. The first thing that happened was that a bee managed to fly up inside my sleeve and get himself trapped there. He sounded mighty frantic buzzing around in there. I told Dick to look the other way because I intended to do a striptease until I had liberated the bee. I began with the rubber bands. Finally the bee flew away, much to his relief and mine. He hadn't hurt me, and I hadn't hurt him. Fair enough. Meanwhile, standing on the sidelines, Lawrence had stopped reading aloud. He had problems of his own. His shoes had perforations for ventilation; four different bees had found their own special holes and had stung him. We decided to call it quits for that night and to come back with our burning rags and fencing mask another time.

Next day I was on the phone to the county agent. He nearly fell over laughing at me for thinking I should rob the bees at night. The right time to rob bees is high noon, when all the working bees are out gathering honey and spreading pollen among the flowers. So I did it his way. I took off a couple of supers of honey and put them in the little stone house at the end of the arbor. It was fully screened, and I thought the trays of honey would be safe there. But when the bees came home at sundown, after a hard day's work in the field, they were so mad at having been robbed that they set out in search of their winter store. They found where it was hidden.

The next morning, bright and early, the bees got themselves organized and set about claiming their own. They made a million trips but finally got back all that I had stolen from them. I found another beekeeper and asked him please to come take these bees to another location. I would make do with the war sugar ration I was allotted.

At the beginning of one summer, Rabbi Gershon Hadas asked me to let his two teenage daughters stay with me for a couple of weeks while he was undergoing back surgery. It was very exciting for me to have the girls coming, and I busied myself finding young men for them to date. I phoned the naval base, spoke to Chaplain Kalbfleisch, a Lutheran, and asked him to make up a list of Jewish boys on the base. He was careful about the list, and I wrote to a half dozen boys, inviting them for Sunday dinner. Dick Mintz was on the list. We were to pick them up at the drugstore in Olathe. Another boy got off the bus with them and asked if he could come too. What could I say? He wasn't on the chaplain's list, but he was the one that Hedva Hadas fell for. I felt I had failed my trust. It all worked out in the end, but I lost some sleep over what I was going to tell the rabbi.

Dick was a lieutenant in the Navy stationed in Olathe, which had the largest inland installation for training air pilots. They were flying the "yellow perils"—two-seater, open-cockpit planes. He was an instructor. He became our close friend and came to see us often, even after the girls had returned home. He always brought us scarce items of food from the PX. One particular item he brought was Bermuda onions. Out of gratitude for this delicacy, I fried mountains of onion rings. That was the idea. One hand washes the other.

Before I had any children, I went for a holiday to Florida with Lawrence's parents. Lawrence thought I would liven up their stay down there. We read in the paper that Will Durant was going to give a lecture on his latest volume of *History of Civilization*. Kess, as Lawrence's father was called by all of his friends, said he would like to go to the lecture and would be curious to see if Will Durant remembered him.

Many years earlier, before he had begun to publish his books, Durant had lectured in Kansas City, and Kess had been asked to meet him at the train. When Kess saw how shabby Durant's suit was, he took him to a men's store and bought him a new suit to wear for the lecture. Kess pretended that the store owed him some money and that this was the only way he could collect it. In this way Kess made Durant think he was doing him a favor, helping him use up his credit.

Now, Mr. Durant was so prominent and popular an author that Kess rather doubted he would remember him. Kess was too modest. He was not a person that one forgot so easily. Durant was delighted to see him after the lecture and forthwith invited all three of us, Kess, Lawrence's mother, and me, to join him the next day. He was to be the guest of honor at a luncheon given by the Mr. Kellogg of cornflakes fame. Among the other guests, we met Dick and Andrea Simon and Max Schuster. Simon & Schuster published Will Durant.

Kess and Laura treated me as though I were their youngest unmarried daughter instead of their daughter-in-law. They urged me to double-date every night with Max Schuster and the Simons. It was great fun for me. I corresponded with Max for a number of years. He called me his Kansas chronicler because I kept writing him stories of the dreadful drought that was afflicting the Midwest.

The drought we suffered was straight out of Moses' dream. We had seven lean years. Our farm was on the edge of the Dust Bowl. For seven years we had very little rain. Sometimes we would go as long as ninety days without a cloud passing overhead. We were having a hard time keeping our bluegrass alive, and we were renting land on which we hoped to grow grain crops to feed the livestock. We tried a drought-resistant sorghum that grew well enough to fill the silo. We got water from Olathe, through two miles of our own pipeline, so we didn't worry about our wells going dry. In fact, we allowed the neighbors to haul tankfuls of water from our wells. Theirs had dried up, and many of them were dairy farmers.

Due to the drought, we also had a plague of locusts. Hordes of them flew in from the north and began to eat everything in sight. When they descended on our farm, it was bad. When I walked across the lawn, a hundred of these grasshoppers of all sizes flew up in the air each time I put my foot down. I wore a hat with a mosquito net pulled down in front as protection because I hated having the bugs hit me in the face. One day I washed a few pairs of socks for Lawrence and hung them outdoors to dry. When I went to bring them back in the house, they were gone. All that remained were tiny shreds protected by the wooden clothespins that held them. Those little bastards had eaten the socks right off the line.

We always had to work some angles, but we were able to make money even during the drought. We formed a working partnership with a man who bought and sold cattle in the stockyards of Kansas City. He was to buy cattle that came to market from the Dust Bowl and were literally skin and bones. He would phone me to say he was trucking us a couple of hundred head, weighing about eight hundred pounds each. In some cases he had paid a cent a pound, but he never paid more than a cent and a half.

I would get ready to feed them, but very slowly. To bring them on to feed without foundering them was tricky. Foundering meant they would overeat and blow up and die. We had to take away all of the salt licks and limit their water intake. If we exercised extreme caution, we could save them all, and they would begin to put on weight again. In three months' time we could usually send them back to market. By then they weighed twelve hundred pounds each and would sell for five or six cents a pound. If you put those figures in your calculator, you will see that by bringing a new herd every month into one of our feeding lots, we could make a nice piece of change. Even though we were making money, we were glad to see the drought end and to find another way of showing a profit.

After the drought was over, we bought a good herd of Hereford beef cows. A strong bull was chosen and brought home in our truck. I was glad to get home safely with him because he kept glaring at me through the dividing window, and I knew he had the power to demolish the whole truck if he got it into his head. When he was unloaded, he couldn't wait to go to work. He made himself at home immediately. With his harem of thirty cows, he felt himself the king of all he surveyed.

After we had a couple of calf crops from the herd, we decided to start a different project, so I ran an ad to sell the herd. A very handsome, white-haired man came to see the cows. He liked them, and we settled on a price. There was one hitch. He had not yet taken possession of his farm and wanted to pay me to graze the cows until he could move them to his place. Judge Rogers phoned one day to say that he was going to bring his son and his daughter-in-law out to see his herd. He asked if I would go with them to the pasture since his cows didn't know him yet. Imagine my surprise when I saw that his son was the movie star Buddy Rogers and the son's wife was Mary Pickford. The scenario didn't exactly match my childhood fantasies, but it was close enough to make my day.

I knew enough to avoid making pets of our animals. The folks in the place next to ours lost their farm because they made pets of their milk cows. They gave every cow a name and talked to them. When a cow no longer produced enough milk to pay for her feed, they kept her in the herd out of friendship and for old times' sake. Finally, they had a worthless herd and couldn't pay their mortgage or their feed bills. I was determined that I would not make their mistake, so I never made friends with the livestock. Ted was our only pet, and even he had better do his job.

We did have a man work for us, for a short time, who made pets of the chickens. When he walked into the henhouse all of the chickens would spread their wings and squat down hoping he would stroke their backs. A lot more important tasks were being neglected while he was playing with the chickens. He couldn't prove to me that his tenderness made the hens lay more eggs, so we parted company.

Raising chickens was another project we had. There was an angle to that too. We kept a laying flock at all times. We made an arrangement with a creamery to test a by-product of making butter. They put alfalfa and soy seeds in the whey and let them sprout. The result was called green milk and was very high in vitamin D. We fed it to our chickens and kept careful records. Not only did green milk increase the number of eggs that the hens laid, but the vitamin D was transmitted to the eggs. We sold them to several hospitals in Kansas City and were paid a thirty percent premium over the market price.

I got the idea of raising broilers. We set up brooder stoves and bought five hundred baby chicks. I had high hopes for this project because I was going to have broilers ready to eat in January instead of waiting until spring. As the chicks grew larger their room became more crowded. I was anxious to send the largest ones to market in order to give more space to those who needed to grow more. I began trying to make contacts to sell the largest chickens. Poultry dealers were very negative to buying broilers in January. They had never heard of anything so unnatural. They were sure the public would not want to eat them before spring. In desperation, I went to the Hotel Muehlbach and spoke to the banquet manager. He would buy eighty broilers, but they had to have unbroken skin and be free of pinfeathers. Maybe professional pickers knew about the hot wax method at that time, but I certainly didn't. My maid and I picked all eighty broilers and cut them in quarters. I guarantee there wasn't a single pinfeather on any of them. My eyebrow tweezers were ruined, but the situation had been saved.

I went to a lecture on raising poultry. There were about forty women attending. In the middle of the lecture the speaker asked if anyone knew how many feathers a chicken had. Again I had my strange feeling of knowing, but I hesitated to say my number. The speaker asked each person in the room, and no one guessed more than a thousand. Finally, I said ten thousand. It was exactly the figure the speaker had in mind. Furthermore, he had been asking audiences this question for twenty years and it was the first time anyone had answered correctly.

Once Lawrence and I were at a small party with ten friends, and I told the stories of my telepathic experiences. My friends decided I should leave the room. They would then chose an object in the room for me to guess. I guessed correctly three times. When I returned to the room the fourth time, I said I wasn't getting any vibes. They admitted they had decided not to choose anything.

I was not by nature a risk taker. In farming there is no such thing as not taking risks. Every time you put a seed in the ground, you are gambling. Once, threshers were due the next day to harvest a field of oats that were ripe. During the night, a hailstorm came from nowhere and flattened the whole field. We tried everything to get in under the oats, to pick them up enough so the mower could get under them to cut. No luck; the crop was a total loss.

Roosevelt had started the Works Project Administration, more familiarly known as WPA. The county agent asked us to think of a project that we needed. The government would share the cost with us. We decided we would like to clean up our ten-acre orchard; it had been neglected by the former owners. This was a very big undertaking. There were dead branches to be trimmed and even dead trees to be grubbed out; that is, the tree's roots had to be cut under the ground and a chain secured around the stump and a team of horses hitched up to pull the tree out of the ground.

The WPA workers were gathered in a truck each morning and delivered to the farm. They brought their own lunches so they could work straight through the day. They put in long, hard hours and did a great job, for which I think they were paid around four dollars a day. These were self-respecting native Kansans who wanted to earn their bread. Welfare had not yet been established. Neither had Social Security or unemployment insurance. When a man was out of work, and one out of four was, he really had his back against the wall. When I needed extra hands for special chores, I would drive to the square in Olathe, go up to a group of men, and ask if anyone wanted to dig ditches that day. Anyone who volunteered came home with me in the truck.

I once got a water bill for twelve dollars. This was high, out of all bounds, so I knew there had to be a leak somewhere along our two miles of private line. I walked the line until I saw a wet spot. Then I went home, gathered up some spades, threw them in the truck, and went to the town square for men. After the men had dug down to the pipe, I went to get the plumber. The repair made, I took the water bill to the town council meeting and appealed to have it reduced. The appeal was deemed reasonable, and the bill was cut in half. I tell this story because it illustrates how hard the times were. One simply did not knowingly or willingly waste anything.

In spite of the general poverty, one never heard of homes being robbed or of anyone taking drugs. We often forgot to lock the doors at night. We did, however, keep a loaded gun on the mantel. It was not for use against humans but for coyotes or marauding bands of dogs that got after the sheep at night. There was a bounty paid for killing a coyote. I think they are now on the list of endangered species, but that is because their fur has become popular. Coyotes were always the enemies of farmers with livestock. They had a rotten habit. Even when they weren't hungry, they would get into a pen of sheep and hamstring one or two. They would bite so deeply into the tendons of the sheep's hind legs that the animal would be unable to walk. Then, when they were hungry, they would check back and finish killing the sheep. That's why I won't send money to a Save the Coyotes Fund. I don't figure I owe them any support.

One night while we were having guests, I heard something sniffing around near the windows. I thought it was dogs, and I kept urging Lawrence to go out with the flashlight and gun and do something. He was reluctant to make a move. The more he resisted and claimed not to hear the noises, the more I insisted. He finally took me out of the room to tell me that one of our guests had a breathing problem. It was he who was making the sniffing noises. Lawrence asked me just to relax and let him do the same.

On his own initiative, Lawrence once decided to go after an animal night prowler. The trusty gun and flashlight came out, and he went on patrol. He had been gone a long time when I heard a shot followed by crashing glass. When he returned, I wanted to know what he had hit. He said he had seen a coyote, but had missed him. The next morning we found what he had hit. Our breakfast room window was all over the floor. We decided it was better to let wild dogs and coyotes do their worst than to run the risk of being protected by such a shot as Lawrence.

The gun came out only once more. I had just told some

friends the story of the window. Lawrence was a bit miffed at my telling it, so he said, "You think it's so easy. Let's see you knock a can off the fence as far away as I was from that coyote." I had never shot a gun, but what did I have to lose? I couldn't do worse than Lawrence had done. I put the gun to my shoulder, aimed, and fired. I knocked the can right off the fence. I turned and took the gun back to the mantel and have never taken another shot. This way I have an accuracy record of a hundred percent. One shot, one bull's-eye, no bull.

Some of the time it was too hot to stay outdoors for more than half an hour. The sun was scorching. There was a ten-day stretch when the temperature went to a hundred and ten every day and stayed around ninety-five at night. It was even too hot to read with pleasure, and reading was my favorite indoor occupation. I had been exploring many fields. At first I was ready to read anything that was put before me. Lawrence's mother was deep into the Italian Renaissance, so I followed her lead in reading Benvenuto Cellini's autobiography, the history of the Medici family, and Mather's *History of Italian Painting*. Kess, on the other hand, gave me such books as a life of Louis Pasteur. On my own I discovered Stephan Zweig's *Marie Antoinette* and A. A. Brill's translation of *The Works of Sigmund Freud*. Reading Freud was very thought provoking. I adopted and embraced all of his theories. I longed to undergo psychoanalysis. Just from reading Freud, I was able to reconnect with my earliest years; but I wanted the whole experience.

Lawrence thought I should learn to speak German. No one believed that Hitler was going to last, and Lawrence had spent so many months studying in Germany that he thought it would be nice to take me there one day. Linguaphone had put out a series of thirty records in German. Since I always liked to learn subjects on my own, this was the perfect method for me. It was a little strange walking around the house talking German to myself, but I didn't feel alone because by then I was expecting our first child.

Lawrence had not wanted me to have a baby until I'd had

time to grow up myself. We had decided that I must reach twenty-one before assuming the responsibility of raising a human baby, our baby. Alfred Adler had dedicated one of his books thus: "To the First Mother Who Raises a Truly Fearless Child." That was a challenge that I would try to meet.

CHAPTER 13

First Born

Since we were in the business of breeding animals and calculating when we wanted them to give birth, it was only natural that we would want to regulate the birth year, month, and day of our own baby. In May of 1936 I went into Kansas City to interview Dr. LeRoy Goodman. I asked him when was the ideal time to have a baby. He answered that a baby born in April would have several months to grow before the hot summer weather. I pressed him to tell me when conception should take place. After answering that one seriously, he threw his head back and laughed. "You really think that you can regulate when you have a baby?" he asked. I saw no reason why I couldn't. I asked about fees. He said it was the first time he'd had a patient make a deal before she became pregnant. I said I thought it was the only time one *could* make a deal. If the patient were already pregnant, she'd have no room to negotiate. By the time I left his office, I knew I was going to enjoy the months ahead and the association with this doctor. He told me to come back when I was pregnant.

I called in August to make an appointment. My due date was April 15th. Lawrence and I could hardly wait. Meanwhile, I found my condition and the changes taking place in my body a constant source of fascination. When LeRoy saw how curious I was, not only about my own pregnancy but about the whole subject, he began pulling books off his shelf for me to read. He was a natural teacher. He had taught at Harvard Medical School before returning to Kansas City to set up his practice. My pregnancy became a nine-months course in obstetrics. It was then that we began giving the sheep shots of estrogen.

In addition to what I read in LeRoy's office, I still relied heavily on government pamphlets. I quoted them so often to the doctor that he finally said, "Am I going to deliver your baby or is the government?"

There were two things that I had decided. First, I wanted no drugs that would knock me out. I figured that having a baby was the most exciting thing I was ever going to do in my whole life, and I didn't want to be asleep when it happened. Furthermore, the government said the drugs sometimes harmed the baby. This was at a time when Twilight Sleep was being widely used.

My second determination was to breast-feed the baby. I had observed on my own that orphan animals raised on a bottle never did as well as the ones who suckled their own mothers. I couldn't resist quoting the government one final time on this subject. The pamphlets said, "The ability to breast-feed a baby is five percent physical capacity and ninety-five percent determination."

I told LeRoy that I had the ninety-five percent, and he was to see to it that I had the other five. He promised to try, but he did admit that I would be the only patient he had who wanted to breast-feed. It was just not fashionable in 1937.

When April 15th arrived, I awoke with a start. I had been having twinges for a couple of weeks, but this was something stronger. We phoned LeRoy and told him we were driving to the hospital but that it would be a half hour before we got there. We hoped he wouldn't go back to sleep. Lawrence drove me to the hospital. I was turned over to the obstetrical nurses and put in the labor room. Lawrence asked LeRoy to let him stay in the delivery room. A sterile coat was arranged for him.

I kept telling the nurses I was ready to go to the delivery

room. They said it was much too early. They would call the doctor when they saw fit. I waited until my next contraction. Then I told them that if they didn't call the doctor, I would. I also said I was capable of making myself heard because I knew how to call hogs and I was in good voice. When the nurses heard that, they got LeRoy to come see to me. He gave very urgent orders to take me into the next room. When we got there, I, too, began giving orders. I wanted the mirrors adjusted so I could watch the progress I was making. I was drunk with excitement. It all went so fast. Two-and-a-half hours after my first pain at home, I was holding our son in my arms.

By 9:00 A.M., I had Ray Ray on the phone and was telling her that I was at the hospital. She said she would be right over. I said not to rush; the babies wouldn't be shown in the nursery before 11:00 A.M. When she realized that the baby had already been born, she said I shouldn't be talking on the phone. A new mother simply did not make her own announcements. It began to seem that I was not in step with my own generation. I was always doing the unconventional thing. It was at least twenty-five years before natural childbirth and breast-feeding and having the father present became popular. I have always been glad that I did it my way.

The custom was to stay in the hospital for two weeks after giving birth. At the end of ten days, I begged to go home. I wasn't sleeping well with all the night patrols that came through the room. Besides, I was anxious to get my hands on the baby and not just have him for a few minutes on a strict schedule.

As a precautionary measure, all babies born in hospitals were routinely X-rayed to see if they had an enlarged thymus gland. The theory then current was that crib deaths were caused by an enlarged thymus. Our baby was diagnosed and given a series of X-ray treatments to shrink the thymus. Now there was nothing to worry about.

Before I left the hospital, LeRoy asked if I would give him the maternity dress I had been wearing. I said I was curious as to why he wanted it. Did he have a patient who was too poor to buy one? "No," he said, "I want to burn it. I saw that same dress all through Selma's pregnancy and all through Ceci's and now yours. I want to take it out of circulation." I told him I didn't think that was a worthy cause and I intended to pass the dress on, but I said I would see to it that the wearer didn't use him as her doctor.

Lawrence wanted to name the baby Paul Nathan. I had always hated double names. I said it should be either Paul or Nathan but not both. We chose Paul. When I saw how happy it made Kess, I was satisfied with the choice. The only sadness I felt was that neither of my parents could share the joy this child had brought into our lives.

Kess and Laura moved into the house with us to help take care of Paul. He was a good baby who cried only when we put him on the scale to weigh him before and after each feeding, to see if he had gotten enough milk from the breast. I don't know whose idea *that* was, but it wasn't mine. The first thing I knew, though, Laura had ruled off the pages of a Red Chief tablet and was writing down every time Paul dirtied his diapers. I couldn't believe that this was how babies were to be treated. Schedules for feeding were very rigid. I used to fake the time by as much as half an hour without telling Laura. Finally, I told Lawrence that it was up to him to rescue me from his well-meaning mother. He simply had to get them out of the house so I could make my own mistakes. I still had it in mind that I was going to meet the Alfred Adler challenge by raising a fearless child. It wasn't going to be possible with Laura around. She had even more fears than my own mother.

Laura thought she was doing her duty when she gave me little housekeeping hints. I had all my mother's oriental rugs on the floor. Laura said I must turn them around every week so as not to wear a path across them. I was killing myself trying to carry out this advice. I then asked Laura where she kept all her own oriental rugs.

"Oh, they are worn out and gone," she answered.

"My mother never turned her rugs, and they are still in good condition," I retorted. "I think you wore your rugs out turning them. I intend to follow my mother's example from here on out." Postscript: The rugs are still in use, still in good shape, and are never ever turned.

I don't know what Lawrence told his parents, but from then on they came to the farm only on weekends. I was happy to have full responsibility for Paul. He thrived even though I no longer weighed him before and after each feeding. When he was awake, I took him everywhere in his carriage. The animals delighted him, and he quickly learned to imitate all their sounds. So far so good—he had no fears. I felt triumphant. He was teaching himself to walk by going from one chair to another. He would fall and get back up. Once he mastered the walking, he began climbing on the jungle gym. He went all the way to the top most fearlessly.

One day when my attention was diverted for a second, I turned around and saw that he had climbed over the fence into the corral with the draft horses. The horses were drinking their fill after having been unharnessed. There was Paul wandering around between their legs. I tried not to show my panic. I didn't want to frighten the horses, and I didn't want to make a sudden movement that would scare Paul. It seemed an aeon before I had him by the hand and was leading him gently out from under the horses. I don't know how much he understood, but I gave a long explanation about how the horse might be annoyed by a fly and—in kicking at the fly—might accidentally kick him if he was in the way. Furthermore, he was not to go into any corral without holding my hand, nor was he to climb fences without permission. Clearly, I was going to have to instill some kind of fear and set some limits if both of us were to survive.

I couldn't wait for Paul to talk. I was sure he would have something interesting to say. He didn't disappoint me. By age two he showed a great sense of humor and loved to make jokes. Once he passed some gas, looked up at me and confided, "If I do that once more, I'll be a flat tire."

When Paul was two and a half, I could no longer resist taking him to Little Rock and showing him off to my friends. By then, Jane and Anne were married and had children about the same age as Paul. We had a glorious time watching the little ones play together. At first, the Southern accent gave him a problem. I had long since lost mine except when talking to a fellow Southerner, so Paul wanted to know why I was talking funny. Ray's date came to pick her up one night and valiantly tried to make contact with this little boy. To make conversation, he asked Paul, "Do you have many books at home?" He misunderstood the key word *books* as *bugs*. He answered according to what he had understood. He replied, "No, I don't have many bugs at home, but I have lots of mousetraps." He was never at a loss for an answer.

Paul liked going to the barn with anyone who would take him. One day, he returned to the house all excited and told me there were some baby pigs in the barn. I innocently baited him for more information by asking, "Where did they come from?" His quick and graphic retort was, "The sow goes unnnh, and they come out of her stomach." No need to explain anything to him; he had seen it all.

There were no bounds to Paul's imagination. He had a dozen different costumes, and when he wore one he became whatever the costume dictated. No one was to address him by his real name when he was wearing an Indian outfit: he was Big Chief. He was anxious to have a Superman suit. Before I had time to make one for him, I simply put some ties around his wrists to hold a bath towel over his shoulders so he could fly around like a soaring bird.

Early one morning, I was rushing to take Lawrence to meet his carpool, and Paul jumped in the car with us. During the few minutes' wait before Lawrence's ride came, Paul, in his bath towel, flew out of the car to watch some men dig a hole in the ground. The two of us then went to the grocery store. I told Paul to stay in the car because I was in a hurry. I dashed into the store and dashed out again and drove home. As I was unloading the car at home I asked the maid where Paul was. She replied that he had been with me. Oh, my God, so he had. I made a quick stop to ask the diggers if I had left him there. They recommended I get in out of the sun. Then I drove frantically to the grocery store. There was Paul, standing on the sidewalk with four or five people around him. They were obviously having a good time. He looked like a cross between Li'l Abner, in his high-top shoes, and Superman in his cape. He was wearing nothing but a pair of short underpants. When Paul was safely in the car, I asked him what they had been talking about. He said, "They were saying, 'Did you have a nice shower, Sonny?'"

Then I asked if he had been worried when he saw that I had left in the car. He hadn't been worried; he had decided that if I didn't come back he would go into the drugstore and ask the druggist to telephone me and tell me where to find him. He seemed to have his head put on better than his mother did.

By the time Paul was three years old, I was finishing my second nine-month course in obstetrics. On a Saturday night, March 30, 1940, I drove the pickup truck to Olathe to meet Kess, who was coming for the weekend. When I got home, I had a twinge. I quickly made out the checks for the men and took them to the barn. I then phoned the ambulance as we had arranged in advance. The driver said he was having his supper and would like to have dessert if I wasn't in any hurry. I agreed but told him not to fool around too long. I phoned Lawrence and LeRoy.

When the ambulance came, I sat in front with the driver. I calmly asked him about speed limits for ambulances and tried urging him to go a little faster. There were laws that prevented the use of sirens on ambulances unless it was a great emergency. I asked the driver if he had ever delivered a baby. He said he hadn't. I asked him if he wanted to deliver one. He said he didn't. I said, "In that case, you had better put on your siren and move out." When we got to the hospital, Lawrence and LeRoy were pacing the floor together trying to have the baby without me. All of us rushed upstairs, and ten minutes later baby Laura put in her appearance.

Her name had been chosen in advance. If we had a girl, she was to be named for Lawrence's mother, who had died a few weeks before. Her death was not unexpected; she had suffered a stroke two years earlier and had been quite ill since then. Kess transferred all his love and affection to this little baby. Her birth helped him overcome the sadness of his loss.

Paul had been prepared for the new baby's arrival with the greatest of care. Everything I'd read about how to ease the pain he would feel from his new rival had been done. I had dozens of presents wrapped up and hidden, ready to give him in case anyone was so thoughtless as to bring a gift for the baby without bringing one for Paul. He was brought to the hospital to help transport us back to the farm. When he got to the hospital, quite by chance he and Lawrence got on the elevator with LeRoy. Lawrence introduced them to each other and Paul said, "Which hand did you use?"

LeRoy, confused, asked him to repeat the question.

Paul elaborated on the question by saying, "Which hand did you use? You *did* get the baby out of my mother's stomach, didn't you? Which hand did you use?" By this time, the whole elevator was in hysterics.

Paul had been put in a grown-up bed months ahead of time. None of these things really worked. There it was, the green-eyed monster of jealousy. He was suddenly afraid to sleep in his big bed and wanted to go back into a crib. I can still see him in his desperate attempt to hold the attention of visitors. He stood in the middle of the living room floor in his cowboy chaps and hat, blowing a whistle, shooting a cap pistol, and throwing a lasso all at the same time. How could anyone ignore such a determined character?

Paul had enormous brown eyes with very thick black lashes. People inevitably asked where he'd gotten his eyes. He always replied, "Out of the raisin box." He knew that was how I made the gingerbread men. There was something else about raisins. He loved to imitate the men on the farm and was a very good mimic. One of the men chewed tobacco. Paul came to me one day carrying a little cloth sack with a string on top and asked me to fill it with raisins. I offered to give him a small box of them. "No," he said, "that won't do." Later I saw why. He didn't want to eat the raisins. He wanted to chew them and spit out like his tobacco-chewing model.

Whenever the farmer was milking our one cow, all the barn cats would gather around to wait for their turn for a squirt in the mouth. I soon found Paul was joining the line and was as skilled as the cats in getting his squirt. The farmer had a small rat terrier, named Buster, who also came for warm milk twice a day. I once found Paul squatting on the floor and squeezing Buster by the testicles. He grinned up at me and gleefully announced, "I'm milking Buster." Buster didn't seem to mind.

If Paul didn't understand something, he felt free to ask about it. He wanted to know how babies got into their mothers' stomachs. I went through the routine about the daddy planting a seed. Later in the day, Paul came to me and said that he was going to have two children when he grew up. I asked how he knew. He had apparently been indulging in self-examination, because he answered simply, "I've only got two seeds." Ah well, he almost had it right.

Paul and I went swimming in a friend's pool. During this era, psychologists recommended that parents not hide their nudity before a child. (They later reversed themselves.) I changed to my bathing suit in front of Paul. He looked at me with great alarm and fairly shouted, "What happened to you, Mama? You've got no buggie." This gave me the chance to explain to him what no one would ever tell *me* as a child—the difference between boys and girls. For a few days, he was busy sorting people out in his mind. Sometimes, in a voice louder than I would have wished, he asked, "Does he have a buggie?" Once he had everyone categorized, the subject was dropped.

A kindergarten was organized in Olathe. Paul agreed to give it a try. The teachers liked to teach the kids little recitations. Occasionally the parents would be invited to watch the children perform. When it was Paul's turn to recite his poem, he went up on the stage. I noticed he was nervous. Then he shoved both hands up to his elbows into his trousers. I wasn't sure what his hands were doing in there. He said his piece just fine. On the way home, he suddenly exclaimed, "She forgot to call on me." I assured him that he had been called on and had recited his poem very well. It was then that I realized we did not have a Hamlet in the making. I avoided telling him that he had no talent.

When we got Laura settled into the crib that had been Paul's, he wouldn't leave me alone with her for five minutes and vice versa. Remembering how I had stood over Junior's bassinet, I had no intention of giving Paul any opportunities to get at Laura's soft spot. He was always there, leaning on my knee, as I breastfed Laura. Sometimes he asked for a turn. I said there wasn't enough for him too. Then he would ask me just to give him a squirt the way the farmer did when milking the cow. He had been brought up *au naturel*. I hadn't been, so I found myself somewhat embarrassed by this free thinker and talker.

One of these awkward occasions took place at a restaurant in Olathe where we went for Sunday dinner. As the owner showed us to our table, Paul asked her, "Do you have lots of kids at home?" She said she didn't have any children, but wanted to know why he'd asked. He was as direct as ever: "Then why do you have such big breasts if you don't have any kids to feed?" He always spoke in full voice. The whole restaurant heard him. I felt a little unwelcome in that restaurant after that. We took our patronage elsewhere.

Paul was good at turning a phrase. I walked in on him one day just after he had pilfered a banana; he had half eaten it. He knew this was forbidden and began to squirm under my glare. Finally, he said to me, "Quit that making faces with your eyes."

Laura was growing cuter by the minute. She was a born flirt. Kess was her adoring slave and would do anything he understood from her gestures that she wanted. Then there was Tom, our jack of all trades, to do her bidding. Worthy Williams had also come to live with us and to take charge of the hogs. Although he was a bit more aloof, Laura had him entranced. She was a sweet, amiable child, quick to laugh when everyone else did; though, on the side, she would ask me if that was a joke. Basically, she was a serious little creature. One Sunday afternoon she was taken ill with vomiting.

She had been well only a half hour before, so I was mystified. When I questioned her, she answered, "You know that man that was smoking a cigarette? He didn't step on it." That was the only time she has ever smoked.

I loved to listen to both children when they talked to themselves. That is how I knew what they were really thinking. During one of my eavesdropping sessions I overheard Paul say, "Oh, shit!" I knew he had probably heard one of the men use the word. First chance I got, I explained to him that though this was a word one could use in the barn, it wasn't nice to say it in the house. A few days later, as we entered the barn together he pulled at my hand and asked, "Can I say it now?" Having forgotten what I had told him, I asked, "Say what?" He gleefully shouted, "OH, SHIT!"

Paul was satisfied and didn't use the word again for a couple of years; at least he didn't say it around me. Then one day he ran into the house in great excitement yelling, "Come quick! Laura's full of shit." I followed him as he led me to his sister. His description was accurate. Laura had been sitting on the seat of the manure spreader that was already loaded to take to the field. She had lost her balance and fallen over backward. She was indeed "full of shit." Paul did not get scolded for using the forbidden word in the house.

CHAPTER 14

Children and Animals

I no longer ran ads when I wanted to hire someone. Word of mouth in Olathe usually yielded several applicants for whatever job I had to offer at that moment. This was how Tom had come to us. Everyone in town knew him as a clever, hard-working fellow, but because they also knew he was an alcoholic, no one recommended him to me. When I interviewed Tom, I was impressed by all the things he knew how to do. He seemed to be a jack-of-all-trades and was willing to fit in wherever he was needed. He would work in the barn, in the yard, in the house, in the field—wherever the work was.

I told Tom that I understood he had a problem with drinking. At first, he began to say that it was all in the past and he was now reformed. Our eyes met, and I told him I was sure that he believed what he was telling me. I would give him the job as a day worker. There was one rule I wanted him to follow. If he got drunk, he was not to show up for work again until he was cold sober. I explained that I never wanted the children to see him except at his best. This arrangement lasted quite a long time. Then Tom asked if he could come to live on the farm. I had no room for him, but he said he could build a room in the basement. If that was all right with him, it was all right with me. He moved in.

Tom's background was interesting. His mother was a white woman, and his father was half negro and half American Indian. Tom was the failure in his family. His brothers and sisters were all scattered. One brother was a colonel in the U.S. Army. One sister had crossed over and passed as white; naturally she did not keep in touch with Tom. We only heard about his real family from time to time. It soon became obvious that Tom had adopted us as his family. There was nothing I asked him to do that he refused. When my maid left, he took over her duties.

Laura became Tom's shadow. If she wasn't trotting along behind him, she was riding on his tall shoulders. He would tell her stories about hunting and fishing and working on the railroad. She sat in rapt attention, just as I had listened when Sally told tales of slavery.

Tom was a good cook, but he had his own ideas of what delicacies were. We never knew what to expect when Tom announced he was making a surprise for dinner. Sometimes it would be squabs that he had been keeping his eye on for several weeks and had captured just before they were ready to fly out of the nest. Sometimes it would be squirrels that he had, as he put it, "shot in self-defense." When he served squirrel, fried like chicken, we were careful not to tell Laura what she was eating for fear of hurting her sensibilities. She had often watched these same squirrels climbing about in the walnut tree behind our house. She was sensitive to our silence, but she enjoyed what she was eating. Then she said, "I want some more of that mouse." We realized that we needn't have shielded her from the truth.

Laura loved all the animals, but the feeling was not always mutual. When she was small, we would put her in a large playpen we had built in the yard. It was made of snow fencing. We would put Ted and all the barn cats in with her to keep her amused. Ten minutes later, they had all vaulted over the fence, and Laura was alone and lonely. At that point we figured she could get her oxygen later, and we'd let her come back in the house. One day I heard her cooing, "Ah, ah, kitty, kitty." I looked to see if by chance one of the cats had gotten into the house. There she was, sitting on the kitchen floor, stroking a mouse that had been caught in a trap. A dead mouse was the only kind of animal that couldn't escape from her.

The WPA workers had done such a good job of cleaning up our orchard that we now had bushels and bushels of Jonathan apples to sell. There was a farm sale about ten miles away (foreclosures were still taking place in spite of Roosevelt's moratorium), and I decided to take a truckload of apples to the farm sale rather than run an ad. After I had sold all of my apples for a dollar a bushel, I walked around the sale to see if there was anything I wanted. There was a Shetland pony all saddled up and tied to the fence. All the children were begging their parents to buy them the pony. I overheard one parent say, "That pony is too old. It might not live until we got it home. If they get twenty dollars for that animal, I'll be surprised." Well, if the pony was going to go that cheap, I was going to stay until it sold. After all, I now had an empty truck and could take it home as a surprise for Paul. He was already four-and-a-half, and Laura was eighteen months old. When the auctioneer asked for bids, I timidly said, "Five dollars." Someone raised me a dollar. It went on like that up to fifteen. The hammer fell. The pony was mine.

When I got home, Paul tried out Beauty. He pronounced her too old and too slow and showed no further interest in her. Laura, who wasn't much on talking, let us know that she wanted her turn on Beauty. She never wanted to get off again. She never went back into her playpen. We would tie her into the saddle with a tea towel, tie up the pony in the shade, and know that they would be there when we came back.

By the time Laura was two, she knew how to use the reins. We no longer needed to tie her into the saddle. All the gates to the yard would be closed, and the two could wander about. Beauty would eventually get tired and try to knock Laura out of the saddle by going under some of the young peach trees we had planted. Laura was very clever at ducking the low branches. When *Laura* got tired, she would slide out of the saddle onto Beauty's rump, grab her tail, slide down to the ground, and go her own way.

I came into the yard once and couldn't find either of them. I noticed that someone had left the gate to the orchard open. To speed my search for the missing twosome, I jumped into the truck. I finally located them in the south forty-six-acre field. Beauty was grazing peacefully, and Laura was standing on the ground pointing first to the saddle and then to the ground. We assumed she was telling us that she had fallen off, but we soon learned that all she wanted was to be put back in the saddle so she could ride home.

As Laura grew older, she made more demands on Beauty. All of us had gone to a circus, and Laura was fascinated by the animal trainers. After the circus, Laura was never without a whip in her hand. Poor Ted was now her lion. He was made to go in and out of his doghouse so many times that he would go in and refuse to come out even when she pulled at his collar. Beauty was being trained to stretch like the show horses. Laura would get Beauty's front hooves in just the right position, then the back ones would move and vice versa. She was never able to get all four hooves planted properly at the same time.

Laura knew how to make Beauty do a slow trot. She also knew how to mount without help. She would lead Beauty over to the wagon scale; this gave her the extra two feet in height that she needed to get her foot in the stirrup. If she was quick about it, she could throw herself in the saddle before Beauty had time to figure out a trick to play on her.

Once the two of them were doing a slow trot around the house when suddenly our half-dozen Belgian horses kicked open the gate to the horse corral and came charging into the yard. They were feeling their oats that day and kicking their heels in the air. They really stampeded around the house. Naturally, Beauty joined the chase. I was terrified, both for Laura and for myself. I stood protected behind the well, waiting to jump out and grab Beauty's bridle the next time she came around. When I stepped out of my hiding place, Beauty shied and Laura fell to the ground. I scooped her into my arms and ran into the house. I yanked her clothes off to see if there were any broken bones. She kept repeating, "Beauty hippity hop." She was neither frightened nor hurt—one of my truly fearless children! All she wanted was more racing around. Never again was she able to get Beauty to run so fast.

Since Laura loved horses so much, I indulged myself in the purchase of a beautiful saddle horse. She was a tall, slim sorrel mare that we called Hedy Lamarr because the movie star's hair was the color of my mare. Friends asked us to keep a Shetland pony for their children at the farm. Laddie Boy was very lively. He was all right for Paul to ride, but he was much too fast for us to let Laura get near him. We would take long rides with Laura in the saddle with me on Hedy Lamarr and Paul riding Laddie Boy. Usually, Paul was in full regalia of one sort or another. He thought cowboy or Indian dress was most appropriate for these excursions.

Even before I had any children of my own, I began holding Easter egg hunts for the children of our friends. I would boil and color thirty dozen eggs. I couldn't hide them until the last moment; when I did, Ted had to be locked up because he thought I was hiding the eggs for his pleasure and would eat any that he found. In fact, for days after the Easter party Ted was still hunting and finding eggs. If we had any lambs that had been born late, we tied ribbons around their necks and put them in the yard for the children to enjoy. They would run like rabbits when a child approached them, so that became a game in itself.

Our only other large parties were usually held on the Fourth of July. We had a creek running through the south eighty, and one of our friends was a specialist in catching crawdads, sometimes called crayfish. He brought all the necessary poles and nets. Raw liver was used as bait. When a crawdad came out of the mud to grab the liver, one shoved the net under it. On a really good day, these shallow-water fishermen could come home with a bushel basket of crawdads. They were washed in the basement shower, and every pot I owned was put into service to boil them in highly spiced water. Barbecued ribs were also on the menu. Tom spent a lot of time getting the coals just right for barbecuing. It was an all-day procedure.

A great deal of cold beer was consumed at those parties. At one party, I was beginning to worry about how I could ever get Paul and Laura to bed while the company was still there. Paul came to me and said that he was very sleepy and so was Laura. Never did two little ones go to bed so sweetly. It was only later that I learned they had been draining all the empty beer cans and had gotten enough from the cans to make them pass out. Oh well, it was only once a year.

I also entertained out of a wish to help strangers in Kansas City. Refugees from Hitler's Germany were being sent to many cities throughout the states. Otherwise they would all have liked to stay in New York. I had maps drawn of how to drive to our farm, and an announcement made at each meeting of the Council of Jewish Women stated that anyone wishing to bring refugees to our farm would be welcome any Sunday afternoon. I would sometimes be up until midnight on Saturday baking schneckens, which I knew they would like because Grandmother Adler had made them for me. Once I got the hang of working with yeast-rising dough, it was easy but time-consuming. As many as seventy people might arrive in fair weather, and the weather was usually fair especially during the drought. The Germans were fond of taking long walks on the beautiful roads around our farm. Years later, after they had made new starts in their lives, they would meet me on the street, introduce themselves, and thank me for having received them in my home. It made me happy to think that it had mattered to them.

There was a committee to find jobs for the refugees. Lawrence and I volunteered to hire a German who had been a horse-and-cattle dealer before fleeing his home in southern Germany. I was willing to teach him English and to let him learn how we raised livestock in America. I have never encountered anyone like him. He had bought a book of English phrases that he insisted on using as a textbook; he would have no other. This book listed phrases such as, "I am in clover" and "I'm over my head in work." I didn't think that he needed to know those phrases when he couldn't even ask the price of a loaf of bread. He was just as stubborn about learning cattle feeding as he was about learning English. After a six-week trial period, I asked the committee to find him another placement. I don't know where they sent him, but wherever he is I hope he's in clover.

He left a souvenir to remember him by. During his brief stay, he insisted on making a crockful of sauerkraut, or rather he insisted on teaching me how to make it. Since we had a lot of cabbage in the garden, I fell in with his scheme. About the time I sent him back to the committee, I had to throw out the crock of kraut too. The smell had gotten unbearable. It was so bad that I didn't even feed the sauerkraut to the pigs for fear it would give the pork a peculiar flavor when we butchered. We dug a big hole in the ground and buried all of it far away from barns and houses.

Next we hired an ex-house painter—mainly so his wife would work for me. She was a fine cook, but he wasn't worth much as a worker. He did, however, have a great interest in making home brew. I said I didn't mind if it didn't smell up the house. We had just gotten it aired out from the sauerkraut. He promised that the home brew wouldn't smell; it would be bottled. I also stipulated that I wouldn't have to drink it if I didn't like it. Having very little else to say to this man, I used to inquire about the progress of his beer. He would report that he had been forced to throw out a few bottles because of leakage. I thought I knew where the leakage was going, but I was too polite to insinuate any such thing. Besides, his wife was too good a cook to lose.

One night we were awakened by loud explosions. My first thoughts, as I jumped out of bed, were that Hitler had decided to bomb America. Never mind that his attack planes would have had to cross half the nation before arriving at our farm. When we calmed down and began to investigate, we found that a lot of beer bottles had exploded, shattering themselves and their contents all over the basement. I did not help in the cleanup. I suggested to the ex-house painter that he might like to paint the cupboards to get rid of the beer smell, but he now declared himself allergic to paint. I know what he was allergic to—WORK.

As long as I'm on the subject of culinary accidents, I am reminded of the time when Lawrence's mother was still alive and she decided to make marinated herring. I had tasted some at the Fred Harvey restaurant and had thought it was good. Lawrence's mother was always anxious to be helpful, so she bought all the ingredients and went to work on the herrings. It took a long time for them to marinate, but finally it was time for the unveiling of her masterwork. She watched my expression closely as I took the first bite. I couldn't make any comment because I couldn't talk. It wasn't that I was speechless with admiration; it was simply that I had gotten hold of something I could neither swallow nor spit out. Everyone else tried a taste. The vote was unanimous. Something had definitely gone wrong. Perhaps she had doubled the amount of spice. All the barn cats were called to the house, a rare occurrence in itself. We thought they might like fish instead of their usual diet of mice. We were wrong. As they tasted this unusual delicacy, each in turn let out a little scream and ran for the safety of the barns. I had a hard time ever getting them to the house for any more goodies.

Several times we had been invited to Rabbi Hadas' home. I was beginning to be embarrassed that we had never reciprocated, but I worried about not being able to serve a kosher meal. I hit on the idea of getting a government pamphlet on how to kosher-kill a chicken. It didn't sound too hard. The idea seemed to be to draw the maximum amount of blood from the bird. The farmer and I worked it out together. Since I came from the South, fried chicken was my one sure, successful meal; I felt confident whenever I served it. When Gershon and Anne Hadas arrived, I was bursting to tell them they had nothing to fear about the dinner. I had personally kosher-killed the chicken.

Gershon led me to describe how I had done it. After I told him all the details, he smiled and said, "You did everything right. The only problem is that you are not an authorized person, but never mind." He went on to question me further,

"And just what did you use to fry the chicken?" Without any hesitation I replied, "Lard." There went the ball game. That night he and Anne dined on boiled eggs. There was no error I could make there. I understand Gershon told the story from his pulpit as an example to his congregation of someone who had been sincere but misguided.

After this meager meal, we walked them around the corrals and showed them the animals we were taking to the Kansas State Fair the following week. Lawrence asked Gershon to pray that we would win. Gershon said something to the effect that he wasn't really qualified to bless pigs but that he did wish us good luck.

Just one more cooking story. When the team of men came to fill our silo, I had to cook for their noontime meal so that the minimum of time would be lost. There were about a dozen men who made the circuit, exchanging labor with each other. Usually, they spent only two days at our farm. Even though I had no kitchen help at that moment, I decided to show off a bit with what I gave them to eat. There was always a competitive spirit between the women who had to feed the men. No one wanted the men to go away saying they had not enjoyed their meal. One would lose face.

I got up at five o'clock in the morning to bake six pies before I had breakfast. Then I cut up and fried eight chickens. This time it didn't matter if I used lard; in fact it was the only way to get the chicken crisp enough. The men ate heartily, and when ten drops of rain fell shortly after lunch, they decided to call it a day. For one reason or another, they found an excuse to stop work AFTER lunch each day. They managed to drag the job out for five lunches. I was so tired the fifth day that I told them if they didn't plan to finish that day, they should bring the next day's lunches from home or I would have to send them to a restaurant in Olathe. They got the message and finished up shortly after two o'clock.

CHAPTER 15

Pigs and Ribbons

We decided to try our hand at raising purebred Poland China hogs. In Independence, Missouri, there was a famous breeder named Wayne Williams, who had been showing and winning prizes for many years. I went to him and told him that I knew nothing about pigs but wanted to try. He was willing to give me free consultations over the phone if I bought my seed stock from him. Furthermore, he would let me hire his youngest son as my herdsman. With Wayne's help, I selected five brood sows that were due to farrow in a month. We loaded them into the truck. Wayne's son, Worthy, got in the truck cab with me, and we were on our way to many new adventures. Worthy was to stay until after the farrowing and until the piglets were neutered and had their tusks cut off with pincers. I would then be on my own until we were ready to try our luck on the circuit of livestock shows. Worthy would come back to us at that point and get the animals into prime condition.

The farrowing went splendidly. Instead of a herd of five sows, we now had fifty-five piglets scampering all over the place. Each sow had her own pen, carefully provided with guardrails about a foot off the ground. This was done so that the piggies would have a place to run when their big, fat mothers started to lie down. The sows were so big they couldn't see where all of their babies were, and they were apt to mash them accidentally if the little fellows didn't have sense enough to get out of the way. Maybe this is what is called "survival of the fittest." The dumbest ones died young. We lost very few from their own stupidity.

In order to sell breeding stock, one had to show and win. From our first crop, we carefully chose five male pigs that we would not cut. We would let them grow up to be boars. It's very difficult to judge the contour of their bodies when they are so young, so we partially selected them according to their markings. A Poland China must have five white marks and the rest of him must be black. The five white points are usually the hocks, just above the hooves, and a part of the muzzle above the snout.

Wayne also came over to help with these important decisions. We evidently chose well, because these boars grew very rapidly and were beautiful examples of their breed. When they were six months old, they weighed about three hundred pounds each. We chose three boars and a pen of three sows to show. Our young sows took first prize, and one of our boars named Top Row Special took the blue ribbon as junior champion. We were ecstatic. This meant we could use him for breeding and could advertise the pedigrees of his offspring.

We had to keep track of the pedigrees very carefully because it was sometimes beneficial to breed closely related pigs if you were trying to set a certain characteristic in the line. At times we deliberately bred a young sow with her own grandfather; at other times we wanted to introduce new blood lines for various reasons.

Soon we had weanling pigs to sell through ads. We shipped them to six farming states. The price we got for these thirty-pound pigs was as much as we would have gotten had we fed them several more months to the weight of two-hundred-and-fifty pounds. We had found our angle for making pigs profitable at a time when ordinary pigs were selling for a nickel a pound live.

Whenever a farmer came to choose a boar or a sow, I asked

how he wanted me to price the animal. I would say, "Shall I name a price, so we can discuss it for a while, or shall I tell you the bottom price right at the start?" Farmers always said they wanted to hear the bottom price. After I told it to them, they always wanted to negotiate. This was a tough situation because it is quite impossible to say that one animal is worth two hundred dollars and another, that looks almost the same, is only worth one hundred and seventy-five. I always gave the farmers a choice of several animals and a range of prices. Invariably, they wanted to buy the highest-priced animal at the price I had set for the cheapest one. I would remind them that I had offered them the chance to haggle and they had chosen not to.

I spent two hours hanging over the fence with one farmer. He wanted to buy the two-hundred-dollar boar for one hundred and fifty. Finally, by slow stages, he got his offer up to one hundred and ninety-five dollars, and I let him walk away. Keep in mind, the big Depression was still on. I went into the house and burst into tears. My nerves were shot. I had blown it for a lousy five dollars. The next week, this same farmer came back and announced, "I'll take that damn boar at your price." I said I was very sorry, but I had sold him. He would have to choose another. This time, he gave me no argument. He remained my customer for many years. I had gained his respect, and I had established a reputation for straight dealing.

A farmer once returned a boar to me claiming that the boar had refused to mount his sow when she was in heat. With the boldest face imaginable, I told him to leave the boar with me. I would teach him whatever he needed to know, and the farmer could come back for him in a week. He was satisfied with that arrangement. Little did he know that my confidence was all front. I didn't have the least notion how I was going to teach this boar what nature had failed to instill in him.

I was on the phone to Wayne as soon as the farmer drove away. Our phone was on a party line, and the neighbors were in the habit of listening to my conversations. If they failed to understand what they heard on the phone, they would drive by the next day and ask what they had missed. No one ever asked me about this particular consultation on the boar who wouldn't breed. Wayne wanted to know if I had a sow in heat. If not, he would bring one of his. I said I had a sow ready; I just had to put her in a private pen. Wayne would have his lunch and then come over. He could not explain this case to me over a party line.

After lunch, I went to the barn to get the sow into the pen. I wasn't having much luck getting her to move in the right direction. Both she and I were confused. I didn't want to bring out the electric gad, but she was exasperating me. Finally, I gave her a good slap on her rump with my bare hand, not really hard enough to hurt such a thick-skinned animal. She froze dead still in her tracks. She wouldn't budge one way or another. She was a living statue of a pig.

When I heard Wayne drive in, I ran to tell him what had happened. He wanted to know how long she had been like that. I said it had been close to a half hour. He reassured me that he could straighten out my blunders. First, I should have led the sow with a bucket of feed rather than trying to drive her from behind. Second, I should never have touched her on the rump; she mistook this gesture as the sign that a boar was going to mount her, and that is why she was so patiently waiting. Wayne predicted that the sow would be ready to move in another few minutes, and she was.

Once we had the sow in the pen, we wanted to freeze her. When she had gone through the laying-on-of-hands ceremony and was properly statuesque, we placed a bale of hay on either side of her. We positioned a man on each bale. Then the reticent boar was brought forth. His reticence was overcome by the assistants on the bales. Each one grabbed him by a front hoof and they dragged him. My assigned task was to twist his tail so he would step forward. We finally had him in perfect alignment with the sow. He still didn't know what was expected of him. Gradually, his corkscrew penis came out of its sheath and he hit the mark. Apparently, he liked it once he'd tried it, because he hung in there for a half hour. He was happy; the sow was happy; we were happy; and his owner was happy. My promise to the farmer had been fulfilled, not entirely without outside help.

We liked to have as much publicity for our hogs as we could get. When the *Poland China Journal* called to say they were sending a reporter to our farm to interview me, we were pleased and flattered. The reporter came, camera and all. He wanted to take a picture of me with Top Row Special. I grabbed the protection board I always carried when I went among the boars. It was a simple panel, with a handle, that I kept between me and the animal's head in case he got rambunctious. The two of us posed for our picture, and the reporter went away content. Imagine my surprise when the magazine came out with the picture on the front page under the caption, "Beauty and the Beast."

We were even more amused when my first fan mail arrived. I received a letter from a farmer that said, "You are just what I have been looking for in a wife. I want a good looker and someone who knows all about pigs. From your picture and the article you seem to be both of these. I am interested in marriage." He went on to describe his qualifications. They seemed pretty good. I wrote back and told him I was sorry he had assumed I was a widow but that my husband was very much alive. I thanked him all the same.

A year after Top Row Special had won the junior championship, we decided to show him again in the senior class. By that time, he had grown to be an enormous, eight-hundred-pound animal. His contour was still excellent, but because of his great weight his hocks had weakened and he tended to walk a little back on his haunches. In humans, he could be compared to an older person whose arches have fallen a bit. We hoped the judges wouldn't fault him too much for this minor defect. Worthy moved back to our farm to get him ready. His coat was brushed twice a day until it became lustrous. He was in the pink when he was loaded to go to the fair. Wayne and I drove down the next day for the judging.

We went to say hello to Worthy just as he was putting the finishing touches on Top Row. The boar's white points had been talcumed, and any bare spots in his coat had been blackened with lamp soot. He was majestic. Wayne and I went to our seats to watch the grand entrance of all the competitors. Just as Worthy crossed the threshold, I saw him draw a small container out of his pocket and rub its contents below Top Row's tail. I asked Wayne if there was something wrong with Top Row. In no uncertain terms he told me to shut up.

I then whispered to him, "Is something wrong?"

His only reply was, "Watch that pig strut."

Sure enough, he was no longer walking back on his haunches. He was up on his hooves, looking for all the world like a cross between Pavlova and Miss Piggie. Never did a pig look more like a ballerina on point. This high-stepping pig was named grand champion boar of the state of Kansas. That meant he was the champion of all the boars in all of the different age classes. We showed him later at the American Royal in Kansas City, and he was the grand champion there too. Eventually, we sold him to the Kansas State Agricultural College for their breeding herd. It was years before I could get Worthy to tell me what he had put under Top Row's tail. It was a simple concoction of cold cream and red hot pepper.

CHAPTER 16

Joining Clubs Again

In 1936, there was a scandal in Washington. Marian Anderson, the great Negro singer, had been scheduled to sing in Constitution Hall, which was owned by the Daughters of the American Revolution. According to newspaper accounts, when it was discovered that the DAR had booked a black artist, they canceled the concert. Miss Anderson did a very dramatic thing. She gave a free concert from the steps of the Lincoln Memorial. Throngs of people, both black and white, attended this great concert. Mrs. Roosevelt, as first lady of the land, resigned her DAR membership in protest.

Just as I believed it was right for Mrs. Roosevelt to resign, I thought that I should join the DAR in order to make my voice heard from within the organization. I knew that I was qualified for membership, because Mother had already done the research necessary to trace our ancestry to a soldier in the Revolutionary War. All I needed to do was let the Olathe chapter know that I wanted to join and give them Mother's membership number. After a few weeks, I was accepted to full membership.

Each member was responsible for delivering a talk once a year. Most gave interesting historical papers. I wanted to talk about what was happening in America at that time. When it was my turn, I gave a book review of Louis Adamek's *My America* which described America not as the traditional melting pot, but as a "symphony" in which each culture played its part, hopefully in harmony with the whole. I liked this concept, and I wanted to share it with the other members.

I didn't have much time for writing papers, so the next year I polished up a paper I had written for my art class at Kansas City Junior College on the bronzes of the African country of Benin. This was by way of introducing the subject of black culture and its influence in America. I had already given the paper before an assembly in a Negro high school in celebration of Negro History Week. I felt good talking about the accomplishments of blacks. It made me feel that I was making a down payment on a debt I owed Sally.

During the war, when it was my turn to speak, I made up a test of twenty questions. All twenty-eight members agreed to take the test provided that their individual answers would not be revealed. I was only interested in the totals. I don't remember all twenty questions, but I do remember that I started off in the least controversial way and gradually led up to more contentious material.

Question one: Would you object to sitting next to a Negro on the bus? (There were still Jim Crow laws in Missouri but not in Kansas.) No one would object. Question two: Would you object to sitting next to a Negro in a movie? Five people would object. (Negroes could go to the movies in Kansas, but they had to sit in the back rows. In Missouri, they couldn't even go to the white movie theaters.) I also asked if they would object to being cared for by a Negro trained nurse in a hospital. No one would object to that. This was at a time when the U.S. Army had just turned down the services of two thousand black nurses on the supposition that the soldiers wouldn't want to be cared for by black nurses.

In the discussion that followed my reading the tabulation of the answers, the members began to discuss the inconsistencies in their own prejudices. This was definite progress. Years earlier I had met Roy Wilkins in New York; we were introduced by a mutual friend. I decided to send this questionnaire and answers to Wilkins for his comments. By that time, he was head of the National Association for the Advancement of Colored People. He wrote me a very cordial letter in which he said, "If all of America was as liberal in their thinking as your group of members, we would be satisfied."

I had another club affiliation. Because Lawrence's mother had been national president of the Council of Jewish Women, I was invited to be on the Kansas City chapter's board of directors. I didn't know what I had to contribute, but it was an honor I couldn't refuse without offending people. It was a big effort for me to attend meetings because it meant spending a day in the city. I tried to plan other things that I needed to do there on the same day. I remember one particular day when I combined a trip to the stockyards in the pickup. When I came rushing in to the Council board, I forgot to take off the galoshes I had worn in the stockyards. The ladies were too polite to comment, but finally even I noticed: there was something that didn't smell quite right. I realized that the smell was coming from me. I excused myself, much to everyone's relief, took the galoshes to the truck and left them, then returned to the meeting.

One of the more interesting posts I held on the board was that of program chairman for the monthly open meetings. The meetings were usually attended by two or three hundred members. I was given a very small budget for hiring speakers, so I had to cajole members into being on the programs. That was free labor.

I practically blew my whole budget on one speaker, Thomas Hart Benton. He had just returned to his native Missouri, after spending many years studying and painting in Italy. I wanted to be the first to have him speak in Kansas City. He pleaded that he was a painter not a speaker. I pleaded that he was a public figure and said he could have free rein in his subject. He accepted the invitation to speak. It was the best-attended meeting we had under my chairmanship. In the process, we became good friends. The Bentons' daughter

Jessie and our daughter Laura were the same age. Their visits to our farm were fun for all of us. Tom and his wife, Rita, admired the portraits of my Ramsey ancestors and thought that perhaps they had been painted by Caleb Bingham. I've never gotten around to checking with the Metropolitan Museum to see if they were right. That's a project for my old age.

There was another board of directors that elected me as a new member. I was the first woman to be chosen in their history. The Young Men's Hebrew Association was the real cultural center of the Jewish community. It brought some of the finest speakers in the world to Kansas City. For the first time, I was to sit on a male board. It was a very different experience. When the board made a decision to spend money for a project, before the meeting closed, enough men had sent notes up to the chairman—to say how much they would donate—so that the membership at large did not have to be asked for contributions. This could never have happened in a board made up of women. The money controls were still solidly in the hands of the men.

The YMHA had brought a new executive director from New York. He was wonderfully trained for his job and was very interested in bringing a wider variety of activities to the center. When I proposed that we get Langston Hughes, the great Negro poet, to read some of his own poems, the director backed me up. I was still trying to use every opportunity I could to foster acceptance of the Negroes. With Hitler persecuting their people in Germany, the Jews felt they couldn't afford to take on the unpopular cause of Negro rights as well. Often I felt like a minority of one. Nevertheless, we did bring Langston Hughes, and his evening was a big success, judging by the number of encores he was forced to give.

In Olathe, one election day, Lawrence and I were standing in line at the courthouse waiting to vote, when we noticed a hesitant group of blacks huddled together across the street. Lawrence said he thought they wanted to vote but were afraid to get in the line. We got out of line ourselves and went over to encourage them. One black followed us. Then we were disappointed to see that he had left the line. We watched to see where he had gone. A few minutes later, he came back with about a dozen friends. Lawrence and I signaled our approval. His face burst into a broad grin. He too approved of what he had done and what he was about to do. He was about to vote for the first time in his life.

CHAPTER 17

Paul

Because the war was on and there was gasoline rationing, we had to limit our driving. When Paul was five-and-a-half years old, we enrolled him in Pembroke Country Day School in Kansas City. We sent him by public bus; Pembroke assigned an upper classman to take him off the bus at school. Whenever Paul returned home in the afternoon, I saw the whole busload of sailors from the Naval Air Base waving good-bye to him. I asked Paul how everyone on the bus happened to know him. He said, "I take messages for them to the girls." It seems he was social director of the bus, providing introductions whenever they were requested. He loved playing the role of Cupid.

Paul's first report card was glowing. His teacher wrote that she had asked if anyone wanted to tell a story for the class. Paul volunteered to tell the story of Robin Hood. Lawrence had read it to him in the adult version. His teacher gave us a quote from Paul's version as told to his class. He said, "You saucy knave, I'm going to lambaste you with my trusty quarterstaff." She thought that was pretty funny language for a kindergartner, and so did we.

All of Paul's sailor friends from the bus knew where he lived. From up in the air, the farm stood out because we had a two-hundred-foot concrete barn. When they were up in their "yellow perils," they would fly very low over our fields, doing what they called hedgehopping. They would swoop low and go straight up again. They always leaned out of the cabs and waved to their little friends on the ground. Sometimes they tossed notes to Paul and Laura. I thought the sailors were homesick for their own brothers and sisters and so adopted my children to fill that need. At first, Paul would run to me with the notes they threw and ask me to read them aloud. Then he got to figuring them out for himself and didn't need me as his reader. Laura was awed by her brother's new knowledge of reading and would ask him to read to her. He wasn't really good at it, so he faked a lot. He would "read" the most outlandish scary tales until finally she covered her ears and said, "I don't want to hear any more of that story." Then she would go off and find Tom to see if she could join in whatever he was doing.

When Paul was seven and had entered the second grade, he began to complain at night that he had a backache. I found it hard to take his complaints seriously because he was so active in his play all day. A few nights passed like this before I phoned for an appointment with the doctor. Our pediatrician took his symptoms seriously enough to send him to a radiologist for X-rays of the back. It looked as though he had a compressed fracture of the fourth and fifth thoracic vertebrae. A brace was ordered by the orthopedic surgeon who was consulted.

Everyone was baffled because Paul had not had any injury. Then Paul began to be unsure of himself in walking, even stumbling and holding on to the wall. At our insistence, further tests were done. After spinal taps and more X-rays, it was decided that there was a spinal cord tumor and that a neurosurgeon had to operate immediately. By that time, Paul was already incontinent from the pressure on the nerves in his spine. He found this so humiliating and so hard to understand. I tried to explain the anatomy of the body and of the nervous system. I made comparisons with electric circuits and explained, as well as I understood it myself, what the doctors hoped to accomplish with the operation. It was not easy to explain to a seven-year-old active boy the reasons why he had lost all sensation in his legs and could not even stand up.

The day Paul was operated on, Laura broke out in a full-blown case of measles. My sister came to Kansas City to help out; but since she hadn't been around children much, Laura found it easy to talk her into permitting all kinds of nonsense. Lawrence and I were terribly torn between being with Laura and running the risk of carrying her measles to Paul. The doctors didn't think we could be carriers, but they weren't really reassuring. Nowhere were there any guarantees on the outcome of the surgery, either for the short term or the long term. The pathology report came back. The tumor that had been removed was a rare type of cancer never before seen in a child.

Lawrence and I continued to shuttle between our two sick children and hardly ever had more than a few seconds' exchange of vital information as we traded posts. Laura recovered first, and we found a kindergarten for her. Since it was 1944 and the war was still on, there were kindergartens that kept children of working mothers almost twelve hours a day. It was a great comfort to drop her off and know that she would be cared for by well-trained teachers. She was a good sport about being shunted about like this.

Paul began to show some small signs of improvement. One day I noticed that the hairs on his legs were standing up, the way they do when one is cold. Without being seen, I reached over and plucked one of the hairs, and he felt it. I was ready to skip down the hall and shout for the doctors to come see what miracle had happened. Sensation was returning. Another month, and Paul was begging to go back to school even if he had to be in his wheelchair.

The school and his teacher were marvelous. They said they could handle Paul if I came to school two or three times a day to take him to the toilet. Paul was so thrilled to be back with his friends that I would have done anything to make it possible. His classmates must have been well taught both at home and at school; they all accepted him back as if nothing had changed. The only difference, as far as they were concerned, was that instead of playing football with them, Paul was now their coach from his wheelchair.

During Paul's stay in the hospital we had rented an apartment in Kansas City in order to avoid the twenty mile drive each day. Some of the boys would come to our apartment after school to play. I marveled at how inventive Paul was. Since he couldn't walk, he devised games of war in which he would drag himself around on the floor as though he were a soldier trying to keep low in order not to be hit by the enemy bullets. He was better than his friends at this type of crawling because his arms had developed strength from pushing the wheels of his chair.

It became obvious to us that this was going to be a long illness and that it would be better if we didn't have the responsibility of running the farm. It seemed easier for us to part with it altogether than to rent it. We made the decision to sell the farm and all the equipment and livestock in order to be free to go with Paul to wherever there was a possibility of finding treatment for him.

First we sold the farm. The buyer wanted some of the furniture, and the rest was sold to individuals. I still held on to the pieces that had been in our home in Little Rock. For the second time, I was supervising the crating of the grandfather clock. Then we held a farm auction. It was embarrassing because the equipment brought almost double the price that we had paid for it years earlier. There were such scarcities due to the war.

We didn't want to sell Beauty. We felt she deserved to be put out to pasture, and the new owner agreed to give her a good home free of work. Tom was placed with friends of ours. The farm manager decided on a job in a war plant in the city. There was nothing more to be done but pack our remaining clothes and drive away from the home where we had spent ten happy years.

The first summer after Paul's operation, we had a friend rent an apartment for us in Far Rockaway, New York. There we could be close to the sea and also close enough to take Paul for consultations at Memorial Hospital in New York

City. It was a good summer. All four of us were together most of the time. There were lots of children in the building where we lived. They would vie with each other as to who could push the wheelchair and who could ride in it with Paul. We had an inner tube that we blew up at the beach. Paul could float around in it and feel as though he were a normal boy again. We didn't want the summer to end. What we had at that moment was acceptable, and the future was so uncertain.

In the fall, Paul went back to school. He was now in third grade even though he had been absent for more than half of the time in second grade. Everyone thought it was important to keep him with his group of friends and no one felt it was too important whether or not he could keep up with the class. He did keep up.

In the spring, more X-rays showed that the tumor had had an extension into the chest cavity and that part of the tumor was still growing. Our pediatrician heard of a research project at Lankenau Hospital in Philadelphia. They were working with polysaccharides that made tumors disappear in laboratory rats. Lawrence took Paul to Philadelphia. A panel of doctors examined him and then debated the pros and cons of accepting him as an experimental patient. All their other patients had tumors that could be biopsied after a few treatments to see if any of the cancer cells were dying. In Paul's case, they couldn't get at the tumor to follow the progress. After days of discussion, they decided to take him into the experiment, not because he was a suitable case but because he had so charmed them that they wanted to do everything they could for him. They knew he had no other chance.

Lawrence and I took turns living in Philadelphia in the hospital with Paul. Lankenau was a Lutheran hospital staffed by Lutheran nuns. They were among the kindest people I have ever known. The polysaccharides were administered by intravenous drip. Because the substance was so highly toxic, they were afraid to give Paul dosages that were the equivalent of the doses given the lab rats. Even with this great caution, he twice shot a temperature of a hundred and seven. All of us looked forward to the weekends, when there was no treatment. We were free to take Paul for small excursions in the city.

One of the most amusing trips was a Sunday afternoon when Sister Ruth said she would like to show us the zoo. We ordered a taxi and loaded ourselves and the wheelchair into it. The taxi driver fell into our holiday mood and sang songs about monkeys that got drunk. We were sorry to part from our driver. I think he would have been happy to park his cab and come with us. Later I regretted not asking him to join us. We visited all the animals. Paul thought the gorilla was making faces at him and he in return made faces at the gorilla. He sang him the song he had just learned from the taxi driver:

> The monkey he got drunk
> And sat on the elephant's trunk.
> The elephant sneezed
> And fell on his knees.
> So what became of the monk, the monk?

We were having such a good time that it was almost closing hour when we decided to go back to the hospital. There was not a taxi in sight. Panic struck. Sister Ruth and I held a quick decision-making conference. We would hitchhike. How could we fail to get a ride? Who could pass up a corpulent nun, a seven-year-old in a wheelchair, and a not unattractive young woman? The answer is that plenty of people could. I must admit that most of the cars were already filled with families and didn't have room for us. Finally, a blessed soul with an empty car came to our rescue. He went miles out of his way to deliver us to our door.

After a few months of treatment, the doctors decided that they would like a surgeon to try removing the tumor in the chest cavity. We took Paul to Hahneman Hospital there in Philadelphia. The day he underwent surgery was the day the Japanese surrendered. At the end of the five-hour operation, the surgeon came to us in the waiting room. His voice quivered as he told us that he had removed the tumor, which was the size of a baby's head, but that he had been forced to leave a tiny piece, no bigger than the size of the nail on one's pinky. In order to have removed it, he would have had to cut the aorta; the technique for doing that had not yet been developed. He was sure this tiny remnant of the tumor was going to give us trouble. None of us felt like celebrating the victory over Japan. We had met our own personal defeat. All of us wept together, dried our eyes, and went in to be there when Paul came out of the anesthesia.

There was one more operation done at the University of Pennsylvania Hospital, an attempt to remove the portion of the tumor that had grown back on the spine. After that, Paul said it was the last try he wanted us to make, and we agreed with him. As soon as he was strong enough to travel, we all went back to Kansas City.

Paul wanted to go back to school, but we all knew that this time our luck had run out and that he was too weak to make it through even a couple of hours in class. Sometimes as a surprise, Laura would help him get dressed so that when we entered his room the two of them would be giggling with glee. Christmas came, but there was not much joy in it. All I remember is a small white tree that we set up in the apartment. A few days later, the doctor wanted us to take Paul to the hospital. He was too tired to make the effort of reading to himself, so I read to him. He told me to turn off the radio because they were playing music and music meant dancing and he knew now that he would never dance. For some reason, he loved the stories of Sherlock Holmes, so I read those to him for much of the night. Lawrence and I alternated nights with him in the hospital.

One day Paul noticed that his arms were beginning to feel numb. By then, he understood better than any of us just what this meant. He begged me to give him enough pills to put him to sleep forever. The one thing that he wanted from me, I did not have the courage to give him. It was torture to watch him weaken and diminish hourly and to be so powerless to help him.

I decided that I needed help myself to face the inevitable. I began to see Dr. Sylvia Allen, a psychoanalyst, who was very supportive during this period. She persuaded me that Laura also needed me to be with her more and that Lawrence and I needed to have some time together too.

One afternoon, Lawrence's father went to see Paul. He hadn't seen him in nearly a week and was so shocked by the change in him that he could barely get home. After a few hours at home, Kess had a massive stroke and died two days later in the room next to Paul's in the hospital. Paul was beyond caring when we told him. He just said, "He's lucky to be dead."

All of us were reaching physical and emotional exhaustion. Paul was willing for Lawrence and me to spend the night in our own beds. We told him to phone us if he wanted anything. He reassured us that he would be all right. He said that since his doctor always came to see him around midnight anyway, he wouldn't be alone very long. He was more cheerful than he had been for a long time. He called me back in the room for another good-night kiss.

The next morning the phone rang at six o'clock. Lawrence answered it. He came back and simply said, "It's over."

I was sure of one thing. I did not want any flowers. Flowers fade. I only wanted to have boughs of pine because they are evergreen and I wanted to keep fresh memories of this courageous child who had brought so much joy into our lives and who had now left us, three months before his ninth birthday.

CHAPTER 18

Triumphs and Disasters

I had learned a great deal in the past two years. For one thing, I learned that the things we worry about happening probably won't. Conversely, the things we could never imagine happening sometimes do. Ever since I had seen my mother have a nervous breakdown, I had harbored a secret fear that if it had happened to her, maybe it could also happen to me. Now that I had been through this unimaginable trial, I felt that I had misplaced my concerns. Nonetheless I wanted to continue the work I had begun with Dr. Allen.

At the beginning, Dr. Allen could see me only once a week. As some of her patients "graduated," she was able to increase my appointments to three times a week. Having read Freud, I was inclined to try doing my own analysis. Dr. Allen had a hard time teaching me that I was the analysand and she was the analyst. Learning to free-associate was difficult. I eventually realized it was like a game we had played as children, where someone says a word and everyone then has to say the first thing that comes to mind. Free association is letting one image stimulate another and without censorship; in this way, one thought can lead to another until you find yourself at the brink of a revelation. Sometimes you pull yourself up short and wonder how you got to that point considering where you started. Since intellectualization was my strongest defense, it was months before I could break through and stop using it.

Psychoanalysis is really controlled regression. One goes back in time and place to earlier events in one's life that have caused trauma. Each time one revisits the event, a new dimension is added. At first, I would remember an early happening, and it was as though I were telling the story of someone else about whom I had read. In some ways it was like peeling the layers of an onion: take one layer away and the next one looks the same, except that in removing each layer you are coming closer to the core. You eventually sense that you are not telling the story of someone else, but are reliving the event, and all the emotions you felt at the time come flooding in. I use the word flooding because frequently lots of tears accompany these early memories.

I remember one particular session when I was recalling my mother's callousness as she flushed my dead goldfish down the toilet. I allowed myself to weep copiously on the analytic couch. When my fifty minutes were up and I was pulling myself together to go back into the world of the present, my analyst said to me, "My, haven't we had fun today?" I was ready to swing at her. Wasn't she being just as callous as my mother? I couldn't dismiss her remark from my mind.

Finally, I got her message. I had been wallowing in my sorrow. I had been enjoying feeling sorry for poor me. I had come face to face with the masochistic side of my nature. Looking at myself at such close range had dissipated the fun of self pity. I could no longer enjoy it. Thank God, I learned that lesson. There were many more lessons I had to learn, slowly and painfully.

There was a memorable session in which I discovered the way I had been using Junior. He now preferred to be called Nat. He was married and was a pilot in the U.S. Air Force. I'll never forget the pride we all felt when we went to the Kansas City airport to watch him pilot a B-17 bomber plane to a safe landing. He was then sent overseas to England. At first, the Air Force required the pilots to fly a total of only fifteen missions. When Nat had flown fourteen, it was announced that pilots would have to fly twenty. Each time he was about to reach his quota, more missions were added on. Nat was finally up to twenty-nine when his plane was badly hit over Germany. He stayed in the plane until all of his crew had parachuted. This extra time on the plane meant that when he was captured he was sent to a different prisoner-of-war camp from the rest of his men.

Nat only talked about his experiences when he was pressed to do so. He didn't seem bitter about his treatment as a prisoner because he knew the Germans themselves didn't have food. Each prisoner was in the habit of saving a little piece of bread to eat during the night. This small cache sometimes attracted a nocturnal thief. The prisoners were determined to catch the culprit; when they did, they were going to hold a mock court-martial. At last they caught the rat. They held their trial. He was condemned to death. Then they cooked him and ate him. Justice had been served.

The prisoners also saved little bits of food or toothpaste and compacted them into what they called their escape cakes. They talked constantly of ways to escape and of food. One of the senior British officers, also a prisoner, suggested that it was not good for morale always to talk about food. Couldn't they focus on other things? He suggested that they could talk about what kinds of cars they would buy when they got home. They agreed that he was right. The first speaker announced, "I'm going to buy a four-door Buick, and its steering wheel will be made of licorice. It will have marshmallow tires covered with chocolate." So much for their morale lesson.

Nat's stalag was quite far east. When they heard that the Russians were coming, the Germans decided to evacuate all prisoners. Having no means to transport them, they made them walk. These were later called the "death marches." Nat said the escape cakes worked: the survival rate of those with cakes was much higher than the rate of those who hadn't made them.

After long days of marching, they were loaded into an empty cattle car on a railroad siding. They were packed in so tightly that when a poor soul expired there was no space for him to fall and no way to remove him. They were not surprised when American planes began flying low over them. But when our own airplanes began to strafe them, trapped as they were in this cattle car, they were terrified. Later, Patton arrived and assured them that he was going to fly them out right away. To celebrate, they ate up the few remaining crumbs of their escape cakes. Patton kept his promise, but it took another week. Meanwhile they were without food. When Nat got to France, he weighed eighty pounds, a little more than half his normal weight.

The Air Force decided to fatten the men up before sending them home. Nat had regained forty pounds before any of us saw him. He and his wife, Lucile, went on a second honeymoon before Nat was to be discharged from duty. When the Army doctors examined him, they told him he now had a healed TB lesion that he had not had when he entered the service.

In the fall, Nat enrolled in the Harvard School of Architecture. He and Lucile had an apartment just off campus. Nat designed and built all the furniture himself. The bookshelves were stacks of bricks with lumber laid on them. He made Calder mobiles out of coat hangers and painted Picassos that even Picasso would have authenticated had he been asked. He was creative in another direction, too, and soon son John was born. I visited them once and was enchanted with their life and their friends.

Two weeks before his final project was due, Nat had a massive lung hemmorrhage. Instead of going to his graduation, he went to a veteran's hospital for a year. His classmates petitioned the school to give him his degree in architecture even though he had not quite finished his project. Nat got his degree, but he never used it. His doctors advised against it when he was discharged. Nat, Lucile, and John moved to Santa Fe, New Mexico, because of the dry climate. They bought a wonderful adobe house, and Nat set about building furniture again, this time a more permanent kind.

What I started out to say was how, in my analysis, I discovered that all my life I had tried to make Nat live out the aggressive side of my nature for me—the part of me that had always wanted to be a boy. Remember how hard I tried to kiss my elbow? That ended when I unconsciously adopted Nat to act out what I would have wanted to do had I been the boy in the family.

When I made this discovery, Dr. Allen said to me, "Your brother is going to feel so much better now that you have freed him." I thought she was carrying things too far. How could I still be controlling him? We lived halfway across the country from each other. I only wrote him every six months. The last time I had been aware of trying to influence him was when he was choosing his undergraduate college. I had pushed for Harvard, and he had gone there.

Years later, Nat described to me how he'd suddenly had a feeling of coming into his own. He felt that he no longer needed to do things to please me but was free to please himself. I pressed him to try and pin down the time when he got this strong feeling. He worked it out, and the time coincided precisely with when Dr. Allen had said he would feel free from my control. Was this more extrasensory perception?

Speaking of extrasensory perception, I had been through a particularly sad session with Dr. Allen and was having difficulty shaking off the mood. I drove to pick up Laura at school. We rode in silence. She was evidently sensitive to how I was feeling because she quietly said, "I'm so sorry about your father dying." It was exactly what I had been dealing with in my psychoanalytic session. It was not a subject I had ever discussed with Laura. When I told Dr. Allen about the incident, she agreed that it was probably still another case of ESP.

My friends, who knew me before and after my analysis always said they couldn't see any difference in me. No doubt they couldn't. Only I knew the difference in how I felt about myself. The French have a wonderful expression that I can apply here to describe what was going on inside me: "*Je me sens bien dans ma peau*" or "I feel good in my skin." I have been at ease with myself ever since. I only worry about the things I can do something about. I have abandoned the heavy baggage that I carried from the past. I consider that my analysis was successful, and in the end I am the only one who can make that judgment.

While I was undergoing analysis, I worked with Lawrence in his retail women's wear store. Without his father, he had lost his appetite for running the business. I came into the store knowing nothing about retailing, but soon we were back in our earlier roles: he was the teacher and I was the pupil. We worked well together, and the store recovered from the two years of neglect during which we had spent all of our time in hospitals.

I would leave the store early each day to pick up Laura at school. Her favorite pastime in the afternoons was going to the pony ring. I doled out quarters with a cautious hand, and three times around the ring was not very fulfilling for someone who would have liked to ride for hours. We had a great piece of luck. The pony ring owner bought a bunch of young ponies that had never been ridden before. He was too heavy, himself, to break them in to carry a saddle and rider. Laura was the only child he knew who would be able to ride the untamed ponies. When he asked, she was jumping up and down, hoping I would agree. The owner wasn't afraid that they would buck or rear; he knew they would just run as fast as they could until they finally exhausted themselves and slowed down. They would then be ready to carry the usual pony ring riders. My six-year-old daughter and Mr. Curley formed a perfect partnership. His ponies were well trained, and she got hours of free rides at breakneck speed.

Mr. Curley bought a show pony, which he asked Laura to ride in the American Royal Horse Show. They trained together for weeks. We sent to Best and Company, in New York, for a brown tweed riding suit with a brown velvet derby. She was going to be the sharpest rider in the show. Laura didn't want to tell us, but she had developed a knot on her leg from so much practice. When she finally told us, it was too late to clear it up before the big show. She missed her one chance to ride in the American Royal. In this there could be no second turns, and there would be no ribbons. We all knew she was a champion and told her so. It didn't matter what we thought; her dream of glory was shattered.

In the spring of 1947, I enrolled Laura in Sunset Hill School in Kansas City for the fall term. I thought it strange that they didn't ask me to bring Laura for an interview. They said it wouldn't be necessary. The school had the reputation of being the best private girls' school in town. All of Lawrence's cousins had gone there, and now their daughters were also going. I heard nothing from the school and decided to telephone the director of admissions. When I reached her, she was full of apologies. She had forgotten about Laura's application and had accepted two other girls in the second-grade class. I said I hadn't realized that their classes were so small. No, they weren't *that* small, but they could have only two Jewish girls in each class. She freely admitted her mistake and was willing to rectify her error by asking one of the other children not to come.

I made an appointment to see her in her office. There she elaborated on the school policy. She told me which two Jewish girls had been admitted. I knew them both. They were nice little girls, and I knew it would disappoint them not to go to Sunset Hill in the fall.

"Would the school have a place for Laura if she weren't Jewish?" I asked. The answer was clear. Yes, they would.

"Would my being an active member of the Olathe chapter of the DAR matter to the school?" I asked. The admissions director wanted to know why I hadn't mentioned that before. Of course, it made all the difference in the world, and the school would be happy to have Laura. I said I wanted to discuss the situation with my husband and that I would let her know.

Together Lawrence and I decided not to place Laura in this uncomfortable situation. Besides, something was brewing that meant we might move to New York in a year or two, and Laura was happy enough in her public school. We wrote a note to Sunset Hill saying she would not be entering the second grade. This happened in 1947, and I feel sure that the school has changed its admission policy since then. I write about it only because that is the way it was then.

There was a course being given at Columbia University, in New York City, by Professor David Dodd, dean of Columbia's School of Finance. Lawrence was anxious to attend, and I urged him to go. By then, I felt confident I could run the store without his daily presence. He could use his time in New York to do buying for the store as well. Air travel had advanced to the point where he could fly home to be with Laura and me for the weekends. My analyst, Dr. Allen, also thought it was a good idea because Lawrence was inclined to interfere with the analysis by trying to keep me from having a firm transference to her. There being no dissenting votes, Lawrence enrolled for the course. It would change our lives.

Lawrence worked very hard. He wanted to learn as much about investments as he could. The text for the course was a book called *Security Analysis,* written some years earlier by Professors David Dodd and Benjamin Graham. This book is still considered the Bible of the investment field. Dodd arranged for Lawrence to meet Benjamin Graham. The two of them hit it off from the beginning. Graham was a general partner in an investment partnership called Graham and Newman. Lawrence persuaded Graham to let him invest some money in this partnership. He also told Graham that he was considering moving to New York.

Lawrence was in the right place at the right moment. Graham and Dodd were working on a revision of their book, and they needed someone to supply fresh examples and in general oversee the mechanics of getting it into shape. If Lawrence could move to New York permanently within the next six months, he could be Benjamin Graham's man Friday. Who wouldn't have jumped at such a chance?

There were only two real opponents to our move, Dr. Allen and Aunt Ray. They weren't enough to stop us. The timing was right; the lease of the store building was ending. We announced we would be closing the store after fifty-seven years in business. Lawrence himself had been a merchant for twenty-four of those years, and he felt it was time for a change. He had gone into the business to please his father. Now there was no longer a reason to stay.

We almost made a game of the closing-out sale. A number of dealers had offered to buy all the merchandise that was left. We jokingly told them we would file their cards, but they were not to be too hopeful because we intended to sell the last item directly to our customers, who had been loyal to us over the years. As our stocks diminished, we literally moved the walls forward so the store wouldn't look empty. The final day, we sold out of the display windows. There were two dresses, size fifty-two, that remained. A very stout lady came in and bought both of them. That was it! We were out of business.

We took Laura to a camp in Pearl River, New York, so she would have a good summer while we looked for an apartment in New York City. Lawrence had provisionally chosen one on the west side. I took a look at it and saw that the ceilings were too low for the grandfather clock. I had been without the clock for three-and-a-half years, and I missed it. We would have to look further.

Part Three

CHAPTER 19

New York, New Life

Lawrence and I were together when we saw an apartment on East 78th Street between Madison and Fifth Avenues. We had to hunt down the building superintendent because it was a Sunday and the apartment was in a brownstone, only recently converted from a private home. Even from the street I could tell that the ceilings would be high enough for the clock. It was a nice, tree-lined block of low buildings. (Although I didn't know it then, the large house on the corner was one of Doris Duke's homes.) When we finally rooted out the super and saw the apartment, I was enchanted. The ceilings were not only high, they were graceful, and there were two wood-burning fireplaces. One of the mantels was marble. Lawrence was more inclined to be practical. He pointed out that the kitchen was only six feet by six feet and the refrigerator was so small it fitted under the sink. I assured him that it didn't matter; I would manage.

The next day, when Lawrence went to the landlord's office to negotiate the lease, he made me stay in the car. He knew I was ready to pay any price that was asked in order to have this apartment. My obvious enthusiasm would have handicapped him. When he came back to the car, we had a home in New York.

We phoned the warehouse in Kansas City and told them to find a truck coming east and put our furniture on it. We had to wait a good ten days before the truck arrived. When it came, there were problems to be solved. The elevator was only thirty by twenty-eight *inches!* Everything had to be taken out of the crates in the lobby. It was a miracle, but when the clock was disassembled we were able to load it in the elevator. The truckmen had to stop everything and help me put it together. By the time all the rest was unloaded, I had the clock running and chiming its old, familiar Westminster tune. It was Christmas in September. It was a resurrection. Its tick was the heartbeat it had always been for me. The truckmen were duly reverent and admired its Gothic carving and its mellow tones. I slept well that night. We were reunited.

The rest of the furniture gave me more problems. The dining room was okay, but the bedroom was a mess. None of the draperies I had brought were long enough. I needed to learn something about decorating in order to turn this hodgepodge into something livable. I found a course I could take at the New York School of Interior Decoration. After six months of study I would know what to do to improve the looks of our apartment. I had agreed to the inconveniences of the kitchen, but could I live with this incomplete décor for six months? I could hire a decorator. Maybe the decorator wouldn't respect my wishes. I'd rather make my own mistakes. I enrolled.

It was a wonderful course. It began with the history of architecture and included the history of furniture. It gave me the background I needed to be able to pull together all the lovely museums I had seen on our honeymoon in Europe some sixteen years before. I couldn't wait to learn what I now so urgently needed to know. Four months into the course we were sent to the fabric houses and taught how to mix paints to match fabrics. That was coming closer to what I needed.

Since I had taught myself to sew, when we lived on the farm, I was particularly interested in the lectures on styles of draperies for different periods. I realized for the first time that my dining room furniture was Federal and that I should make draperies to carry out that period. I cut muslin patterns for swags and jabots. Then I was ready to tackle them in red satin. I found a material in red and white stripes for the chairs. I covered them myself. I painted the walls in Williamsburg blue. All that was lacking was a chandelier. This could wait until I knew more. I had solved the easiest of my problems. There was still the bedroom. I stalled for time, awaiting an inspiration.

The school assigned us the project of designing a living room. I used the measurements of my room and began drawing the furniture layout to scale. I used twin sofas facing each other and put a partner's desk at one end of the room. The problem bedroom was no longer a problem when I conceptualized it as a living room. I couldn't wait for the course to end so I could devote myself to shopping and executing the design that had earned me an A plus.

My oriental rugs were the wrong sizes for my rooms, so I had to learn the oriental rug market. I found a pair of large, matching Bokhara rugs from the estate of J. P. Morgan. They were to be the basis of the color scheme. I was having fun now that I knew what I was doing.

Through his work, Lawrence was meeting a great number of people; we were invited to many dinner parties. Entertaining was on a different scale from what I had known before. I was glad I had saved Mother's best dishes. Now it would be appropriate to use them. I finally found a cateress who didn't faint when she saw the size of the kitchen and the refrigerator she had to work with. We had a few small dinner parties to reciprocate. Evidently, our guests liked what I had done with our apartment because they began calling me for advice. Lawrence said that if I was going to take on the responsibility of helping people with decorating, I must get a resale license and keep books and run the buying and selling like a business. There was too much money involved for me to act like a dilettante; either I should become a professional or I should stop handing out advice. I knew he was right, so I turned pro.

It was more fun spending other people's money even though I exercised the same care I would have if it had been mine. I found my own method of working with clients, a technique of educating them to look at details. When shopping for a certain piece of furniture, I narrowed down the selection before taking the client with me. I then pointed out the different features of each piece until the client could choose for herself. I was usually involved with the wife on a day-to-day basis, but the husbands all reserved the right of veto. They could veto on two levels, from the standpoint of either taste or cost. Even though I insisted on having a budget allowance before beginning a job, and though I adhered to the budget with firmness, it was usually the husbands who decided to exceed the budget when they saw something they really wanted.

No one who knew me as a decorator would believe that I had raised pigs, and no one who had known me when I raised pigs would believe that this sophisticated decorator was the same person. What was the common denominator of both professions? I think it was what Sally had taught me with her picture-reading: Look at details. The same eye that had enabled me to differentiate between a two-hundred-dollar boar and a one-hundred-and-fifty-dollar boar also helped me select a fine antique rather than one that was less worthy.

My clients usually stayed with me for years. They would start by doing only one room. As that was completed, they would begin to talk about doing another one. Sometimes I felt they were stretching out the decorating in order to have someone to lean on. I was meeting their dependency needs as well as their decorating needs. I did not deliberately foster dependency in my clients, but there are people who like to have someone else tell them what to do. I was lucky that in ten years I never had a serious complaint from a client who was surprised by the room we created together. Clients were usually delighted when they saw it all come together on the day of installation.

The best part of being a decorator was that it gave me control over my time. I could always arrange to be home when Laura's school let out. The first year we were in New York, we sent Laura to a very progressive private school that was just a half block from our apartment. The school was housed in a converted mansion that had been the home of Jock Whitney. The study of Chinese was obligatory. The theory behind teaching Chinese seemed a good one. At that time, we were still friendly with China and half the world's population spoke Chinese. In addition, the school had a wonderfully creative drama teacher.

As the term progressed, I began having doubts about what Laura was learning in the fourth grade. For one thing, she felt deprived. She was the one person in her class who had only two parents. Nicky had six. Why couldn't she? It seems that Nicky knew how to get an auction going with all six of his parents bidding for his affection. They bid with high stakes, and Nicky profited from this competition. He got whatever he wanted. I asked if Laura wanted something that she didn't have. Yes, she wanted a better harmonica. We felt that was a reasonable request, and it was much easier to give her a harmonica than an additional four parents. She got the harmonica and dropped the other request.

In some respects, her school reminded me of the artsy, quixotic one that Auntie Mame's nephew Patrick attended. Maybe this was New York. At the end of the year, Laura came to me and said that if I expected her to learn anything I had better find another school for the next year. She was only confirming what I suspected. The year hadn't been a total loss; after all, she could count to ten in Chinese.

The next year Laura went to P.S. 6, which was supposed to be the best school in the New York public school system. It was only three short blocks from our house.

Laura was happy at P.S. 6. She had lots of boyfriends because she was able to meet the boys on their own level. She was a big Yankee fan. We teased her, saying she wanted to be the first woman on the Yankees. She was a better pitcher than most of the boys. She also played basketball. One day she came home with a very sad face. What was the matter? She had missed being elected captain of the boy's basketball team by one vote. We empathized but couldn't help wondering how she had gotten herself nominated in the first place.

In seventh grade, Laura showed me a paper returned by her teacher. She had an A for the paper, and there were no marks of correction on it. I read it, expecting to be very proud. Instead, I was shocked. There wasn't a complete sentence in the whole two pages. Without telling Laura that I was disappointed, I made an appointment to see her teacher. When I confronted him with her ignorance of what a sentence should be, he smiled, shrugged his shoulders, and said, "Your daughter is a very attractive young girl. She will grow up and marry a rich man. What's the difference if she can't write a sentence?"

I felt sad that this could happen in the school with the best reputation. However, unprepared to tackle reforming the public school system, I went in search of a private school that believed in solid, old-fashioned teaching methods.

Laura entered the Lenox School in the eighth grade. They had finished teaching grammar and were ready to start teaching literature. They began with Beowulf and moved forward chronologically. Chaucer came next in their curriculum. We were planning to take Laura to England and Paris for her first European trip. She was excited at the idea of seeing where Chaucer's pilgrims had traveled. I considered we were lucky she didn't make us walk "The Pilgrim's Way." In Winchester Cathedral, the guide mentioned that a rest home close by had been one of the pilgrims' inns. If we went there and asked for the "Wayfarers' Dole," we would be served ale in a cattle horn and bread on a board that still had an inlaid crusader's cross in the center. This was the perfect link to Laura's studies.

We visited all the tourist places, including the Shakespeare theater at Stratford-upon-Avon and John Harvard's house. I can't think why we went to Chichester, but we did, much to our regret. Our hotel was next door to the church, and the chimes sounded every quarter hour. We were accustomed to sleeping through our own clock chimes, but this church defied us to sleep. In spite of this one night's lost sleep, the trip was a big success.

When Laura was fifteen I thought it would be nice if she again met some of the children of my friends from Kansas City and other parts of America. There were so many of them going to school in the east. I decided to invite them for Thanksgiving dinner since none would be going home for the four-day holiday. In this way they could all get together, and Laura could renew friendships with people she hadn't seen for seven years. I hardly knew what I was getting into. First I had to write to their parents for their college addresses. The parents would write asking if I knew that so-and-so was in the east and whether I might like to include him or her too. The list was long. Invitations went out promptly. Replies came in slowly, if at all. Everyone said this was characteristic of teenagers but that I had better count on the entire list showing up and then add twenty percent for friends of the invited guests.

With my two-and-a-half-cubic-foot refrigerator, it was a question of careful planning. I bought a frozen turkey and calculated how long it would take to thaw so that it wouldn't have to go in the refrigerator at all. It was many years since I had baked enough pies for harvest hands, but I still knew how. By eleven-thirty guests began to arrive. All told, there were twenty-five people who shared our turkey that year. Allan, who went to Williams and lived in Memphis, had brought his cousin, a freshman at Yale who lived in Fort Smith, Arkansas. He introduced us to Randy. I could barely acknowledge the introduction because I was so struck by Randy's resemblance to our Paul. He was the age that Paul would have been and had the same large brown eyes, round face, and dark hair. He looked exactly as I imagined Paul would have looked at the age of eighteen. I said nothing about what I was thinking. There was plenty to occupy me with feeding so many starving students.

It was late afternoon before all our guests went their separate ways. Just as I was thinking that it had been more trouble than it was worth and that I would probably never do such a party again, the departing guests said they hoped they could all come again next year. How could I reply, "God forbid"? Instead, I acquiesced, and a tradition was born that lasted several years.

As I washed dishes for hours, I concluded that I really should do something to modernize the kitchen. With all my decorating experience, I still had a block in my mind as to what could be done so I could have a full-sized refrigerator, a stove with two ovens, and a double sink. It was Lawrence who set me on the right track and found the solution. He thought it was time to put my own project at the head of the line, in front of my clients. Once I got started, it didn't take more than a few weeks, and it made a great difference in our comfort.

The Tuesday after Thanksgiving two letters arrived in the same handwriting. They were postmarked New Haven. One was for me, the other was for Laura. Randy had written to thank me and to ask Laura for a date. How nice! One could see that he was a well-brought-up young man. Laura tried not to get too excited about having a date with an older guy because she knew that Randy was going with a girl who was a freshman somewhere in the east. Laura had doubts that she, as a fifteen-year-old, could compete successfully with a southern belle who was three years older.

We decided to spend the Christmas holidays with my sister and her husband, Foster Cochran, in Little Rock. There were always lots of dances and much gaiety there at Christmas. Elsie Stebbins promised that at least one of her three sons would see to it that Laura got around. It ended up with all three of them adopting her and seeing to it that she had the best time an out-of-towner could possibly have. Laura had the easiest adolescence of any girl I ever knew. The transition from playing on the same baseball team to having dates was so smooth that no one noticed the difference.

By February, after mid-semester exams, Laura and Randy were beginning to date regularly. Randy was a member of one of Yale's famous singing groups, the Baker's Dozen. The group had singing engagements at all the colleges, and Laura went along for every performance, getting a close look at the various schools as a bonus.

Late in the spring, I developed phlebitis in my left leg. It was painful and had to be treated in hospital. Through a number of medical misjudgments I lost practically the whole summer. Every time I was treated for one thing, something else went wrong: a real series of mishaps. Meanwhile, we sent Laura to the Chatelaine School in Gstaad, Switzerland, so she would learn French. She ended up teaching the German girls English.

Gstaad was the location for an international tennis tournament. Laura and her schoolmates were kept busy entertaining champions from all over the world. It was quite an experience for a sixteen-year-old.

As my summer in the hospital dragged on into months, it became obvious that my days of being a decorator were over. Decorators who cannot shop the market may as well put away their licenses. My leg was not going to permit me to do the necessary running around. With time on my hands, I began to fret over what kind of preparation Laura was making for her college board exams. When she came back from Switzerland, I began to nag her about her studies. Finally, she turned to me and said, "Get off my back. You're the one who wants the education. Why don't *you* go back to school?"

Laura had really hit on something. The next day, I was standing in line to register at the Columbia University School of General Studies. I was forty-two years old, but why not give it a try?

CHAPTER 20

Change of Life

When I registered at Columbia, I caused quite a stir at the registration desk. The commotion wasn't because of my advanced age but because of my credentials. I had brought with me my diploma from Central High School of Little Rock. This was in 1957 at the very moment when President Eisenhower called out the federal troops to ensure that a few black students would be conducted safely into this same school. The people at the registration desk were so curious about the origin of my diploma that they took no notice of its date, twenty-five years earlier.

There were academic decisions to be made. I was afraid to take advanced French, having forgotten what little I had learned, so I opted for starting a new language. Spanish could be helpful if I was going to become a social worker. There had been an influx of people to New York from Puerto Rico, and it would be nice if I could speak their language.

The reality of going back to college after so many years was just beginning to hit me. What about all those requirements in statistics and science and mathematics? What did I remember of high school trigonometry or solid geometry? Nothing, though I had been able to help Laura with plane geometry. I could see I was going to have to approach my studies one thing at a time instead of worrying about the courses I would have to take that year or the next. Once I adopted that attitude, I felt better. I knew how my grandfather must have felt when he entered first grade at the age of twenty-one.

Freshman English was obligatory. After a few minor themes, we were told we would have to write an original research paper using primary sources. I kept submitting subjects to the professor, and he kept rejecting them. Either too much had already been written on my proposals, or it would be impossible for me to write anything original on something as vast as the "Origin of European Porcelain." Finally, in desperation, I submitted the subject "The Pineapple as the Symbol of Hospitality." That one he liked. If the professor wanted original research he was going to get it; nothing had been written on the subject.

This paper had me pouring through books in the architecture library, where I found copies of Christopher Wren's original drawings for St. Paul's Cathedral in London. Wren's first plan was to make the central dome a huge pineapple and have two smaller pineapples atop each of the front towers. In his final plan, only the two small pineapples remained, and the center dome was built as it is today. Since this dome became the prototype for so many of our state capitol buildings—even for the U.S. Capitol—I ask myself even now what would have happened if Wren's original plan had been used. Would there be pineapples all over the country? That paper taught me how to seek and find in the hidden stacks of libraries.

A paper I wrote for a course in philosophy was less of a hit. We had been reading Plato's *Republic*. It seemed to me that the government changes Plato described were brought about by young sons rebelling against their fathers. I decided to look into Plato's life to see what gave him such rebellious feelings against his own father. Sure enough, I found an answer. Plato's mother had remarried after his father died, when he was tiny, and his stepfather was very hard on him. I gave the paper a psychoanalytic twist, going into why Plato thought as he did. After all, Freud had written a paper analyzing Moses. Why shouldn't I do the same for Plato? The professor was not pleased. He grudgingly gave me a B. Four years later, in graduate school, I submitted the same paper for a course in Freudian psychoanalysis. I hadn't changed a comma, but this time I got an A plus. So much for differences of opinion!

In my course in music appreciation there was a young man of twenty-two who was a real character. He had studied for two years at MIT and had decided to take a year off and more or less hitchhike on a trip around the world. When he returned from his sabbatical, he came to Columbia University to finish his studies. He wore the souvenirs of his trip: a sleeveless embroidered vest from Afghanistan, barefoot sandals from Greece, a karakul lamb cap from Russia. He was handsome enough so this odd assortment looked well on him. He rode a disreputable-looking, old bicycle. He explained that he had chosen a bicycle no one would want to steal. He had achieved his purpose.

Just before the Christmas vacation, this classmate handed me an invitation to a party he was giving in his apartment. He invited Lawrence too and added a note saying that his parents would be there. Until the invitation came I had known him as Stewart. Now I learned that his last name was Mott.

Lawrence and I were a little nervous about going to a basement apartment in the nineties on the Upper West Side. We decided, however, that this was as close as we would ever get to a hippie party, so we went. Stewart greeted us at the door wearing kilts of the Stewart plaid. Hanging above his piano was an oil painting of him in these same kilts. When his parents arrived, we were a bit surprised. His father looked just like the grandfather (C. Aubrey Smith) in the movie version of *Little Lord Fauntleroy*. All that was missing was the Great Dane at his side. Bit by bit we got the whole picture: This was Charles Stewart Mott, former Chairman of the Board of General Motors and still a very active member of that board and of the Dupont-Nemours board. At that time he was over eighty-five and as energetic as a man thirty years younger.

Stewart had done all of the cooking himself. After dinner

he played the piano so everyone could sing Christmas carols. It wasn't exactly the hippie party that we expected, but it was certainly a memorable evening.

The course in statistics nearly put me six feet under. Only one person in the class really understood what was being taught. He was a brilliant Japanese student, and I asked him to be my tutor. Without him I never would have made it. One day, he told me that he was to be married when he got back to Japan the following year. He showed me a picture of his fiancée. When I asked him questions about her, I noticed a certain vagueness in his answers. He finally told me that his parents had submitted photos of three young ladies, among whom he was to make his choice. He had never met any of them. I hope it worked out well for him, because without him I would never have made it to the Columbia University School of Social Work.

Getting into a graduate school the following year was very different from getting into the undergraduate college. A lengthy questionnaire had to be completed, and there was a three-hour interview. I was concerned with the line the questions took. It was all right as long as my examiner quizzed me about why I wanted to be a social worker, but when she began to ask about Paul's death, I thought she had wandered into territory that shouldn't concern her. I knew she was angling for something. When she wanted me to describe his death, I responded by asking if she wanted me to tell it with or without tears. I said I could do it either way. I was feeling very hostile by then. She said I should decide. I gave her the briefest version possible.

I was told to come back on an appointed day to find out whether or not I had been accepted. The admissions officer was cordial in her way. She said, "I want you to know that you have been accepted as a student, but I also want to go on record as saying that I think you have very little chance of success in the school." I stammered a thank-you for her frankness and got the hell out of there before I said something that would blow the whole project.

In social work school a student does classroom work two

days a week and has a field placement in a social agency in the community three days a week. When I heard where my field placement was to be, I began to understand why the admissions person had thought I would fail. I was assigned to the Department of Welfare on Staten Island. I was to be there at eight o'clock in the morning. There was "easy" access to the department office. Forty minutes by subway, followed by a half-hour ferryboat ride and a ten-minute walk, would get me there. After I got to the office and checked in with my supervisor, there would be a bit more travel as I made home visits to the clients.

My first client was a woman with three children; her husband was in prison. On my initial visit, she said she had received a letter from her husband telling her he did not intend to come back to her when he got out of prison. We were required to do what the school referred to as "process recording." This meant we had to write down everything the client said and what we responded. I dutifully recorded my first visit and turned it in to my supervisor.

She read it and called me to her desk. She said, "I see where your client got some terrible news from her husband, but I don't see what you said to her. What did you say?"

I told her that I had said "Huhhmmmmm."

She was incredulous and said as much, "You mean to tell me that this poor woman poured out her heart to you and all you said was 'Huhhmmmm'? Why on earth would you say a thing like that?"

I mumbled something to the effect that I was sure that's what Dr. Allen would have said.

To this she replied that I was not treating my client with psychoanalysis; in the therapy that I was expected to learn, I would have to be more involved in order to help the client.

Deferentially, I asked what she would have said to the client.

Her ready-made answer was, "I would have asked her how she felt about that news."

My supervisor had just given me the password. If in doubt about what to say, always ask the clients how they feel about any given subject. I also learned never to answer a direct question. One must always answer a question with a question. If I could master that, there was hope of my becoming a good social worker.

I had requested that I be assigned Puerto Rican clients because I was very happy to be able to speak Spanish. In fact, we had spent two summer vacations in Spain so I could polish up what I had learned in class. The clients were pleased to have someone who could understand them. They could more easily make their special requests for extra grants of money. I was learning the ins and outs of the welfare department in order to serve my clients better.

They knew the rules better than my supervisor did; that is, they knew the loopholes better. It seems that if you showed your worker a stained and torn mattress, you would get extra money in your next check to replace the mattress. Several of my clients lived in the same city housing project. One of them showed me the worst-looking mattress I had ever seen. I turned in a report at the office so this client would get extra money. A few weeks later, I asked her if the mattress had been replaced. She assured me she had bought a new one. She didn't offer to show it to me, and I didn't ask to see it. After all, I was a social worker not a detective. Nevertheless, I had certain lurking suspicions. Time passed, and another client took me into the bedroom to show me how much he needed a new mattress. By then, I recognized this disreputable piece of bedding and asked the client where he had gotten it. He swore it was his, so I took out my pen and wrote my initials on it. I told him he was the last person to whom I would have money issued on the basis of the same mattress that was making the grand tour of all the housing project tenants who were on welfare. I don't know how many other social workers fell into this same trap. I felt very sad to think that people on welfare had to resort to this kind of petty chicanery.

Welfare would not issue money for television sets, and yet all of my clients owned TVs of some kind. It was almost their only form of recreation. However, once I was in the awkward position of making a home visit when the project prostitute arrived to make her own home visit of a different kind. My client told her to come back in a half hour. She wasn't sure she could make it back that quickly. That was their problem to work out without benefit of help from this social worker.

One of my clients had seven children. Her husband was a busboy in a restaurant, but what he earned wasn't enough to feed such a large family. One of the problems this little mother confided to me was that her children were having a hard time with their teachers at school because they didn't know when their birthdays were. I wanted to know if she knew their birthdays. Of course she did. Then why wouldn't she tell them? She thought that if she told them, each would want to have a birthday cake. She didn't know how to bake one, and she couldn't afford to buy one. The next week I arrived with a box of ready-mix cake and icing. Together we baked her first cake. We discussed how she could afford these cakes even on her budget. She was so happy she decided to tell her children when their birthdays were. Although the client was happy, my supervisor was furious with me. She didn't see cooking lessons as proper social work technique. I fought back on this. I saw anything that helped clients in their miserable lives as being appropriate work.

Another client was pregnant for the seventh time. There had never been a husband in the picture. Each of her children had a different father. She had never lived with a man. She just occasionally broke loose and went to a bar where sailors hung out. She must have been the most fertile female on this planet, because each encounter always meant a new baby. She was a very timid person and terrified of childbirth. She asked me to arrange to have her baby delivered by caesarian section. When she heard that I had asked to have her tubes tied so she wouldn't have any more unwanted babies, she was ready to kiss my feet. It took a lot of arguing to get this procedure done, since her confinement was going to be in a Catholic hospital. To its great credit, the hospital cooperated.

The second year, my field placement was at Manhattan State Hospital on Randall's Island, just off the Triborough Bridge. This year, the emphasis was to work with families of patients who had been in the hospital a long time. We were supposed to get the families involved with taking patients out for weekends and becoming interested in rejoining their lives with those of the patients. The patients who were assigned to me seemed a most unlikely group for reuniting. One was a young girl of twenty who had already been in the hospital for three years; her mother lived in Florida. This involved a lot of letter writing. I decided to work just with the girl, and I got her into a school that would train her as a beautician.

Another patient, a woman in her thirties, had been hospitalized with a postpartum depression after her baby was born. Her baby was now thirteen years old. Her policeman husband consented to see me once, but he had reconstructed his life, and it did not include her. I was able to get the patient a job as a cashier, and she commuted to work every day from the hospital.

Another of my assignments was a sixty-two-year-old Irish cleaning woman who had spent the past twenty years in the hospital. I was to find her family and bring them into the picture. They had managed to move without leaving any address. Maybe I was in training to be a detective after all. When I did succeed in locating the family, they wanted no part of Sis. I therefore devoted my attentions to getting a set of dentures for this totally toothless woman.

I had great antipathy for my second supervisor. I thought she had deliberately assigned unreachable families to me. I knew she was personally unhappy because one of the doctors, on whom she'd had her eye, had married someone else. In February, I was called to the office of Dean Mitchell Ginsberg. He had bad news. My supervisor had written a devastating report about me. I was allowed to hear its contents. It was a fabrication from beginning to end. I asked if I was allowed to respond in writing. Or could I verbally reply on the spot? The dean said that I could do either or both. I chose both. I focused on telling him the things I had done rather than emphasizing the things I had not done. I could read the dean's face as I spoke. I sensed that I had been given a reprieve. They decided to offer me a new field placement at Psychiatric Institute. I was overjoyed with this assignment. I had heard that P.I. was the crown jewel of the whole New York State system of mental hospitals. I would have to work throughout the summer, however, to make up for the semester I had lost at Manhattan State. I was ready to agree to anything that was proposed in order not to give the admissions person the satisfaction of seeing her prediction fulfilled.

It was a long and hot summer. Lawrence was deprived of our usual trip to Europe. He didn't complain. He had always encouraged me to do whatever I wanted, and he didn't want me to fail to get my master's degree in social work.

At Psychiatric Institute, I was assigned to work with families who were genuinely interested in helping the patient in their family. They willingly kept their weekly appointments. Usually, due to the trauma of having a sick family member, the relative was in need of support. In one case, I was seeing a young man whose mother was in the hospital. He was very bright and doing extremely well in his third year of college, but he needed a job for the summer. I made a few phone calls on his behalf. I was then given to understand, by my supervisor, that unless I could do the same for all my clients, I should not involve myself in getting a job for this student. I asked if she wanted me to call up and tell his employer to let him go. She didn't believe that would be necessary, but I was never to do it again.

The job I got for this young black man was doing research for a psychologist. He became so interested that he wanted to become a psychologist himself. I encouraged him to aim even higher, try to get into medical school and become a psychiatrist. There happened to be a fine black psychiatrist on the staff at P.I. I arranged to have them meet so that my client could hear at first hand what kinds of difficulties he was likely to encounter. I was reprimanded for this too. I began to wonder if perhaps I had chosen the wrong field.

Years later, I had a letter from this young person. He thanked me for the moral support I had given him and told me that he was now a full-fledged psychiatrist. That letter made all of the rebukes I had suffered seem worthwhile.

Another of my clients was the father of a brilliant young student who had suffered a psychotic episode during her senior year in one of the Ivy League colleges. When the student became a patient in Psychiatric Institute, I was assigned to work with her parents. I saw the father and mother separately. The father was a very depressed person and had been all his life. He had been threatening to commit suicide for thirty years. On one occasion he had taken rat poison, made himself thoroughly ill, and then recovered. That had been many years earlier and, though he constantly talked about killing himself, he had never made another attempt. One week, I became alarmed because during his session he said he wanted to live only until he had a grandchild. The alarming part was that his son's wife was expecting a baby momentarily. As soon as he left, I wrote up my process recording and left it on the desk of my supervisor so that she would read it before I saw her for supervision.

When I went to her for supervision, she was very sarcastic. Hadn't I read his record? Didn't I know that he had been talking like this for thirty years? Why did I think he meant it this time? Didn't I know that barking dogs don't bite? I could only repeat that I was worried because of the impending birth of his first grandchild.

Less than a week later, his grandchild was born. He went to the hospital to see the baby, and then he went home and killed himself.

When Psychiatric Institute got word of this, a large conference was set up to examine where it was that we had been remiss and had failed to save this depressed man from destroying himself. My supervisor called me into her office. She began by saying, "Don't you know that if any patient ever talks about killing himself, you must prevent him from leaving the building? You must go immediately for help."

I said, "No, I did not know that, but it makes sense. Why didn't you tell me this rule when you supervised me on this case a few days ago? Why didn't you ask me to bring the client into the hospital? If I had phoned him, he would have come. Why were you so sarcastic when I said I was alarmed about him? When is this conference to be held? I want to be there to tell them the full story as I see it."

If they held the conference, I was excluded. Perhaps only my supervisor was allowed to attend. I was not able to find out. I did not know if I had again put my degree in jeopardy. I thought I had, but on the other hand maybe the supervisor didn't want the school to hear me defend myself.

I was awarded my Master of Social Work degree in September 1962, a few weeks before I reached forty-seven. My target had been to have it before I was fifty. I was ahead of schedule.

I was in no hurry to look for a job. I needed time to pull myself together. Whereas most students spend their adolescence in college, I suddenly realized that I had spent my menopause there. I hadn't had time to notice.

While all of this higher education was being poured into me, other aspects of my life were going on simultaneously.

CHAPTER 21

Other Parts of My Life

Lawrence continued at Graham and Newman for many years after he finished helping to revise *Security Analysis*. The partnership had plenty of financial experts, but Lawrence added another dimension: he was a business person as well as a financier. He soon became their troubleshooter. Whenever the partnership had a sizable investment in a company and the stock was not living up to its potential, Lawrence would be sent to interview the company management to see if he could help straighten out its affairs. Often he was invited to become a member of the board of directors. Over a period of years, he was on twenty-nine boards of companies listed on the New York Stock Exchange.

Lawrence would sometimes serve as president of the company while trying to effect a merger or a sale. For a year, he was president of Cockshutt Farm Equipment Company in Brandford, Ontario. White Motors eventually bought them out. He was also president of Adam Hat Company, a national chain of retail stores. Learning about diverse businesses was exciting, and what better place to learn than sitting on the board of directors. He ran the gamut from railroads to manufacturing of giant printing presses, machine tool companies, motion picture chains, knitting mills, magazine publishing, and life insurance companies. He was a pioneer among the merger men. Lawrence really enjoyed problem solving. Management found it helpful to have his objective point of view. The sicker the businesses were, the more satisfaction he got out of helping them back to a state of good health and joining them with stronger companies.

I was glad that Lawrence was enjoying his work, but most of the time I wasn't too involved. He was careful to explain what he was doing, but I'm afraid I sometimes listened only with the left ear; for me it was more fun to hear about Laura's weekend trips with Randy and his singing groups. Randy was interested in helping Laura find the right college. Sometimes the four of us took excursions together to look at schools. Randy wanted to make sure that her school would be within easy driving distance of Yale.

In September 1958, Laura became a freshman at Briarcliff Junior College. During the week Randy frequently came and stayed with Lawrence and me when he had an important paper to write and needed privacy to think. He brought his typewriter with him. Lawrence and I would proofread his work if he wanted. We were like surrogate parents and were both delighted that he was willing to give us this role to play. We knew he wasn't really our son yet, but all of us behaved as though he were. Laura and I had both visited his parents in Fort Smith, Arkansas. We'd had a wonderful time.

In Randy's senior year, he was chosen business manager of the Whiffenpoofs, the most famous of all the Yale singing groups, open only to seniors. After four years, Randy was ready to graduate from Yale. He got seats for his parents and his grandmother and for Lawrence and me as well as Laura, of course. It was the first time I had seen that magnificent campus with all of its Gothic buildings in cut stone. The weather was perfect for an outdoor ceremony under the large, old trees, which lent so much to the institution's look of stability. Since both families were together, Lawrence and I half expected Laura and Randy to announce some future plans. We were aware that there had been considerable discussion of whether Randy was going to join his father in the family retail chain of stores or was going to stay on in New

York and accept an extremely attractive offer that he had received.

There was no announcement. Late in the afternoon of graduation day, back in New York, Randy came into our living room and said to Lawrence and me, "Laura says it is all over between us. Do you think she means it?"

My reply was, "I'm as surprised as you are, Randy, but if she says it I guess she means it. Do you want to tell us any more about it?"

He mumbled, which was not his habit, something to the effect that he had decided to join his father in business and that Laura didn't want to leave New York. She had chosen to make a clean break rather than simply drifting apart because of geographic separation.

Randy asked if he could at least keep the friendship with Lawrence and me. It was hard to hold back the tears as I explained that I was sure Laura would be suffering as much as he was and that she would need our full loyalty and support in the months to come. Therefore, I didn't think it would be a good idea if we continued to see him. We went through some formalities thanking each other for the joys of the past four years, and then Randy walked out of our lives through the same door he had entered on a Thanksgiving Day. Now there were no thanks to be given. Someone very dear to us had gone home to his real parents, and there was a great void where he had been.

We hastily planned a trip to Spain and Portugal, where we would be out of reach by telephone. Laura showed no outward signs of suffering, and certainly there were plenty of distractions on the trip. The men in Spain liked Laura's type. She had blond hair and clear, dark-brown eyes. Her skin looked good enough for a Palmolive soap ad. Evidently, when a Spanish man wants to flatter a woman, he tells her she looks like the Madonna. Everywhere we went, men compared her to the Macarene, a beautiful Madonna in Seville. Maybe that's what they tell all the girls.

CHAPTER 22

On the Job

I did not rush to look for work after my Columbia graduation. I was tired, having spent that whole summer working at Psychiatric Institute, where there was no air-conditioning. Now that I had my masters degree, I was going to take my time and catch up on things that had been neglected at home.

In looking through my textbooks, I selected those I knew I would never open again, packed them up, took them to the library at the School of Social Work and told the library to give them to a student who was pressed for funds and needed the books.

Mission accomplished, I was waiting for the bus when I started talking to a woman who was also waiting. We were both admiring a baby in a carriage. I asked if she was new on the school faculty. No, she had been supervising students from the school for many years. Her primary job was head of the social work department at Albert Einstein College of Medicine in the Bronx. When she learned that I was a graduate and was available for work, she set a date for me to come to her office. On the bus between 92nd and 78th Streets, we practically had it settled that I would work in her department.

After I left Agnes Lauga's office in Jacobi Hospital, there was still the question of where in the division of psychiatry I would be placed. During the next week, I was interviewed by three of the best psychiatrists in New York. First, I was seen by Dr. Israel Zwerling. I couldn't help but contrast this interview with the one I'd had before entering the School of Social Work. Dr. Zwerling made me want to talk about myself and my concerns in taking a new job. The admissions woman at Columbia could have learned from him, and so could I. He was obviously a master.

Next I was interviewed by Dr. Ed Hornick. He had me come to his New York office so he could conduct the interview while driving up to the medical school. Dr. Hornick was a very flamboyant character who delighted in shocking people by his way of dressing. Much of the time he wore an opera cape and anticipated fashion by wearing a single earring. He drove a camper minibus in the middle of New York. I almost needed help to climb into it. I don't remember what questions he asked or how I answered because my eyes were glued to the road. I wasn't sure that his were.

The final interview was with Dr. Jack F. Wilder. I was apparently going to be hired as his assistant. This was another sort of interview. He did all the talking. He described a certain task he wanted done and asked if I thought I could do it. When I answered that I believed I could, he proceeded to describe another job he wanted done. Could I do that also? Yes, I could. At the end of an hour, we shook hands, and he said that he was going to have a desk put in the corner of his office for me and that we would be working very closely together.

When I got home and began to tell Lawrence what my duties were to be as assistant to the director of rehabilitation of the Department of Psychiatry, I became physically dizzy. What had I promised to do? How could I possibly have thought I could do all those things? And what was the time frame for accomplishing these feats? I was expected at work on Monday morning at 8:30, and I had the impression that Dr. Wilder would like to have everything done and running by Tuesday. That's what was making me dizzy. I had promised to establish a sheltered workshop to employ the emotionally disturbed clientele of the Day Hospital. Furthermore, I had promised to start a halfway house in which patients could be placed for varying periods of time, from one day to six months.

The thought went through my mind that maybe I didn't need a job. Maybe I needed to go back into psychoanalysis myself! I had to be crazy if I thought I could do all that I had promised. And yet I had just been interviewed by three eminent psychiatrists who thought I could cope. I would just have to give it my best effort and see what the outcome would be. Lawrence was, as usual, very supportive, and he pointed out that I should take each project in its turn. He was sure Dr. Wilder would understand if I didn't have a full-blown plan on his desk by Tuesday.

The Monday morning subway ride wasn't at all bad. It took only fifty minutes, and, because I was traveling in the opposite direction from the main traffic, there was no crowd to jostle me. Since I had allowed more time than I needed to get to work, I wandered around Westchester Square to get a feeling of the neighborhood. Finding this was a prosperous business area, I walked two blocks to Glebe Avenue, where the Day Hospital was located. This hospital was part of a research program to determine if patients could be treated during the day and returned to their homes at night instead of having to be in the hospital twenty-four hours a day. It was a whole new concept of treatment that subsequently became popular but was innovative in 1962.

I arrived at the office expecting to find my own desk in the corner of Dr. Wilder's room. Neither Dr. Wilder nor my desk was there. I strolled the halls and introduced myself to anyone who looked curious about me. Eventually, Dr. Wilder showed up. My desk never did. As students we had learned to write notes on our laps. This skill came in handy. Dr. Wilder said I could use his desk whenever he wasn't there. That gave me an idea. I would just use any vacant desk I saw and carry a briefcase packed with all my pencils, tablets, and phone numbers. I would keep the telephone operator informed of my whereabouts in case people tried to return my phone calls.

Because I had no real base, I mingled with the patients on the floor a great deal of the time. There was one particularly interesting patient. The police had brought him to the hospital when they found him chopping down trees on Pelham Parkway. He spoke a language all his own. When patients talk like that, it is called schizophrenese, which means they are using their own private code of symbols to express themselves. One has to listen very attentively to get the trend of thought and crack the code. I had the time, so I listened.

One day I answered him in his own language. He looked very startled. We went on talking to each other in schizophrenese for a few more days. Gradually, as he felt himself better understood, he began to let his guard down and speak in a more normal way. Also, his medication was beginning to take effect. Dr. Zwerling called on me at grand rounds to tell the rest of the staff how I had been able to understand and answer the patient. As I talked, I could see Dr. Zwerling smiling and nodding his head in approval. One of the registered nurses sat there fuming. I hadn't known that this particular patient was someone in whom she had taken a special interest. I had been poaching on her preserve. I took no notice. I felt I had helped the patient, and that was what counted.

I was assigned a social work supervisor and a full caseload of patients. There was no money in the budget for the sheltered workshop or the halfway house. I would have to hold them on a back burner for the present.

Then Jack set up an appointment for the two of us to meet with Bertram Black, the executive director of Altro, a sheltered workshop and training center for handicapped people. Altro had originally been founded to train recovering tuberculosis patients. As tuberculosis was brought under control, Altro had begun to train people who were emotionally disturbed. They prepared people to go into the needle trades. They also taught secretarial skills. Our meeting with Bertram Black included a tour of their large operation. We saw the type of contracts on which they were working in their sheltered workshop. We concluded that it would be mutually beneficial to start a branch of Altro at our Day Hospital. They would supply us with work, and we in turn would send our patients to them as they got better and became more stable. This proved to be a good arrangement all around. It lasted more than twenty years.

We started our workshop in one room. It grew to two, then bulged into a third later. By the time we needed even more space, a number of changes had taken place at the top level of management. Dr. Zwerling had left, to become the director of Bronx Psychiatric Center, and Dr. Wilder had become our director. We were no longer Day Hospital; that research project had ended. We were now established as the first Community Mental Health Center in New York. We had become the model for the city. We had to hire someone just to take visiting dignitaries around, explain to them what we were doing, and try to help them set up a replica of our clinic.

We appealed to Dr. Zwerling to lend us space in his huge hospital for our sheltered workshop. He negotiated a deal. We could have a splendid, large space on the ground floor near a trucking platform if I would train his staff in setting up a workshop for his inpatients. There were no papers to sign. We just shook hands and moved into our new quarters. Perry McFarland was in charge. He was a young black man who was great with the patients and made them all feel new confidence in themselves. For many, it was the first work they had ever done. We had to adjust their work schedules because many patients could not sit for even an hour. All were gradually able to expand their periods of concentration.

While Dr. Zwerling was still director of the Day Hospital, a real estate speculator had just finished building a couple of two-family houses diagonally across the street from what had been Day Hospital. I had my eye on them as being ideally located for our purpose. I was trying to think how it would be possible to get the money for a down payment when a strange and fortuitous thing happened. Jack Wilder asked me if I knew Mrs. Peter I. B. Lavan. Using my best social worker technique of answering a question with a question, I replied, "Why do you ask?"

Jack said, "She has just been in my office, and she said she had read about our work here and thought we should have a halfway house to shelter some of the people who should not be living with their families while they are in treatment. I wanted to know if you knew her and if you thought she would be willing to help us financially."

I then told Jack that I had not known she was interested in the field of mental health but would certainly discuss it with her and her husband. Lawrence and I would be spending the weekend at the Lavan's summer house in Croton.

It was a wonderful weekend. We swam, we lounged around the pool, we talked at great length. Fay and Pete hadn't realized that I was working at the Sound-View Throgs Neck Community Mental Health Center. All of us marveled at the coincidence: their idea of establishing a halfway house would be placed in my hands to carry out. We decided that I was to go with Dr. Wilder on Monday morning to look at the two houses across the street and find out the asking price.

At grand rounds, before all the staff had assembled, I asked Dr. Zwerling what he thought of the idea of buying the two houses. He replied, "Dreams are cheap, reality costs a bit more." I told him we already had the benefactors lined up and asked if he would like to join Jack and me on a tour of inspection. The three of us could hardly wait for grand rounds to end so we could meet the owner and see the two houses.

They were built of red brick. The ground floor of each included a large recreation room, a powder room, a garage, and the usual furnace room. There was plenty of space for washing machines and so forth. The houses had two apartments apiece, each apartment having three bedrooms, a living room, a large kitchen with dining area, and a bathroom. We figured we could easily house sixteen patients plus live-in staff.

I returned to my office and phoned Pete Lavan. He was a senior partner in the prestigious law firm of Stroock & Stroock & Lavan. I told him that we had seen the houses and that the asking price for the two of them was eighty thousand dollars. I gave him the owner's name and phone number. Pete said he would take it from there. First, we needed to form a not-for-profit corporation and get it approved by the state of New York and the federal government. He asked if I had any preference for the corporation's name. Things were happening so fast, I couldn't think of anything. Pete explained that if we wanted approval quickly we must choose a name that no one else had. He knew cases in which four or five names had been turned down because they were already in use. I left it entirely up to him but asked him please to hurry. I didn't want to miss out on the houses just because we had no name. We got our not-for-profit status in record time.

One month after application, we were approved, and I learned for the first time that our name was "Pibly Fund, Inc." No wonder there was no other corporation with that name. Pete had simply taken his own initials and added a y to make them pronounceable. The lawyers in Pete's firm arranged a mortgage for us. Jack had a friend who owned a mail-order business. He was generous enough to send us his catalog and tell us to order whatever we needed for each building; it would be on the house. I spent days writing the order: four tightly typewritten pages by the time I got the courage to mail it. A huge trailer truck arrived. We had it unloaded into one of the recreation rooms. Tables had to have their legs screwed on. Everything had to be uncrated and assembled.

My old skills as a decorator were being called into service again. No two rooms were to be alike. Curtains were color coordinated with the bedspreads and chair. My farming skills were also being used as I wielded screwdrivers and pliers in assembling the furniture. Perry McFarland and I rented a gasoline-driven garden plow, and together we got the soil prepared for laying sod. I was in my element.

In the midst of all of this unpacking and plowing, I had a phone call asking me to see Agnes Lauga in her office at Jacobi. When I got there, she said she understood I was spending all my time setting up a halfway house. I confirmed that what she had heard was true. She asked, "Do you think this is proper use of a trained social worker's time?" I answered, "Do you agree that we need a halfway house?" She certainly did agree that it was needed. I further asked, "Do you know anyone else who can set it up?" No, she didn't know anyone. I then answered her original question by saying, "In that case, I think it is proper work for a trained social worker."

Jack and I visited two halfway houses in Boston and one in Washington. We wanted to learn the kinds of rules they had, what the pitfalls were, and what they would do if they were in our position of just starting. Joan Woodruf, in Washington, told us something that we were to quote often. She said, "I always tell the tenant that I don't know what the rules are but I know when you break them." It was much easier to operate that way.

We opened in September 1963 and have been running ever since then, with certain changes. During our first year of operation, we received tenants from seventeen different hospitals. We took this as proof that there was a great need for our type of home for recovering patients. Despite the fact that we were located in an all-white neighborhood, we decided that we would be desegregated. Knowing what had happened in desegregated public housing, we informally decided to keep the ratio of blacks at around twenty-five percent, at least until the neighbors got used to our presence.

We did have one very serious rule. No one was allowed to commit suicide. This was difficult to enforce. What could you do to a person who broke the rule? In fact having such a rule did act as a deterrent to a genuine attempt. It eliminated the kind of gesture some people make as a means of communicating to others that they are feeling miserable.

I don't know if it was because of our rule or not, but no one in the apartments has ever committed suicide while living with us. That's not to say there were no attempts, but they were caught in time by our alert staff. There was the case of a young college student who had landed in the psychiatric ward after jumping off a roof and breaking both his legs.

When he left the hospital, he came to our halfway house. He was a model tenant, and we made an exception in allowing him to stay more than six months because in the fall he was going back to college and would be living in the college dormitory. In August, he took an overdose of pills and was hospitalized. I visited him in the hospital and asked why he had taken the pills. His answer was, "Because they were there." He made a solemn promise that if I let him return to the house for the three remaining weeks before college, he would not attempt suicide again for one year. I broke my own rule and let him return. He went to school as scheduled. I later learned that one year and one day after making his promise to me, he killed himself. It still gives me gooseflesh to think of that tragedy. He had not broken his promise to me.

There was a beautiful girl in her early twenties who had been hospitalized when she began giving away all her clothes and money. Maybe she figured they were ill-gotten gains because she had earned them by being a prostitute. When she was released from the hospital, she came to live with us, and we got to know her better. She had been guilt-ridden all her life. Her mother had died in childbirth, and her family had treated her as though she were responsible for her mother's death. We accepted her but required her to get a suitable job. After she was with us a few months, I began to suspect that she had returned to her old profession. She denied it but confessed to having suicidal thoughts. We persuaded her to go back to the hospital in order to be more protected from herself. The hospital began to give her weekend passes in the custody of her sister. One weekend in May, while she was on pass, she managed to give her sister the slip at 42nd Street and Fifth Avenue. The next day, she was found dead in a Philadelphia hotel room. It was Mother's Day.

We had thought that six months of living in our apartments would be long enough for the tenants to adjust to taking care of themselves outside a hospital. This was an error in judgment. What happened was that when we began trying to help the patients find their own apartments so they could move out, they became sick again and had to be re-hospitalized. Several people were approaching the six-month deadline, and we explored what they would like us to do to help them further. From these discussions came the idea that the Pibly Fund should rent satellite apartments in the community and furnish them. In this way, the ex-residents could come back and see the staff whenever they wanted, and they would not have the burden of dealing with a landlord. Pibly would be their landlord. They would continue to be under our surveillance.

We had found it cumbersome to keep in contact with doctors who were located in many different hospitals; therefore, we began giving preferential acceptance to people who had originally come from the Bronx. We were not rigid about excluding others.

Again, we were considered to be a showcase model, since we were the first in the city. Professionals visited us from all parts of the country. I spent a lot of time explaining how to get started, knowing full well that all of them would be hard pressed to find another couple as generous as Pete and Fay Lavan.

While I was getting the sheltered workshop and the halfway house started, I was carrying a full caseload of patients and attending all the training conferences. Because medical students rotated through our clinic, as part of their training in psychiatry, we had specialists who came to us on a regularly scheduled basis. Any staff member was privileged to sit in on these training sessions. We had what we called the "one-way-screen room." One wall was glass that turned into a mirror when the viewing room on the other side was dark. The spectators were seated in the darkened room, and the microphones were fixed so we could follow every word spoken on the other side of the mirror.

The world-renowned psychiatrist Dr. Nathan Ackerman came to us once a month to demonstrate his technique of family therapy. Since he lived only two blocks from me in Manhattan, I was frequently asked to drive him up to the Bronx in my car. This gave me a private hour with him, which was an extra bonus. Dr. Edrita Fried came once a week to teach group therapy. I ran a group of patients just in order to be supervised by Dr. Fried.

After Dr. Zwerling went to Bronx Psychiatric Center and Dr. Wilder became our new chief, we began to detach our clinic from Jacobi Hospital. Meals, which had previously been sent over for the patients, were no longer available. It was necessary to work out a means of providing lunch for the clinic clients. Jack asked me to set up a canteen. We chose the room for it on the second floor, and I selected a stove, a refrigerator, and a second-hand cash register. I was friendly with the building superintendent, who agreed to work with an assistant over the weekend and install the necessary equipment. A nearby factory had already built us a serving counter. I had advanced the money myself because I knew that this was the fastest way to get started. I was so sure the canteen would be a financial success that I didn't worry about being paid back.

When Jack came to work Monday, there it was: his canteen. Instead of just serving food, we incorporated it into a training program to teach our clients to work in short-order restaurants. It was hard work for the person chosen to train these novices. The food was so good that the staff began to eat there also. It didn't take long for me to recover my loan money and be able to buy a soft drink dispensing machine.

Since we were no longer a day hospital, the registered nurses were having a tough time finding their role in the new setup. They couldn't see themselves running activity groups. That was not what they were trained to do. Again Jack called on me. He asked if I thought I could get the social workers to run activity groups every Thursday afternoon. I canvassed all the social workers and got them to sign up for whatever kind of group they would enjoy running. Jack was delighted with the list that resulted. There were to be a current events group, a makeup and grooming group, a furniture-refinishing group, a sewing group, and a cooking group.

I had taken on the cooking group. I watched for recipes that I thought would be easy to make. To get started, we made brownies and then ate them. Word got around that in the cooking group you could eat the goodies you made. We were flooded with people wanting to join. We couldn't fit that many people in the canteen, so we decided we would cook enough to send someone around with coffee and the day's specialty on a cart. We were never stuck with leftover merchandise. When I walked through the halls, no one even said hello anymore; they just greeted me with, "What are you going to bake on Thursday?"

Running that group was fun, but it also had moments of despair, such as the day when I was reading out loud from a recipe that said, "Add a whole egg." One of the group followed the instruction to the letter; she tossed in the egg, shell and all.

CHAPTER 23

T-Groups

There was no modality of treatment started in the field of psychiatry that we didn't have demonstrated to us by an expert—including a new therapy called psychodrama. Most of our staff assembled to see how it worked. We had read about it, but seeing adds to one's understanding. The expert asked for volunteers. No one was willing, so I said I'd give it a try. She set the "stage" by giving me two chairs. I was to sit in one when I was playing the role of myself. I sat in the other chair when I was playing the role of one of my patients. I was to imitate the patient's voice and movements.

I chose not one of my own patients but a "floater patient" who went from office to office, wherever there was an open door, and said he just wanted to ask one question. Behind his back, he was nicknamed "The Pest." Beyond that, I had privately given him the facetious diagnosis of "nudge." From my opening line, "No, you can't come in; I'm very busy now," everyone knew who the patient was. I made up the script and acted it out as I went along. At the end, I went to the door and put The Pest out; he kept pushing from the other side until I finally ended up with my knee against the door to keep him from pushing his way back in. The staff applauded. I had dramatized a fantasy with which all of them could identify. In the psychodrama I had acted in a totally unprofessional way, a way in which no therapist would behave vis-à-vis a client. Yet it had given me great relief. Better than relief, I felt I had triumphed over The Pest. In future encounters, I was able to tolerate him more because I had let out all of my resentments.

This was my first acting experience. Many people told me I had missed my calling and should have gone on the stage. That was one profession I had never envisaged for myself, but that single performance was enough to give me the feeling of what an actor must experience in psyching up for a role.

Dr. Bill Schutz, a well-known psychologist, came to work at Sound View-Throgs Neck Community Mental Health Center (SVTN) for a couple of years. While he was with us, he wrote his famous book, *Joy*. He lead large groups of patients and also offered to run a T-group for the staff. It was decided that the T-group would be held in a conference center owned by Columbia University. It began on Friday night and ended late Sunday afternoon. We had all of our meals together. We didn't go to sleep before one or two in the morning and started again at eight in the morning. Bill wouldn't tell us if T-group meant training group or therapy group. To this day, I'm not sure. There were about twenty of us, representing all the disciplines. In general, participants were encouraged to air their feelings about themselves and about each other. At one point, I began to wonder if this marathon T-group would help people work better together—or was it going to make rifts wider so that they could never again be bridged?

The registered nurse who had borne a grudge against me, ever since I learned to speak in schizophrenese with "her" patient, was bound to hit out at me sooner or later. She was a long time getting around to it; but when her feelings finally surfaced, she could hardly talk she was so choked with tears and sobs. She hated me, really *hated* me. It seems I was the same age as her own mother and yet I looked half her mother's age. I was slim, her mother was fat. In sum, I was what she wished her mother would be like. After this very sincere disclosure, she burst from the room sobbing, went upstairs, threw herself on the bed, and cried. I sat there flabbergasted.

Everyone thought I should go and comfort her. I wasn't so sure she would want to be comforted by the "enemy"; nevertheless I went. She threw her arms around me and clung to me as though I were her mother and she was my infant. I sort of rocked her in my arms for a while, and then we pulled ourselves together and went back downstairs to join the group. Neither of us ever spoke of it again, but we became fond of one another. The rest of the staff all felt that the weekend had drawn them closer together and that thenceforth they would be able to work together in more productive ways.

As Jack Wilder moved into the top position at SVTN, I also moved up a notch. I was now director of rehabilitation. We began making plans to build a workshop that would enable us to move out of our shop at Bronx Psychiatric Center and into our own more spacious quarters. I talked it over with Lawrence and with the Lavans. They agreed to back the project financially and gave me enough money right away to buy some land with industrial zoning. I bought two plots: one for the workshop building and the other for parking employees' cars. We had architectural plans drawn up.

Perry McFarland, the supervisor of the sheltered workshop, was being groomed to take charge of this much larger operation. He was included at every step of the plans. He was valued by patients and staff alike for his intuitive and sympathetic qualities.

One day, one of the black rehabilitation counselors, whom I had hired, asked me when we were going to have the building ready. It was the first sign of interest this man had ever shown in the workshop. I asked him why he was inquiring. His reply was fast and belligerent. He said, "Because when you get it built, the blacks are going to see to it that I am put in charge of it."

My response was slower but equally hostile. I said in measured tones, "In that case, it will never be built."

That was the end of the conversation, but I knew I had a

new enemy. I reported the incident to Jack. He was not as alarmed as I was. I decided to drag my heels awhile and see what would happen. I certainly didn't want to get the Lavans and Lawrence any further involved financially if we were going to have a racial problem on our hands. This was a time when racial questions arose in many places where they had not previously existed.

Another staff weekend was planned to take place in the same Columbia University conference center. This time the participants were not volunteers but selected, and it was to be a leaderless group. After all, everyone there was a trained group leader. When we assembled, I realized that I was the only female. I was also the only social worker, and I was in the midst of seventeen male psychiatrists. If you think this got me special attention, you are right.

Most of the psychiatrists were undergoing didactic psychoanalysis and no doubt had some unresolved sentiments about their relationships with their own mothers. It soon came out that many of them looked on Jack as their father and me as their mother. That is to say, they had transferred to Jack and me many of their feelings toward their real parents. One after another said that he saw me as the most powerful female he had ever encountered. This did not accord with my image of myself. I did not think in terms of power. Whenever I had a job to do, I just plowed ahead and let nothing stand in my way. Was this power?

Toward the end of the two days, I began using my best soft-spoken Southern drawl. I told them how I had been brought up to subjugate myself totally to the wishes of men and their opinions. Was that how they would like me to behave? There was a loud and enthusiastic chorus of yes. Then I dropped my Southern accent and stood up, slammed my fist down on the table, and declared, "I spent three and a half years in analysis to become accepting of my own aggressive nature and put it to use for my own good and the good of others. I have no intention of reverting to the sweet, mild person you would like me to be. I have listened patiently for two days to your complaints about me. I suggest you go back to your own analysts and work hard on your feelings about your real mothers. Come talk to me in a few years when you have worked through your feelings. I'm sure you'll find that I am not as powerful as you now think, and that you are not as weak." As I drove home, I kept thinking of more things that I wished I had said.

When I got home, Lawrence couldn't understand why I looked so tired and why I didn't want to talk about the weekend. How could I explain what it felt like to sit for two days taking a verbal beating from sixteen psychiatrists. (I don't include Jack, because he was also taking a beating.) Years later I saw many of these men. They always came over and put their arms around my shoulders, saying something to the effect that they now realized what a rough time they had given me and that I had not deserved it.

Jack was going to a convention of the American Psychiatric Association in Miami. Besides hearing some interesting papers and discussing mutual problems with his colleagues, he was going with his mind made up to find a black psychiatrist there. He returned to SVTN feeling elated. He had found two highly qualified black psychiatrists and had persuaded both to come and visit our whole operation and to meet the people with whom they might be working. Schedules were made out for each of them to meet the members of upper management. The time I spent with each convinced me that we should hire both if they would come to us.

Everyone who was supposed to give an opinion of the two men felt as Jack and I did. Then we heard very negative rumblings from a different quarter. The rehabilitation counselor who had threatened me with taking over the workshop when it was built had now managed to have an unscheduled meeting with each of the two men. He wanted us to hire only one of them and to make him associate director as well as a staff psychiatrist. We never knew what he said to the psychiatrist that he hadn't liked; but suddenly, from being enthusiastic about the job we offered, that psychiatrist lost his zeal and told us not to give him any further consideration as a candidate. We were all disappointed to lose him, and I was furious at the presumption of authority that this rehab counselor had taken upon himself. He had set himself up as a kind of spokesman for all the black employees. This was his first move.

The week was drawing to a close. Friday morning, we had a meeting of a dozen heads of services to discuss the job description for the new psychiatrist. Where was he needed the most? Was our racial problem serious enough for him to be given the additional duty of trying to work toward improving staff racial relations? I personally felt that we had only one troublemaker, and I was surprised he was getting anyone to follow him. I knew in my heart that if I had ever shown racial discrimination in hiring or promoting employees, it had been, if anything, prejudiced in *favor* of black people. This did not mean that I was willing to look the other way if someone needed to be disciplined.

After the Friday morning meeting, the rehab counselor flew into a rage on learning that we had decided not to make the newly arriving psychiatrist an associate director. We had never *had* an associate director, and we saw no need for one now. There was time enough for that if he proved himself.

The rehab counselor demanded that the morning meeting reconvene with an additional number of black employees plus himself and a worker from the drug abuse division who was his chief henchman. At that time, it was believed that ex-addicts were best able to understand and help current addicts to break the habit. The henchman had been hired because he was an ex-addict. I had never seen him before, though I had been aware of his presence on the staff.

Ten minutes into the meeting, the shouting began. It would be inaccurate to call it a shouting match. No one was answering back. All the shouting was being done by the rehab counselor and the ex-addict. At one point, the rehab counselor stood up and moved toward Jack in a very menacing way. He was shaking his index finger very close to Jack's face, so close in fact that his finger accidently caught under the bridge of Jack's glasses, catapulting them into the air and onto the floor. Someone retrieved them and handed them to Jack. As he put them back on, he looked straight at the rehab counselor and said firmly, "Now don't do that again." With this admonition, the rehab counselor deliberately reached over and plucked the glasses from Jack's nose and threw them across the room.

The charged and violent atmosphere was very uncomfortable. There was a lot of name calling. The two of them sort of went around the room, screaming at each person, using names they thought suitable. When it came my turn, the ex-addict stood in front of me and shouted, "And here you have this rich, white Southern bitch giving orders." This from a man I had never seen before. This from a man who, as far as I knew, had one accomplishment in life: he had managed to kick his drug habit. I stood up and glared at him without saying anything. I walked out of the room. I had no clear idea of where I was going or what I was going to do when I got there.

Once I got out in the hall where I could think more clearly, I paced up and down a few times. Should I call the police? I rejected that idea because I didn't know what one could charge these troublemakers with. Disturbing the peace? They were certainly doing that. I knew I was going back into that room because I didn't want them to think I had left because I was afraid of them. I wasn't. I just wanted to think. Finally, I knew what I would say when I returned.

I went back into the meeting. I stood in the middle of the floor and waited for silence. When it came, I said in my loudest and most commanding voice, "I propose that we move this meeting to the one-way-screen room. Are there any seconds to the motion?" Now there was total silence. Each person looked at his nearest neighbor, and no one made a move. No one questioned why I wanted to move the meeting. There was no discussion. They just went back to their abusive shouting.

I wanted to move the meeting because there was a video camera in the one-way-screen-room, and I wanted to have the meeting recorded. I knew that one of two things would happen in front of the camera. Either the attackers would calm down, so we could have a sensible discussion of the job description for the new psychiatrist, or the violence would continue. In the latter case, we would have perfect evidence for firing the two troublemakers.

At four o'clock, I had to leave. Lawrence and I were going to Connecticut for the weekend. I understand the meeting went on for another two hours after that. Afterward, I asked some of the people who had been present why they had not seconded my motion. They claimed not to have heard me. I believe them; the tension was so great that people had psychologically tuned out.

On Monday morning, a number of employees, including blacks, asked me if I was going to fire the rehab counselor. When asked, they all said he deserved to be fired. I then told them it was not up to me to do the firing. One very responsible black man, who had sat silent during the meeting, came to me in secret and said that some weeks before he had borrowed two hundred dollars from the rehab counselor. If I would lend him the money to repay the loan, he would again be a free man and would not feel forced to support this false "leader." He further told me that many employees owed money to the rehab counselor and this was the source of his power. If this were true, it would explain his hold on his followers, although not the source of the money that he loaned so freely. I wondered if he had been hired to do this agitating.

I went to Jack and related what I had been told. I asked him to fire the two men. Jack was scheduled to go to Boston to take a two-week course in systems analysis in order to set up a computer system at the center. I asked him not to go right now when the center was in so much turmoil. He told me he was going to have lunch with the rehab counselor, and he guaranteed to establish calm before he left the next day. After his lunch meeting, Jack called me into his office and assured me that he and the rehab counselor had come to amicable terms. There would be no further trouble.

Jack appointed Dr. Gabriel Koz, a South African psychiatrist, to be in charge of SVTN during his absence. Gabe had not been at the fiery Friday meeting as he had been at his regular post at Jacobi. We were all surprised when we heard that he was scheduling a meeting in Jack's office for that afternoon. As soon as I got the notice, I went to try to dissuade him from holding the meeting. He was confident that he could keep it calm.

The room was filled with most of the same people who had been there on Friday. The rehab man was sitting with his hands folded on his lap and looking quite composed as he was called on to say why he had wanted Dr. Koz to call us together. He opened with, "I understand that Dr. Wilder is spreading the lie that I threatened his wife. Did any of you hear me threaten his wife?" I said that I did not feel comfortable in discussing this accusation since Dr. Wilder was not present. Everyone else said they felt free to talk about it in his absence, so Dr. Koz went around the room asking each person if they had heard any such threats. No one had heard anything like that. When it was my turn, I said that I had heard him say, "I don't give a damn for my life." Could that be what had been heard? No one thought so.

The rehab counselor was emboldened to go further. He drew a breath and said, "Furthermore, I hear that Marie Kessel has been saying that I didn't win any contract advantages for the new psychiatrist." I was glad I was present to answer him.

I said, "For once you heard something right. I said it because it is true. If on Friday you had ever stopped your ranting long enough to let anyone tell you what we proposed to put in his job description, you would have learned right away that we had already included everything that was in the final contract." He was visibly shrinking from my attack. I definitely had the upper hand at that moment. Then one of the PhD psychologists pulled the rug out from under me by saying, "I'm not so sure we didn't give in on some points."

The rehab counselor left the meeting, and we continued with an agenda that was posted on the blackboard. Among the agenda items was the filling of vacancies. The empty places were listed. I silently stepped up to the board, picked up some chalk, and added to the list my own title, director of rehabilitation.

Over the weekend Jack and I talked in person. I gave him some of my reasons for resigning. They were emotional. I was unable to give whole-hearted support to carrying out a policy I believed to be wrong. In my opinion it was a mistake to reward violence by making concessions. I had lost respect for many of my colleagues. My conviction was strong that we should fire the rehab counselor, and yet I was not permitted to get rid of him. I felt my authority in my own service division to be diminished. I felt betrayed by the black employees whom I had considered to be my friends. I did not feel guilt over how I had treated black employees. I knew that I had been fair.

Under these difficult circumstances, I did not want to continue with the project of building the sheltered workshop. I knew I would be able to sell the land I had bought. We would leave the money in the Pibly Fund for future projects. The sheltered workshop was never built, but we have just finished a project that used the money for an innovative new teaching center headed by Dr. Wilder.

Officially, this was the end of my career as a social worker.

CHAPTER 24

New Adventures

While I had been leaving our apartment every morning at seven-thirty to go to my job in the Bronx, there had been a good deal of activity on the home front. Living in a brownstone is different from living in a large apartment building. For one thing, you know who all your neighbors are. Just riding together in our tiny elevator gave a certain intimacy to the relationship. Also, we formed a cohesive group because we had a common enemy—the landlord. We held frequent phone conferences to work out strategies for getting better service.

On the floor below us lived Ted Rousseau, who was curator of European paintings at the Metropolitan Museum of Art. One night we rode down in the elevator together; between the third floor and the first floor, he dropped his apartment keys three times. He was obviously very nervous. The next day I read in *The New York Times* that Rousseau had bought Rembrandt's *Head of Socrates* at Parke Bernet's auction for the record-breaking price of one-and-one-half million dollars.

Woody Allen lived overhead. Just as we sat down to dinner each evening, he would begin to practice his xylophone. He was in his apartment, and we were in ours, but the acoustics were such that it sounded as though he were playing in our apartment, just for us. We are probably the only people in New York who can brag that they dined nightly to Woody Allen's live music.

One night while coming home Ted Rousseau was assaulted in the outer lobby of our building. His assailant was vicious. Even after Ted had handed him money; he hit him over the head with a bottle, knocking him to the floor; he kicked out a couple of teeth. There had been four other attacks, within two square blocks, in the preceding ten days. The descriptions of the assailant sounded as though it was just one person who had targeted our neighborhood. We all became very suspicious of anyone we saw on the street. Suddenly I was fearful when I walked to the subway at an early hour. The street was usually deserted, and now I began to see disreputable-looking men lurking in doorways. They obviously did not belong there, loitering and waiting for likely prey.

The eight tenants in our building had a couple of meetings on how to increase security. We asked the tenant who lived on Woody Allen's floor why she left her door ajar. Wouldn't she feel safer if she kept it locked? She said she was leaving it open to let the rats out. It was the first any of us had heard about rats in the building! The more she talked, the clearer it became that this affair had completely unhinged her.

Woody Allen took her statement about the rats quite seriously. He was going to buy some traps. I was sure she was hallucinating. Before I could decide on action to find help for her, she resolved it in her own way. She took an overdose of sleeping pills, had second thoughts, and phoned the police. The first we knew about it was when we heard the police stomping around in her apartment. An ambulance took her away. We tried to check on her recovery but didn't get far. She never came back to that apartment, and soon someone else moved in.

A couple of weeks after Ted Rousseau was beaten, the police caught the man who had attacked him. After that, all the strange characters hiding in doorways disappeared. They turned out to be plainclothes policemen dressed to look like bums. They had certainly fooled me. I was relieved when they departed. I had begun to fear that I was becoming paranoid.

By the time Woody Allen moved out, Laura had been graduated from Briarcliff and was living at home while going to Columbia University. We offered to rent Allen's former apartment for her, and she accepted on condition that she not lose her eating-at-home privileges. I assured her that she could come for dinner any time she wished. If she wanted to have company, though, she had to do her own entertaining. It worked out just fine. We had great fun decorating her new apartment. She was living away from home, at home. Everyone's privacy tripled.

After Laura's graduation from Columbia University, she worked at Tiffany's in their executive training program. Every day she told us of some exciting new adventure. She loved waiting on the celebrities who bought there. She was full of enthusiasm for the store, its management, and its merchandise.

Laura was asked to be chairperson of a fund-raising dance for New York City Center. The hope was that she would be able to interest young adults in the community in supporting City Center. The dance was a huge success on two levels. First, it made a nice financial contribution to C.C., but more importantly it added a great new interest to Laura's private life; she met and fell in love with Boris Shlomm.

Boris had been born in Paris to Gregory and Raissa Shlomm, who were both Russian émigrés. When he was two years old his parents and maternal grandparents fled Paris only days after Hitler's army arrived. His father was exceptional in being able to establish himself in his own business. He started a company in specialty fibers: vicuna, camel's hair, and cashmere. After graduating from Yale, Boris had joined his father's firm and was being groomed to head the company whenever his father retired.

Since Laura was living upstairs in her own place, Lawrence and I didn't really get acquainted with Boris until they became engaged after a summer and fall dating period. On

March 14, 1966, they were married at the Plaza Hotel. There were two hundred and forty guests. Laura and Boris paid attention to every detail, including what I was to wear.

Half a dozen of my girlhood friends from Little Rock came with their husbands. There were also family members from Boston and Kansas City and friends from Detroit and Memphis. The Shlomm's guests were more cosmopolitan: They came from Switzerland and England. Since the Shlomm's main plant for cashmere was in Charlotte, North Carolina, many of their executives came to the wedding from there.

We were so happy to see Laura settling into married life. We now felt we had more freedom to travel. Lawrence and I had a wonderful trip the next year to Japan. We saw and enjoyed all the major sights of that wonderful country, except that we never got a good view of Fujiyama. Every time our driver shouted, "There it is!" we leaped from the car, field glasses and all. By the time we got ourselves in position, the clouds covered the mountain. We would climb back into the car, once more disappointed.

The day before we were to leave Japan, we went to the arena to watch sumo wrestling matches. The wrestlers had been fattened up to weigh around three hundred pounds, and the rules for the fight are very strict and formal. The best seats we could get at the last moment were high up under the rafters; there were only two rows above ours. Each pair of competitors fought one round. We watched the wrestlers come out and display themselves, showing off their bodies, doing knee bends to show how supple they were. This was done so the people who wanted to bet could chose their favorites. Lawrence and I watched the first fight without making any choice. By the second match, I made a selection, and my wrestler won. There were a lot of young Japanese men seated behind us. When my man won, they bowed politely to me. Although no words were spoken, I realized they were congratulating me on picking a winner. I saw nothing remarkable in my win; after all, I'd had a fifty-fifty chance.

By the time I had picked three winners in a row, I noticed that the men behind me were waiting for me to make my choice. They would then run to place their bets. After I had picked thirteen winners straight, my neighbors were exceedingly happy. I decided to quit while I had a perfect score, as I had done at the farm after shooting the can off the fence. When we stood up to leave, all the Japanese men put their hands in a praying position and bowed very low before us. I wasn't sure what the gesture meant. Were they begging me to stay and give them more tips, or were they deifying me for what I had already done for them? Was this another case of my ESP?

I was easily persuaded to go on a photographic safari to Africa. Lawrence wouldn't consider it; he didn't want to be out of touch with Wall Street. It was a three-week Lindblad Wing Safari for ten people.

We flew from one wild animal reserve to another. Each place was different, and the animals we saw were specific to each location. We traveled in Kenya, Uganda, and Tanzania. Our group was the first to visit Lake Rudolph since it had been forbidden to tourists some years before. My plans had been made so hastily that I hadn't had time to do my homework. When we arrived at the lake, I heard for the first time the story of why it had been out of bounds. It seems a tribe of Somalis had gone on a rampage; they had crossed the frontier, entered the camp, and massacred everyone. We now had an armed guard, but I didn't feel particularly reassured when I saw him. All he wore was a loincloth, and he carried a dull spear. He was drunk besides.

The next day a fishing party was organized. We went out in an open launch to a small island half an hour away. The water was like glass—it was a pleasant trip. We were fishing for wide-mouth bass that were supposed to weigh around a hundred pounds. Our tackle was chunks of wood about eight inches long with three large hooks at one end. The fish would have to be mighty big to swallow anything that large. A couple of people got strikes but failed to sink the hooks into the fishes' mouths fast enough. Then I got a strike and was able to hook the fish. He started to swim back and forth frantically. I tried to get the boatman to move the boat so we could drag the fish, to tire him out. That's the way I caught a forty-three-pound cobra fish once in Florida. The boatman couldn't understand what I wanted, so when the fish got smart and swam under the boat I knew he was going to break the line and get away. The owner of the camp felt so sad that he wanted to stay and try some more.

A strong wind had come up, and we could smell rain. The sky began to darken. We urged them to turn back. We could still get home before the storm reached us. By the time they finally agreed, it was too late. The waves were so high that our small launch could not make any progress. Our motors were just strong enough to keep us from being dashed against the small, rocky island. The boatman was afraid we were running out of gas. Yet if he shut off the motors in order to fill the tanks from the ten-gallon cans on the boat, he would not be able to restart them. Much to my horror, he and the owner decided to refill the tanks with the motors running. We were lucky we didn't explode right then.

I was hanging onto the side rails. Every wave that hit the boat got me full in the face. Someone felt sorry for me and fixed a director's chair in the middle of the boat for me. I had nothing to hold onto from that position. The first wave that came tipped the chair over, and I started to float out the side of the boat. Someone grabbed me by the legs and pulled me back. After that, I clung tenaciously to the side railing. The refrain kept going through my mind, "Why did I have to spend so much money to get myself killed?" It took us three and a half hours to cross the same distance that had taken a half hour on the way out. By the time we finally reached the dock, the storm had dissipated, and the rest of the group members were standing on the pier, curious to see what we had caught. We only hoped we hadn't caught our death. I dashed to the shower so I could stop shaking from the cold—and perhaps from fright.

The trip included enough adventure to last the rest of my days. When we got to the hotel near Murchison Falls in Uganda, we learned that a leopard had killed one of the hotel employees the night before. At the Nagora Gora crater, a tree lion killed a native from the village the day we were there. At Tsavo Tent camp, a herd of elephants came thundering through the dry creek bed just after dark and a spitting cobra spat in the eyes of the camp dog. He howled in pain most of the night. At Treetop, a water buffalo got stuck in a mud hole and kept slipping deeper and deeper into the mire until it disappeared altogether. The elephants liked to scratch themselves by rubbing against the tree trunks that held our hotel up in the air. When an elephant had an itch, our whole hotel swayed until it had scratched the right spot. I'm glad I took the trip, and I'm equally glad I never have to go again.

CHAPTER 25

Two New Homes and a Grandson

In 1968 we rented a house in Atlantic Beach to be near Laura and Boris, who spent their summer weekends there with his parents. Since I was still working in the Bronx, this meant an hour's drive over the Whitestone Bridge to get to work.

Lawrence had left Graham and Newman when Ben Graham retired. He'd formed his own general and limited partnership and was investing the funds that all the limited partners had contributed. It didn't matter to Lawrence where his base was. His office could be wherever he kept an inventory of his partnership holdings and where he had his telephone. He could work anywhere and everywhere, and he did. I liked the idea of having parties for Laura and Boris and their friends on weekends. This at least got Lawrence away from his desk for a few hours.

Atlantic Beach is a narrow island off the southern coast of Long Island. It is only two blocks wide, with the bay on one side and the Atlantic Ocean on the other. There is a long boardwalk, and we used to ride our bicycles up and down after dinner. We rented the same house for ten years, from Elmer and Anita Block. Elmer always left me a wonderful vegetable garden, which I enjoyed watering and weeding.

I only commuted to the Bronx from Atlantic Beach for two summers. By the third summer, I'd resigned from my job and led a completely idle life. There was a lot of turmoil in the city. We were happy to be away. Mayor Lindsay made his famous walk through Harlem to cool racial tensions. A lot of publicity was given to the pending uprisings. Everyone was reading *Soul on Ice,* by Eldridge Cleaver. I found it very moving, well-written, and very frightening. It ended with the statement that if the blacks couldn't have a bigger piece of the action they were going to burn the place down.

The general atmosphere, coupled with what I had just experienced personally, made Lawrence and me begin to think about having a small place to which we could escape in case the predicted "long, hot summer" came to pass. In the spring of 1970 we went to Switzerland, rented a small car, and toured the country looking for a place where we might like to have a pied à terre. We were fortunate to find an apartment, still being constructed, that we could rent. It was in Montreux, at the opposite end of Lake Léman from Geneva. On the lake side was a long balcony, and the view included the lake, the Savoy Alps, and the Dents du Midi, one of the most beautiful snow-capped mountains in all the land.

The dollar was very strong at that time, equal to four Swiss francs and twenty-nine centimes. The apartment, with a garage for our car, was going to cost us around one-hundred-and-fifty dollars a month. (At the time we were paying one-hundred-and-thirty dollars a month just for garaging our car in New York.) We no longer needed a car in New York, since I wasn't working, so for a difference of only twenty dollars we could have this delightful place in Switzerland. I didn't see how we could afford not to take it.

I took all the apartment measurements back to New York. I still had the drawing equipment from my days as a decorator. After making a scale drawing, I set out to shop for furniture. I looked only at pieces that were imported from Europe, pieces I knew I would be able to buy in Switzerland. It was such fun to start with a new apartment again and have complete freedom to furnish it in any style I wanted. This had never been the case before; I had always had some inherited pieces to which I was tied by sentiment. The architecture and the scale of rooms seemed to say "go modern." Also, Breuer and Corbusier had designed lovely pieces. Lawrence had been fond of modern furniture since his student days in Germany, when the Bauhaus school was in full swing. He left the choice to me. I collected photos to show him, and also to show whichever Swiss decorator I hired to order the furniture.

After our summer in Atlantic Beach, we flew back to Montreux to see if our apartment building had been finished as scheduled. We found a decorator, Henri Pernet, to help us. With our feeble French and his equally feeble English, communications were difficult. Thank goodness I had the pictures and the scale drawings. Pernet didn't trust the accuracy of my drawings, so he made his own and was surprised that the two coincided, his and mine. Selection of the fabrics and rugs and curtains was all that needed to be done. It was agreed that Pernet would place all the orders and that when we returned, in May, everything would have been installed. How nice to have someone else assume the responsibility of coordinating all the deliveries. When we returned in the spring, we just moved right in. I had brought drip-dry sheets with me because Europe had not yet heard of such things.

We had purposely not bought any bibelots or pictures for the apartment. We wanted to have the fun of looking for those things together. Needlepointing was all the rage, and I thought I should find a design to do for the living room. I had definite ideas of what I did not want to do—I did not want to copy Marie Laurencin—but I didn't know what would lend itself to needlepoint. We had plenty of time to make these decisions. It didn't matter if the walls were bare as long as we had our view.

Laura and Boris were expecting their first baby. She wanted me to keep her company when she did her constitutional walks in New York. Even in her last weeks, I had to run to keep up with her. Once I counted ninety blocks that we had walked in a day. No wonder I was feeling tired. The baby was in no hurry to leave its snug inner space. Two weeks past term, December 13, 1970, Alexander Shlomm was born.

Alexander was precocious. He did everything long before Dr. Spock said he should. The pediatrician said there was an old wives' tale that every extra day spent in utero is equal to a week's development in the outside world. The pediatrician told the story for what it was worth; he didn't necessarily believe it himself. After watching Alexander develop, I am convinced the theory is correct. He could turn himself from stomach to back when he was two weeks old. Spock said you can expect a baby to do that at two and a half months.

We left New York in mid-May to spend a month and a half in Montreux. About five months earlier we had visited the Matisse Chapel in St. Paul de Vence and I had known immediately that I wanted to copy Matisse's collages in needlepoint tapestry. It was just a question of getting books and finding the right Matisse for my purpose. His cutouts had everything I wanted. The design was superb, so were the colors, and they would both translate well into another art form. After much thought I chose to copy *Blue Nude IV* in its original dimensions, thirty-six by forty-five inches. I had it drawn on number ten canvas, which worked out to 162,000 stitches. I set myself a daily quota in order to be able to complete this mammoth undertaking in four and a half months. I wanted to take the finished tapestry as a "house present" for the new apartment.

Now the *Blue Nude* was hanging in our living room. I didn't know it then, but I was eventually going to make everything that would be on the walls of that apartment. I would wait for inspiration to strike, then enter into frenetic activity, finally sit back and admire my handiwork. I hadn't had so much fun using my hands since the days on the farm when I was making all of Laura's clothes and learning to do tailoring.

I found a wonderful old lady to teach me conversational French. She had the faculty of being a good listener and of making me feel that I was bringing the outside world to her. I would get so involved in what I was saying that I forgot to be self-conscious about speaking French. I spent at least an hour a day with my teacher, and she usually kept me for two hours.

My confidence was soaring. It was rare that I had to look for different ways of expressing myself in order to be understood.

It became our pattern to spend one-and-a-half months in the spring and again in the fall in Montreux, while we passed the summer in Atlantic Beach. After Alexander was born, Laura and Boris rented a house for themselves at the beach. We led separate, but commingled lives.

Alexander made his first trip to Switzerland when he was nine months old. Laura and Boris had decided to spend their Christmas holidays skiing. They asked Lawrence and me to come with them and look after Alexander while they were skiing. I had entered my fifth career: I was now a professional grandmother, and I loved it. On his first trip, Alexander spoke his first word, "cookie." It was a word well chosen; even then he loved to eat. He also learned to run during that stay. He never learned to walk, he always ran. We thought it was momentum that held him upright; if he had slowed to a walk, he would have fallen over.

We rented a beautiful four-bedroom chalet in Crans-sur-Sierre for December. Alexander had his first birthday there. We bought a sled with a seat and pulled and pushed Alexander up and down the mountains. He was aware of all the sounds around him. The birds, to my surprise, were chirping away even in mid-winter, and he listened to them all. The squirrels in Crans were much cuter than those in Central Park. They were black, with pointed, alert ears. They were so fast that one had to look quickly to catch a glimpse of them.

The year 1971 was one of the happiest in our lives. It was our first year in our apartment in Switzerland. Greatest of all, it was our grandson's first year, and Laura and Boris had been generous enough to let us share in their joy.

CHAPTER 26

Lawrence

After Christmas in Crans, Lawrence decided to stay in Montreux and make business trips from there to Germany. He had exclusive rights to sell an American company to a foreign investor. I was ready to go home. We kept in touch by phone. One day he called and said he'd been poisoned by something he'd eaten but had recovered after taking medication. In a few days, he came home. Somehow he never felt a hundred percent after that.

We went to Islamarado to get away from the cold and bake in the Florida sun. Since Lawrence wasn't feeling himself, I wouldn't let him carry any luggage. We rented a car at Miami airport and drove down to the Keys.

I unpacked all the suitcases and went for a swim. When I returned, Lawrence proudly showed me how he had placed all the empty cases on a very high shelf so they would be out of the way. I scolded him for not waiting for the maid to do it the next morning. I had been protecting him, and now he deliberately strained himself. We had an early supper at the hotel and went to bed.

Around five-thirty the next morning, Lawrence woke me to say that he was in pain and needed a doctor. The motel helped me telephone a hospital some twenty miles away, to say that I was driving my husband up immediately. The staff was ready when we arrived and began treating him for a heart attack. It was a small hospital with telephone supervision by a heart specialist in south Miami. After a few days, the specialist thought we should get an ambulance and bring Lawrence to his hospital. I followed the ambulance in our car with no idea where I was going. Trying to follow a speeding ambulance on a highway added to my tension. I hate to drive at night. I hate to speed. I hate not to know where I am going. Most of all I hated not knowing what was happening with Lawrence in the ambulance. He had been unconscious when we left the Keys.

He was still out when we got him into the new hospital. The doctor was very grave after examining him. It had been a massive heart attack, and the back of Lawrence's heart was severely affected.

He was in intensive care for a long time. All four rooms had their patients attached to monitors that sounded bells when anyone was having difficulty. I sat in the hall for weeks, listening to those alarm bells go off. From where I was, I never knew for whom the bell was tolling. I didn't have enough concentration even to read the newspaper, but I could do needlepoint. At least my fingers were occupied, if not my mind.

Eventually, Lawrence was allowed to leave the hospital, and we moved into a motel suite. I did some cooking, and we were able to order meals sent to the room. I knew Lawrence was on the mend when he started dictating business letters to me. I was glad, at least, to have the typewriter with us. Lawrence showed me how to record sales and purchases of stock for the partnership. I was okay on the mechanics of bookkeeping. I just didn't want to be involved in making investment judgments. Lawrence should just tell me what to do, and I would do it. In spite of myself, I was learning something about investing.

Once Lawrence had recovered, he resumed his old pattern of working hard. One of Ben Graham's former students at Columbia phoned Lawrence saying he needed help with an investment he had made in a Colorado insurance company.

He had gone on the board to see if he could help straighten the company out. He urged Lawrence to buy enough stock so he too would qualify for a seat on the board. The two of them decided that new management had to be brought into the company. The only way to effect this was to have a proxy fight and to win it. There are companies that specialize in running proxy fights for dissatisfied stockholders, but hiring them to do everything is very expensive. Lawrence decided he would give it his personal attention. He assured me that he knew his limits and would not overtax his strength.

However, when I saw him sitting at his desk until midnight every night, composing letters to the stockholders to solicit their proxies, I decided I had better take some of the burden off him. That is how I became a proxy fighter. At first, we had a dreadful time getting the company to give us a list of the stockholders, the number of shares they owned, their addresses and phone numbers. After weeks of delay, the lawyer we had hired in Colorado was able to ship us the requested material. It was the first computer printout I had ever seen. Nearly twenty-five hundred people owned this stock. Who was going to address that many envelopes? Apparently I was.

I bought boxes of gummed labels so that when I typed an address I had it in triplicate in case a follow-up was needed. I also set up a color-coded card file that I kept updated whenever we had a letter or the return of a proxy card. It was getting to be very exciting. The votes for our side were coming in. It began to look as if we had a chance to win. There were a lot of people out there who had held the stock for many years. They were disgusted with the lack of dividends and were anxious to see something happen.

The last week before the annual meeting, Lawrence and I and the others in our group moved into a hotel in Denver to be nearer our lawyer and to watch the happenings at closer range. I was working the card file. Whenever I found a large stockholder who had not responded, I gave the card to one of the men who would then telephone. We had a box at the post office, and we must have sent people there a dozen times a day. It's hard to believe now, but we didn't have hand calculators in those days, and I was keeping a running tally with a pencil. It was looking better and better. The accountants and lawyers were meeting the night before the open meeting to count the votes.

For some reason, management decided that none of our men except our lawyer and our accountant could be present at the tallying. They also allowed me to be present. What a responsibility that was!

I had alphabetized all the proxy cards so that I could find them easily. Some people were bound to have sent cards to both sides. In such a case, the most recently dated card would be counted. We won some and we lost some. Our opponents challenged a large number of shares that were held in brokers' names. They didn't like the way the officers of the brokerage firms had signed. I demanded the right to telephone the brokerage houses to get it straightened out. Our lawyer backed me in this request. It was late at night when the count ended. Our side had nearly sixty-seven percent of all the shares voted. This was comfortable enough so that I couldn't see how anyone casting a vote in person at the annual meeting could overturn the decision against the current management.

The next day there were few speeches from the floor of the meeting. We had won overwhelmingly. I had done what I had set out to do—help take some of the pressure off Lawrence. I did warn him, though, that if he got himself into another such situation, I wouldn't help him pull his irons out of the fire.

CHAPTER 27

Alexander

I had been away from New York for more than a week. It was time to get back and see what new proofs of genius Alexander had shown. I was not disappointed. He was now sixteen months old and had a vocabulary of three hundred words or more. I know because I made a list, as I did when his mother was the same age. He was far ahead of her. During my absence, Laura had asked a cousin, Esther Gelatt, to baby-sit one afternoon. Esther was writing music for a course she was taking. She handed Alexander a piece of paper on which she had written a large "A" and told him what it was. He was enchanted. He walked all around the room reading his paper out loud. After a while, she gave him another paper with a "B." By the end of the afternoon, he knew the entire alphabet.

The following day Laura bought a set of plastic letters that stuck to a magnetic board. This became his favorite toy. He liked to pull the letters out of a bag and announce what they were before he stuck them on the board. After a week of this, Laura asked if I thought Alexander would be confused if she gave him a set of lower-case letters too. I said they would probably confuse him, but she should give them to him anyway. He was far from being confused; he already knew those letters. We asked how he'd recognized them, and he ran to get a book. He had been doing his homework. The book had large capital letters with smaller lower-case letters next to them. He had simply taught himself to read them all.

It was such fun to see Alexander's mind unfold. He wanted to know the name of everything, and I wanted to tell him. That made us a good team. Laura was generous about sharing him with me. We never talked about what it meant to me to have another little boy, but all of us knew that true joy had come back into our lives. The light was back in my eyes twenty-five years after it had gone out.

Alexander chose the books he wanted to have read to him. He was fond of the usual books for his age, such as Dr. Suess and the Madeline stories, but he loved some that were chance discoveries of his own. He found an old catalog of an Alexander Calder art show. At first, I thought he liked it because the painter's first name was the same as his, but when he dragged that catalog all over the apartment, I realized that he liked the colors and designs. He had two other favorite books. One had hundreds of Buddha photos, the other had colored pictures of fish. His taste certainly was eclectic.

When he was about two-and-a-half years old, I was pushing him down the block in his stroller when he called out in a loud voice, "Look, Grandma, there's an Alexander Calder." Super-sophisticated New Yorkers stopped in their tracks, wanting to know if they had heard correctly. They asked him to repeat what he had said. Happy for the attention, he pointed his chubby finger at the painting in the gallery window and repeated, "Alexander Calder." I shrugged my shoulders as if to say, "What do you expect from a genius?" Very much the same thing happened another day in front of a gallery displaying a couple of small Buddhas. Alexander wasn't particularly interested in what ducks or lambs say; that was old stuff to him. He enjoyed learning words like hexagon and parallelogram. There wasn't a dinosaur whose bones had been excavated that he didn't know by name.

We spent a lot of time at the Museum of Natural History. One of the games we played together we called "Museum." Alexander would build a museum out of blocks and populate it with plastic models of dinosaurs. As for the book of fish species, he just wanted me to read the name of each one to him. In the end, he could correctly identify over one hundred and fifty kinds of fish.

Alexander's teacher told Laura of an occasion when she had shown a movie about a farm to the kindergarten children. She wanted to lead them into a discussion of what they had observed in the film. She asked, "Did any of you notice any differences in the cows?" She expected the answer, "Yes, some of them had spots." Instead, Alexander said, "Yes, the black-and-white cows were Holsteins, the brown-and-white ones were Guernseys, and the brown ones were Jersey's." The teacher didn't know if he was right or wrong, but she was amused at his precision.

The winter that Alexander was two, Lawrence and I met Laura, Boris, and Alexander at the Geneva airport. We were driving to Crans. I caught a glimpse of Alexander as they went through the passport gate, then they all disappeared from view. It was quite a while before they reappeared. Laura told us Alexander had broken away from her and was running back toward the airplane yelling, "I want another turn." He adored airplanes, and no trip was ever too long for him. Characteristically, he learned the symbols of all the airlines and could identify the planes either on the ground or in the air.

That winter he began to go to ski school. The teacher complained to me about Alexander, saying, "That kid is never going to learn to ski. He can't even stop, except by running into someone or something." Alexander kept insisting that he wanted to go "on top of the mountain." One day I agreed to go with them in the telecabine to show Alexander what there was at the top and then bring him back down. It was all and more than he had expected. Bernard Rey, the monitor teaching Boris and Laura, offered to take Alexander with him on his skis. Alexander was to stand on top of Bernard's boots and just relax. It was such a thrill to see how Bernard was able to pattern the muscles of this would be skier. Never again would Alexander go to the ski school. He had had a taste of the top and would not settle for anything less. Every day he had a half-hour ride standing on Bernard's boots. How much better this was than having someone tell him to put his weight on the downhill ski.

CHAPTER 28

Joys and Sorrows

When Alexander was three his brother Daniel was born, on April 16, 1974. From the beginning, Daniel was a very different character from Alexander. He was patient. He could wait to be fed. He had perseverance. He would try a new physical feat over and over until he had mastered it. His tolerance for frustration was extraordinary. He would struggle in his playpen to stand up, only to be knocked over by Alexander. We were never fast enough to intercept those swiftly delivered blows. I don't know what Daniel thought. Maybe he thought it was a game, because he was so good-natured about getting knocked over. He was crazy about his big brother and followed him with his eyes, wherever he went. Maybe he followed him with his eyes so he would know when the next hit was coming.

I was careful not to play with Daniel too much if Alexander was around. I didn't want to enflame his jealousy. During Daniel's first summer, Alexander spent a great deal of time at our house in Atlantic Beach. He adored the tomato and pepper plants. He wanted to pick everything before it was quite ripe. His hands would open and close slowly as he struggled with temptation. Mostly he mastered his instincts, but one day they got the better of him, and he picked a green pepper that we had been watching for weeks. Lawrence, who was near him, gave his hand a quick slap. Alexander blinked a few times. Then he held the pepper out to Lawrence and said, "I picked it for you."

I was jumping waves in the ocean one day with Alexander in my arms when I saw a large whitecap coming toward us. Alexander saw the alarm on my face. He reassured me by saying, "Don't worry, Grandma, it'll dissipate by the time it gets to us." He was right.

His method of learning new words was astounding. Whenever he heard a new word, he asked what it meant if he couldn't guess from its context. He would then repeat it once. Within the next ten minutes, he would use the word. He usually managed to use it once again quite soon. From then on, the word was his. There were only two things that he couldn't say when he was tiny. Helicopter was "hokie" and hippopotamus was "piapi." I never wanted to correct him; it was his only baby talk.

Sitting on the beach, he asked me the word for a doctor who took care of animals. I told him it was veterinarian. He said, "Yeah, that's right." He didn't go through his usual practice of using the word. Later in the day, wanting to see if he had really learned that big a word on just one hearing, I asked if he remembered what I had told him. I could see his mind going through its filing system. He came up with "vegetarian." I said he was very close and gave him the right word again. Then I asked how he knew the word vegetarian. He answered that he knew it because Pepita in *Madeline and the Bad Hot* was a vegetarian. I countered that I remembered Pepita guillotining some chickens. "Yes," he replied, "you're right; but then 'the former barbarian turned into a vegetarian.'" He had given me a direct and accurate quote from the book. He was three-and-a-half years old. He was not going to be an early reader as I had anticipated. Why should he learn to read? It was more fun having someone read to him. That way he had the person's full attention and no competition from Daniel.

This same summer, Alexander learned to swim and plunge. Having spent every summer near the water, he had no fears at all and was thus able to learn quickly. He had used inflated bands around his arms, but now he could manage without them.

Daniel was thriving. Laura breast-fed him for thirteen months, just as she had Alexander. I had the feeling that Laura really wanted to have Daniel to herself. Whatever the reason, I did not sit in the park with Daniel. Sometimes I would keep Laura company when she took Daniel for air, but she was definitely the one in charge.

Alexander never asked for privileges or toys. Perhaps it was because they were given to him before he had a chance to want them. Daniel wasn't like that. He knew what he wanted and asked for it. Mostly he wanted whatever Alexander had. Since Alexander slept in a big bed, Daniel no longer wanted to be in a crib. Because Alexander went to the toilet alone, Daniel trained himself at a very early age. He was anxious to do things for himself. When he didn't want assistance he would politely but firmly say, "Self." Alexander had been happy to have any help you would give him. He'd had no interest at all in learning to tie his shoes. I used to joke that he would have to take me with him to Yale so I could tie his shoes. Daniel wasn't going to need anyone to go anywhere with him. He was master of himself.

When Daniel wanted something, he knew how to negotiate for it. At about the age of eight, he asked if he could use my typewriter when he was twelve. I said I thought it would be okay. He then said, "What about eleven?" I agreed to that. I could see where this was going. Finally he came out with it: "What about now?" I had read about two-year-olds learning to type in an experiment at Yale. According to that experiment, he was behind by six years and had to make up for lost time. I don't know which he loved the most, the typewriter, the calculator, or the message recorder on the telephone. He used to phone me and leave a message then run around the corner from his house to mine to hear it. He was a child of the electronic age.

All of us continued to spend Christmas in Crans. By the time Daniel was two, it was his turn to ride on Bernard Rey's boots. By that time, Alexander was skiing on his own but couldn't quite manage the T-bar lift. This marvelous monitor would come up the mountain on the T-bar with Daniel on his shoulders and Alexander between his legs. Thanks to his superhuman efforts, both boys progressed each year, earning the Swiss bronze medal, then the silver, and finally the gold. This Swiss gold medal is an award coveted especially by the French boys. If they show this badge of competency when they have to do army duty, they are placed in the French ski patrol.

In June of 1979 Lawrence and I made a week's trip to Burgundy, just the two of us. We stayed in a home outside of Autun and made side trips from there. What a wealth of treasures exists in that part of France.

Sunday we decided to rest up because we were leaving Monday for Montreux. We even took a nap that afternoon. When we woke up, Lawrence could not move his left side. He wanted me to help him try to stand. It was no good; he couldn't. I needed to get help quickly. Since no one seemed to be around, I went to my car and honked the horn steadily until some people finally appeared. They phoned the fire department, something I would never have thought to do. Again I found myself following an ambulance at breakneck speed to an unknown destination.

The hospital in Autun had the friendliest nurses I've ever met. They were distressed that they couldn't understand Lawrence. When I left for the night, there was no one to interpret for him. I moved into a hotel in Autun in order to be closer to the hospital.

After about ten days, the cardiologist thought it was a good idea to get Lawrence back to Montreux and into the hospital there, where he could have friends visit to cheer him up. I asked the doctor to order a helicopter. He thought it would be better at the border if the helicopter came from Switzerland to fetch Lawrence. I didn't know how to make such an arrangement. I finally phoned a friend in Switzerland who made all the necessary connections to have him picked up. I still had to figure out how to get our car back to Montreux. I decided to make the six-hour drive alone. I rehearsed the whole schedule with Lawrence, over and over, to make sure he understood what was going to happen. He was still in a confused state, and I didn't want him to have any extra worries.

I left in the car the afternoon before the helicopter pickup was to take place so that I would be in Montreux when he arrived. When I started off, I noticed a peculiar noise in the motor. I stopped at a mechanic's shop, and the diagnosis was a loose, frayed fan belt. They had nothing to give me as a replacement. After several more stops that were equally unsuccessful, I was told just to keep driving. If I didn't kill my motor, the chances were that I would make the drive without incident. What a way to start a trip!

I played the radio, the hours passed, and I came to the Swiss border. The border guards are always efficient, but this time I got one who was a bit too inquisitive. In effect, he asked what a nice lady like me was doing driving around the country all alone. That was too much. I burst into tears as I explained. He was so sorry to have asked, and so sympathetic that at one point I thought he was going to get in the car and drive me the rest of the way. The fan belt held out until I got home. I made myself a supper of peanut butter and crackers and fell into an exhausted sleep.

The following morning Lawrence arrived a couple of hours later than planned. They had sent a small plane for him instead of a helicopter; therefore, he had to be brought from Geneva by ambulance. He didn't seem any worse for having made the trip, and he was pleased to be cared for by his own doctor, who could speak English. Physiotherapy began almost immediately so that the muscles would not atrophy. The therapists had him walking with a cane within a few weeks. His thinking cleared up. The doctor agreed that he could leave the hospital but was to continue his exercises. It looked as if he would come out of this illness not too badly damaged.

Now I had to take full charge of the partnership portfolio. I wrote a letter to all the partners, telling them what had happened and saying it was our intention not to make any new investments. We also told them that as we made sales and generated large amounts of cash, we would distribute it to them. That process finally ended in January 1988.

We had made our last trip together, except for going back and forth to Montreux. There would be no more Christmas in Crans for Lawrence and me. Laura and Boris took their boys there for another seven years.

When we returned to New York, Lawrence began going to the Rusk Institute three times a week for physiotherapy. Although it was an effort to go there, and we both felt the strain, the results made it worthwhile. Lawrence was able to walk across the room without a cane. His therapist told me she had done as much as she could but his progress was hampered by his enormous anxiety about falling. I knew she was right, but I didn't know how to get help for him to overcome this somewhat reasonable fear.

Lawrence still had a lot of drive and determination to recover, but it was like trying to go forward with his brakes on. Fear was his number one enemy, and he was not to conquer it.

CHAPTER 29

The Computer and I

The following summer we returned to Montreux. After a few weeks, Lawrence began to have spells of congestive heart failure. His lungs had to be tapped every two weeks, and he needed to use oxygen most of the time. By chance, I heard a broadcast over Voice of America describing a new experimental medicine for congestive heart failure. It was being tested at Harvard Medical School.

I got the name of the medicine and of a Swiss doctor in Lausanne who could administer it. Dr. Turini had been doing research with Captopril for a year longer than Harvard. Lawrence was the perfect candidate for using it. The doctor was willing to give Lawrence this oral vasodilator only if he stayed in the hospital while his dosage was regulated. Within thirty minutes of his first dose, the quantity of blood that the heart pumped was increased by fifty percent. This increased volume eventually cleared the lungs, and after a few weeks I was able to bring Lawrence back to New York.

I realized that Lawrence was going to be limited in his ability to go out. As a consequence I, too, would be more or less grounded. If I was going to spend that much time in the apartment, I needed a new hobby to occupy me. Occasionally I saw a TV program that showed the use of computers. That was it!

I went shopping. When I look back on that experience, I can't believe that I was so ignorant and yet so daring. I was a fool rushing in where angels feared to tread.

It was not easy to get a salesperson to pay attention to me, especially when I asked such questions as, "Which computer should I buy that will do everything?"

They would counter by asking, "What do you want it to do?"

To this I replied, "Oh, I don't know. What can it do?"

With this they usually disappeared to help someone who was sitting in front of a computer making it draw pictures. After three hours of persistently chasing one salesperson after another, I had narrowed my choices down to the Commodore Pet and the Apple II. By then my questions were becoming a little more focused as I asked which of the two was bought by the most schools and which had the most educational software written for it.

After another hour of catch-as-catch-can with the salespeople, I made my decision. It was to be the Commodore 32 K. I was told it had all the memory I would ever need. I took out my blank check and paid for it. I was buying it partly to prove that I had been serious all along. Delivery would take a week. How could I wait that long to get my hands on something I hadn't even known I wanted twenty-four hours before?

I made up all kinds of reasons to justify this purchase. The truth was, I had suddenly realized that something was happening in the world. I didn't want to remain ignorant of this electronic age. It was going to be exciting and challenging to learn something new.

When the Commodore Pet finally arrived, it took hours for me to get it out of the boxes and connected by cables. The manual threw me into a panic. Maybe I should find a school. They existed only for people who had typing speeds of sixty words a minute or better. I had never passed thirty, so that was out. There was no way but to get a book of exercises and do them. After all, I had learned farming and animal husbandry from government pamphlets. Why not teach myself how to operate a computer? Keep in mind that in 1978 computers were not as "user friendly" as they are today.

After Lawrence went to sleep each night, I would sit at the computer. In my state of total immersion, I would suddenly realize that it was 2:00 A.M. and I was still glued to the screen trying to figure out how to write a program to get the computer to compound interest. I had never come up against anything so frustrating. I thought of throwing the Commodore out the window. I was afraid it would fall on someone. I restrained myself.

Then I met Antonia Stone, a computer expert who was teaching ex-prisoners at the Fortune Society. She had written a number of educational games, but her teaching was hampered because she didn't have a printer. We struck a bargain. I would buy a printer for the Fortune Society if she would come to me once a week to get me over the hump. This worked out well for both of us.

After six months I reluctantly decided that I would not be able to learn computer programming, and I bought my first software. Once I had a spread sheet and a word processor, I regretted the time I had wasted thinking I could write my own programs. Now it was fun! There was still a lot of learning to do, but it was easier. The computer became a tool. Both our grandsons began to use it for writing school papers.

Alexander had transferred to Riverdale Country School in the fifth grade and was very happy there. A strange thing had happened when he took the entrance exams given by an independent group of testers. The examiner had commented that Alexander had no eye for details. It seems he had been shown a picture of a man who had only one hand and had been asked what was wrong with the picture. Alexander had replied that there was nothing wrong with the picture. Just for fun, I asked him if he remembered the picture of the man. He said that he did. Then I asked why he had said there was nothing wrong with the man.

He answered, "They didn't ask me what was wrong with the man; they asked me what was wrong with the picture.

The picture was okay, but the man was missing a hand. They should have asked what was wrong with the man."

I felt justified in my faith in his ability to see details. That is something he had already developed when he knew how to identify a hundred and fifty fish before he went to nursery school. You can't lose that ability, or can you?

Daniel began to come over and use the computer for games. It seemed to me that his eye-to-hand coordination was very fast. He was at ease with the keyboard and totally without fear of making a mistake. Whenever I learned something at night, I would call Daniel to come the next afternoon so I could teach it to him. What had taken hours to teach myself, took me seconds to teach him. Even more important, he would remember it, whereas I was likely to forget in a few days and have to look it up again in the manual. Then I discovered a new trick. Instead of looking it up, I would phone Daniel and say, "Do you remember how I told you to do such and such?" Thinking I was testing him, he would give me the procedure step by step. I would say that I was pleased he had remembered, never letting on that I was really calling for information.

Both boys began studying the computer at Riverdale. When I went for Grandparents' Day, I heard the plans for building a new school library. This stimulated me to think about what libraries were going to be like in the near future.

I had been attending a Columbia University seminar run by Professor Seth Neugroschel and Professor Ray Lorsch. We heard speakers who told us what was happening in the various universities and also in the field of research on computers. Stevens Institute and Brown University were now requiring their entering freshmen to have their own computers. The University of Houston had thirty thousand computers on campus.

Riverdale's computer department was very far advanced both in the elementary and upper grades. The school had a mainframe and many classrooms had computers that connected to the mainframe. I wanted to see the school library's card catalog put on the computer so that it could be accessed from anywhere on campus. This became a project for me. I went to the library at Hunter College to see their installation. I also visited the Forty-Second Street Public Library to see its new way of handling the reference catalog. Everything I saw strengthened my conviction that soon the card catalog would be as obsolete as the buggy whip.

I made an appointment to see the Riverdale librarian and the head of the computer department. I explored with them the possibility of putting their card catalog on a computer. My proposal to them met with enthusiasm. They would do the necessary technical work to bring it to fruition, and I would provide the necessary funding. Lawrence was so pleased that I was enjoying this advanced technology project.

I gave my Commodore Pet to Antonia Stone for her computer center, which she calls, "Playing To Win." She runs it for underprivileged children who would not otherwise have access to learning about computers. I am now on my third computer. It has a hard disk with twenty megabytes of memory. I have to laugh when I think that my first salesperson told me that 32 K of memory was all I would ever need. That's how fast things are changing.

There is another project that I have just completed. In May of 1986 I helped the Pibly Fund buy the house and land next door to our original halfway houses. It is a nice lot with a big, old-fashioned house. We have put in all new electrical wiring and plumbing plus central air-conditioning. Now it is being used as a training center by Dr. Jack Wilder. As always, Jack has many innovative ideas for giving courses to employees who supervise people living in Pibly Residential Program apartments or who are staff members of other Bronx agencies dealing with the emotionally disturbed. Since Pibly now has some fifty employees, this is a very important task that Jack has taken on.

A literacy training course for adults will also use the newest computer technology and equipment, i.e., an attachment for the computer that will read the screen out loud word by word.

A few years ago I took up oil painting. Lawrence couldn't stand the smell in the New York apartment, so I only painted on the balcony in Montreux. It was a wonderful hobby. My walls in New York and in Montreux are filled with my paintings and drawings. I never developed my own style, however. As I was daubing away, the picture would begin to look like one of the Impressionists. I would then start to exaggerate that quality, thus ending up with a poor man's version of Monet, or Bonnard, or Soutine. I finally ran out of walls and had to find a new hobby. That's when I decided to write this book.

CHAPTER 30

Summer's End

Lawrence read every chapter as I wrote it. He laughed and he cried at the memories it evoked. We felt the years slip away and were again young together. He was my strong supporter who praised me and said that what I had written was the way it had happened. Somehow, he turned back into my private tutor. As we left Montreux, we both felt sad that the summer had come to an end. There was always the fear that with his condition so precarious we might not be able to come back the following June.

When we returned to New York, Lawrence's health worsened. There were several hospitalizations. Without the enormous help of our friend Betty Filer, I can't imagine how we could have gotten through the winter. Betty had gone to Switzerland with us for six summers in order to give me moral and physical help in caring for Lawrence.

It was painful to watch Lawrence as he diminished daily. His speech became little more than a whisper. His appetite, which had remained good, began to be finicky. He was always afraid of choking because the paralysis in his throat was getting worse. Still he insisted that I order the tickets for our annual pilgrimage to Montreux. In the early spring I half-heartedly ordered six seats so that he could lie down all the way over. Lola Greaves, who had been his cheerful nurse for six years, was also going with us.

Then in May swallowing became impossible, and he was again in the hospital for a surgical procedure. When we brought him home, he was on tube feeding. Every day he asked when we would be leaving for Switzerland. None of us had the nerve to tell him that we were not going to be able to go. It was the one hope that still remained for him, and we didn't want to take it away. His breathing, even with oxygen, became more and more difficult. He was fully conscious, but his speech was now slurred and incomprehensible. He stopped trying to make himself understood. One day he reached for my hand and took it to his lips and kissed it. Then he squeezed it three times. It came back to me. During our dating days, he had often done that. He had said it was his Morse Code for "I love you." Now he was using it as the only means of communicating left to him. I signaled back to him with three squeezes. I couldn't have spoken then either as my voice was choked with tears. He got my message, and a big smile came to his face. We had been married for fifty-four years, and death was about to us part. That's what we had promised each other, and we had kept our promise.

June 24, 1987, Lawrence died. I did not mourn his passing. He was nearly eighty-four years old and had suffered enough. My mourning had all been done during the eight years that I had watched his frustration at being so dependent and so incapable of doing things for himself. Now I felt I must begin to reconstruct my own life without him.

I brought out a picture taken of Lawrence when he was around fifty-five and still very handsome. I needed it to help erase the memory of the last years. All the furniture was put back to its original location. The fifty-inch TV screen that Lawrence had relied on was sent to Laura's house. The painters were called in and told to paint the walls red. I made a big splash with "Tree of Life" brightly colored chintz at the windows and on the two sofas. It was the first time there was no one to consult. I was both the decorator and the client. Suddenly it occurred to me that there was no one to please but myself. I have sad twinges at not being able to show it to Lawrence and hear him admire it. I know he would have liked it. He always liked what I did.

It's been my good fortune to have had a father and a husband who believed that I could do anything I set my mind to. Their belief has given me the necessary self-confidence to start life anew. I know that however many years remain to me, they will be rich ones.

There has been something very therapeutic about reviewing my life and summing it up. I have relived it.

At last I really understand the Robert Browning poem I memorized in high school nearly sixty years ago. In his poem, *Rabbi Ben Ezra,* he wrote:

> Grow old along with me!
> The best is yet to be!
> The last of life, for which the first was made:
> Our times are in his hand
> Who saith, "A whole I planned,
> Youth shows but half; trust God:
> See all, nor be afraid!"